DEFENCES OF PHILADELPHIA IN 1777

A Da Capo Press Reprint Series

THE ERA OF THE AMERICAN REVOLUTION

GENERAL EDITOR: LEONARD W. LEVY

Claremont Graduate School

DEFENCES OF PHILADELPHIA
IN 1777

Collected and Edited by
WORTHINGTON CHAUNCEY FORD

DA CAPO PRESS • NEW YORK • 1971

A Da Capo Press Reprint Edition

This Da Capo Press edition of
Defences of Philadelphia in 1777
is an unabridged republication of the
1897 edition published in Brooklyn, New York.

Library of Congress Catalog Card Number 71-146145

SBN 306-70140-5

Published by Da Capo Press
A Division of Plenum Publishing Corporation
227 West 17th Street, New York, N.Y. 10011
All Rights Reserved

Manufactured in the United States of America

DEFENCES OF PHILADELPHIA IN 1777

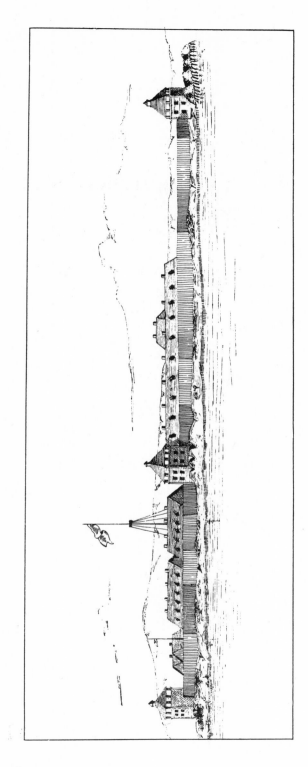

FORT MIFFLIN.

FROM A MAP PREPARED BY CAPTAIN JOHN MONTRESSOR, SIR WILLIAM HOWE'S CHIEF OF ENGINEERS.

DEFENCES

OF

PHILADELPHIA

IN

1777.

COLLECTED AND EDITED BY

WORTHINGTON CHAUNCEY FORD.

BROOKLYN, N. Y. :

HISTORICAL PRINTING CLUB.

1897.

[FROM THE "PENNSYLVANIA MAGAZINE OF HISTORY AND
BIOGRAPHY," 1894–1897.]

One Hundred Copies Printed.

No...............................

NOTE.

WHEN I made a tender to the *Pennsylvania Magazine of History and Biography* of a few minutes of the Councils of War held under Washington, I did not anticipate going outside of those records. Finding an abundance of new material bearing upon the operations in and around Philadelphia in the fall of 1777, the plan was extended until the result is this volume of nearly three hundred pages, containing more than two hundred and twenty letters and opinions, not five of which have before been in print. If only as an evidence of the unused materials for American history, this collection has an interest; and the interest is heightened by the personal touches these buried and forgotten manuscripts give of the writers. It is not so much the importance of the military operations that appeals to us, as the unconscious and therefore free expression these leaders of the Continental army gave to their views and feelings. The campaign of 1777, with its hopes and disappointments, is laid before us with a vividness of detail that no historian could imitate.

In such a wealth of new material it would not be possible to direct attention to the more important pieces. I may, however, be pardoned for believing the record of the Board of War, printed on page 175, to be an important record because of the light it throws upon one of the leading actors in the Conway cabal against Washington.

I wish to express my appreciation of the courteous and untiring assistance rendered by the editors of the *Pennsylvania Magazine of History and Biography* while these sheets were running through that magazine. It is not too much to say that the success of that publication is due to the liberality of the Pennsylvania Historical Society to students of American history, and to the full and accurate knowledge of Pennsylvania history possessed by Mr. Frederick D. Stone and Mr. John W. Jordan, to whom my acknowledgments are specially tendered.

WORTHINGTON CHAUNCEY FORD.

WASHINGTON, D. C., 29th July, 1897.

CONTENTS.

PAGE

Contents. vii

Contents.

Contents.

ON ATTACKING BRITISH IN PHILADELPHIA.

QUESTION OF WINTER QUARTERS.

DEFENCES OF PHILADELPHIA IN 1777.

The following documents form a part of a volume I have for some years intended to complete, a full record of the councils of war held by Washington with his general officers during the Revolution. Such a record would result in many surprises, as the councils were more productive of timidity and caution than of action, and came to be regarded as the easiest method of attaining negative results. Hamilton more than once breaks into indignant speech on the conclusions of the usual council, and in time the instrument was discarded, and the general thrown more upon his own initiative and the advice of a few of his most trusted officers. For action, the advice of many was a hinderance; for information, such advice was of value. It is because the opinions given by the respective officers on the proper defences of Philadelphia belong to the latter that they have an historical as well as a personal value and interest.

On May 31, 1777, Washington wrote to Governor Patrick Henry of the expected sailing of a large fleet of the enemy —estimated at a hundred sail—from New York. What Howe's immediate object was could only be conjectured; but it is believed that he had one of two purposes: either to possess the Hudson River or to attack Philadelphia by way of the Delaware. For either of these operations his command of the sea gave him peculiar advantage, as he could keep Washington in suspense at Middlebrook until his blow in either direction was ready to be struck. On the very day of writing to Governor Henry, Du Coudray, a French officer,

1

came into camp and presented to Washington a contract
signed by Silas Deane, practically giving him a rank above
that of Greene, Sullivan, Knox, and others, and the command of the artillery in the Continental army.   The coincidence is worth noting, as Du Coudray was employed on the
defences of Philadelphia some weeks later.   The situation
early in June is given in the following record:

" At a Council of General Officers held at Head Qᵣ at
Middle Brook, the 12ᵗʰ day of June 1777
   " Present
   " His Excellency, the Commander in Chief

" Majors General	Brigadᵣ
" [Nathaniel] Greene	[William] Maxwell
" Lord Stirling	[Henry] Knox
" [Adam] Stephen	[James M.] Varnum
" [Benjamin] Lincoln	[Anthony] Wayne
	" [Peter] Muhlenberg
	" [George] Weedon
	" [William] Woodford
	" [Charles] Scott
	" [Thomas] Conway.

" His Excellency, the Commander in Chief informed the
Council, that from various intelligence and many concurring
circumstances, it was evident, General Howe had collected
nearly the whole of his Force at Brunswic in Jersey—That
it appeared to him beyond doubt, that General Howe, had
one of two objects in view—either the defeat of the Army
under his immediate command—or to possess himself of
Philadelphia—he stated the importance of the Highland
passes & of the Fortifications on the North River, in & contiguous to the Highlands and then proposed the following
Questions.
   " *Question.* Will it be expedient in the present conjuncture
of things & from the information received, to draw any &
what part of the Troops stationed at Peekskill near the
Highlands, to reinforce this Army?
   " *Answer.* All The Troops should be drawn from Peekskill

to reinforce this Army in Jersey, except one thousand effectives of the Continental Regiments—This Number with the Convalescents & such Militia as are there & can be occasionally drawn in, is esteemed Sufficient to defend the posts there under the present appearances of affairs.

" *Question.* Will it not be necessary to post Troops at Morristown to preserve it, as a post of Communication ?—If it will, what number of men should be stationed there ?

" *Answer.* It will be necessary to maintain that post.—The Detachment of Connecticut Troops under Lieu^t Col^o Butler & the Two Wyoming Independent Companies should be employed in that Service.

" *Question.* What will be the best mode of promotion of Feild & other (inferior) Officers in the Army ?

" *Answer.* All officers below the rank of a Major, should rise regimentally. Officers of that rank superior should be promoted on a larger Scale, Viz on the line of their State. These Rules however, tho they should be observed in general cases, where there lies no objection, should not be established as conclusive, or prevent promotion for particular merit.[1]

" Original Minutes

" ROB. H. HARRISON *Secy.*"

The movement of the fleet, mentioned by Washington to Governor Henry, was premature, and for more than two weeks Howe remained at Brunswick, surprising his opponent by his inactivity, yet developing his plans to attack Philadelphia by water. On the night of June 13 he moved a part of his force to Somerset Court-House, with the object of bringing Washington out of his safe position to a general, engagement. Congress was more affected by Howe's manœuvre than was Washington, and ordered Arnold, then guarding a pass at Coryell's Ferry, to take command of all the militia at Bristol and on every other part of the river to the eastward of Philadelphia. Four days later Howe had

---

[1] See " Washington to the President of Congress," June 20, 1777, in my Writings of Washington, Vol. V. 446.

retired not only from Somerset, but from Brunswick, falling back to Amboy, a step caused, as Washington supposed, by despair at finding the militia of New Jersey and Pennsylvania turning out to oppose them. The mystery of his intention deepened, and greatly perplexed Washington. Burgoyne had appeared on the lake, and so threatened the passes of the Hudson River. Yet the American commander thought this might be only a feint, designed to draw his force to Peekskill, and thus leave Howe a free road to Philadelphia. The activity of the British on Staten Island pointed to a speedy embarkation of a considerable force, but for what purpose could not be ascertained. If it was for the North River, a junction with Burgoyne must be provided against. If it was for Philadelphia, that city must be strengthened. In this doubt, Washington sent a re-enforcement to Peekskill, and moved the main army to Morristown, whence he could the more readily move in either direction as the plan of the enemy was unfolded. Days of anxiety followed, aggravated by the evacuation of Ticonderoga and Mount Independence, under unexpected and suspicious circumstances, by St. Clair.[1] Arnold was ordered to the Northern army, leaving Philadelphia and its defences. "I think," wrote Washington, on July 22, "the works at Billing's-Port well worthy of attention and it is expedient to effect their completion as soon as possible."

At last something definite was obtained in secret intelligence. The sailing of a large fleet to the Hook could be seen; the fact that Southern pilots were on board pointed to Philadelphia as the object. The American army had been edging towards Peekskill, but now moved southward to Ramapaugh. On the 24th the British ships stood out to sea, and the Continental army began a march to Philadelphia. At half-past nine on the morning of July 31, Wash-

---

[1] Landon Carter, of Virginia, on learning of this event, wrote that he never expected much of St. Clair, as he was a Scotchman. The sentence is of interest as pointing to the prejudice among the Virginians against the Scotch, in whose hands the tobacco trade of the colony centred. Glasgow owes much of its importance to this commodity.

ington received an express from Congress announcing the arrival of the fleet at the capes of Delaware, leaving no doubt as to the action to be taken. At ten in the morning Washington and his aides were in Philadelphia and the army close behind him. Going farther to the southward, he was met at Chester by the annoying intelligence of the fleet again leaving the coast, and renewing the suspense. It was in this interval that the general asked for advice on the fortifications of Philadelphia, and received the following replies :

OPINION OF MAJOR-GENERAL GREENE.

[Undated.]

" Philadelphia is an object of such magnitude, the prejudices of the people in the surrounding States so strong, in its favor, as to its importance and consequence, the manufactories and supplies for the army so numerous in that city, that the loss of it would so affect the country and the army that very great injury would arise to the common cause of America. To prevent so great an evil, it is necessary to fix upon some plan to guard the avenues leading to the City both by land and water, and as its security depends upon both being effectually obstructed, it requires a nice examination into the natural strength of each and the force and obstruction necessary for both to be pointed out as far as possible.

" The approaches to the City by land may be made so many different ways, the City so difficult to fortify from its natural situation, that the only security it can have by land is an equal or superior force to that of the enemy. If this be granted as it evidently must, then the plan of fortification upon the river should be so constructed as to draw the least possible force from the land army and render the obstructions on the river so effectual, as to make the approaches that way as difficult or more so than by land. The necessity of dividing your Excellency's attention to both objects is so obvious, and the folly of guarding one of the passages while the other is left open so evident that there need be no arguments to prove howe'er secure the river passage may be rendered, they all must fall of course unless our force proves superior to the enemy in the field.   Having premised these few things, I shall briefly give my opinion respecting the fortification upon the river with some remarks upon strong fortified posts, the influence they have upon the circumjacent country, and the pannick that generally succeeds their loss.

" The Delaware being a long and narrow river, the çhannel crooked and very confin'd, it must be somewhat difficult and not a little dangerous for a large fleet to get up and moor securely in the channel; the fear of the fire ships and fire rafts in such a narrow channel, and quick current, will be consider'd as so many discouraging circumstances to attempt opening a passage to the City.

" There are very different opinions respecting Fort Mifflin; the situation of this fort, as it cannot be injured by regular approaches renders it an object of greater importance and consideration, than a fortification of twice its strength that could be annoy'd by regular approaches; its distance from the Red Bank upon the Jersey shore is such as secures it from any great injury from that quarter; the land upqn Pennsylvania side can be so easily laid under water that it secures the fortress from any approaches from that side; the front is secur'd by three rows of Cheveau de Frize, and it is impossible to approach it in the rear unless the enemy are masters of the river above and the City also.   It appears the fortification is very secure.   The natural make of this Island is not so good as I could wish, neither is the Plan of the Fortification so good as it may be, the plan may be improv'd by an additional battery upon the left of ten or twelve guns, this may be so constructed as to prevent the front Battery being enfiladed and will serve to annoy the enemy if they should attempt to post a ship or floating battery on the left of the Cheveau de Frize to annoy the fort on that quarter.   I should think there ought to be a good enclos'd work to contain from three to five hundred men, and about one hundred and eighty cannoniers.   This is necessary to prevent the fort from being surpriz'd by an attempt with the boats. This fort aided by the Ships, floating batteries, row gallies and fire rafts, I conceive will be full sufficient to secure the passage of the river. Those who profess the greatest knowledge on the strength of the Cheveau de Frize, assert with confidence and I believe with truth, that they cannot be run down by any force; neither can they be rais'd or remov'd from their places, unless two vessels are fastned to each Cheveau de Frize, one on each side, at young flood, and are rais'd by the purchase of the swelling of the water; the fire from the fort, the Ships, Batteries & gallies, must inevitably sink the vessells before they could raise the Cheveau de Frize. But suppose them to be able to resist all this fire; there would be no difficulty in burning the vessels with fire rafts in such a fixt position.

" The xebeques, floating batteries and frigates should be posted behind the upper Cheveau de Frize, because the passage through the Cheveau de Frize must be stop'd to prevent the Enemy from passing. The row gallies as their draft of water is small—may be at liberty to move up and down the river to annoy the enemy as occation may offer.

" The fire ships should be posted in the inner channel from Derby Creek, to Mifflin Fort, they will be secure in this position protected by the row gallies from the Enemys boats from any annoyance of consequence. No ship will dare to approach them in that narrow channel neither will they dare to lay a ship to obstruct the passage out of Derby Creek, for fear of being burnt. These ships must be considered as extra defence; their execution being very uncertain, no dependence should be had upon them for the main defence. The greatest injury I think these ships will be able to do the Enemy is whilst their Ships are below or coming up the river. The only chance of setting the enemys fleet on fire, will be to run the fire ships among them in the night with a good gale and quick tide under foot; favor'd with these circumstances, there is a probability of doing the enemy great injury, provided the person that has the command of the ships behaves with spirit and executes his design with resolution.

" The Commodore and many other Gentlemen, who have
made it their business to examine the River, say the channel
is so narrow that not more than two ships can lye abreast
in it.   If this be a fact, as I have no reason to doubt, from
the concurrent testimony of so many Gentlemen, it will be
impossible for the enemy to bring a greater force up the
river than there is to oppose them.   How they will be able
under these circumstances to remove the obstruction in the
river, when they are constantly annoy'd and threaten'd with
the fire rafts, is difficult for me to conceive.   However it is
proposed in aid to these, to add some fortifications upon the
land, one at Billingsport, one at Red Bank, and one at
Derby's Creek, the situation of all which your Excellency
had an opportunity to see.   I will just examine how far they
will add to the security of the River, and what force it would
take to give this aid, and then see wether the security on
this side, will not diminish the land force to such a degree
as to render the principal object less secure than without
them, not to say any thing about the expence and trouble
attending their construction.

" The plan of the fortification at Billingsport requires four
to five hundred men; Red Bank from two to three, Derby
Creek two hundred and fifty.   Besides these there must not
be less than two hundred cannoniers for the three fortifications; the whole force will amount to upwards of 1200 men,
this is a great dimunition of the land force.   The works at
Billingsport are much superior upon the present plan than
they were upon the former, but I could wish them to be
contracted still if it was possible.   Nay, I could wish them
totally demolished if it was not for the prejudices of the
people, and the reproach it would bring upon administration and the military councils of America.   There have
been prodigious sums of money expended at that place, and
people have been taught to expect great security from its
strength.   To abandon it at this time might alarm their
fears, and give the evil dispos'd a handle to censure the
leaders of the people for subjecting the Continent to such
fruitless and unnecessary expense.   Altho these reasons

urge strongly for holding the work, yet those that offer themselves for abandoning it, operate much more forcibly with me. The situation of Billingsport fortress renders the approaches easy, the enemy can make good their landing a little below the work, the ground is very favorable but a small distance from the fort to open Batteries, the work is not difficult to invest, and once invested it will be difficult if not impossible to keep open such a communication as to take of[f] the Garrison, and it cannot be expected that a garrison without casements, and only constructed to guard against a storm, can stand a regular siege many days, I should suppose not more than three or four at most, when the Cannon and stores, if not the Garrison, will all fall into the enemy's hands. The effect of such an even̈ upon the army and the country, can easily be conceiv'd from the pannick such instances has produc'd. The warmest advocate for this work will readily grant that it cannot resist regular approaches, but must inevitably fall if the enemy seriously invest it. If they do not invest it, the force of the Garrison is lost by being Idle; if they do invest it, the Garrison must fall. This being granted, then the only advantage that can result from this work is the delay it will cause to the enemy, which not exceeding four or five days cannot warrant the expence, and trouble, in constructing such an extensive work; neither will it be an equivalent for the deduction of force, that it necessarily produces from the army.

"The fort at Red Bank may be considered much upon the same footing with that of Billingsport; only less useful and more unnecessary. There runs a creek into the country between Red Bank and Billingsport, eight or ten miles, which is now partly banked out. This being open, the enemy can have no communication with Red Bank without a march of eighteen or twenty miles. If they have a mind to seriously invest this fort, it must fall in the same manner as Billingsport. If there is no work there, they cannot take possession of the ground, but with a very considerable part of their army without laying it liable to be cut off.

"In lieu of these inclos'd works, and strong fortifications,

I would propose having a number of half moon Batteries thrown up, at such places where the ships can come to annoy the shipping &c, appointed for the defence of the Cheveau de Frize; a few eighteen pounders on travelling carriages, to move from place to place, will more effectually annoy the enemy than fixt Batteries. A very inconsiderable force will execute this business. If there are no inclos'd works on the Jersey shore, the Enemy can make no lodgements without a considerable force, which will oblige them to divide their army. If the shores are defended in the manner I propose the parties may be diminish'd or increas'd as circumstances may render necessary.

" If the enemy operates seriously on the Jersey shore, the forts and fortifications must inevitably fall. If they do not, the men appointed to garrison those works will be Idle and useless. That take it in either point of view, those fortifications are unnecessary, and will be a burden upon the state without affording any additional security to the city.

" The fortification of Derby Creek cannot be more useful than the other two. Its situation is upon an Island, and when the land is laid under water to secure fort Mifflin from approaches, this Garrison will have no opportunity to retreat; especially if the enemy takes possession of the Bridge leading to the Chester road. A few troops at this place will prevent any aid coming to the assistance of the Garrison. This garrison, if invested, must fall in the same manner as the others. If there are only a few Half moon Batteries, form'd with a couple of eighteen pounders on travelling carriages, they will afford all the protection and security to the fire ships that a regular fortification will : they will prevent a ship's laying at the mouth of the creek, or in the back channel. This is all that can be expected from a regular work properly garrison'd. It is most probable the enemy will attempt to burn the fire ships with their boats; the Gallies must protect them, and I have no doubt will. They will be able to protect themselves from any other mode of attack.

" All fortifications in America, except for the security of

particular objects, considering the nature of the country are rather prejudicial than useful : the country is taught to expect security, and always loose their confidence upon any unfortunate event. The enemy getting possession of our works, they serve them for strongholds to keep in awe all the circumjacent country—By the assistance of our garrisons, the enemy is enabled to keep a much greater extent of country in subjection. If they had no Garrisons to protect their troops, they would be oblig'd to keep their forces more together. If they were to attempt to erect those works themselves it must necessarily fatigue their troops and delay their operations. The country cannot be conquer'd and held in subjection but by garrisons; it should be our policy, therefore, to have as few as may be. The enemy gains little or no advantage by marching through the country; the inhabitants from their cruelties and abuses, generally grow more obstinate and confirm'd in opposition.

" If we build strong fortifications, the continent must be subject to great expence to support the garrison, besides that of erecting and furnishing the fortress with cannon, military stores, &c. These garrisons only serve to secure a small part of the country, which security is purchas'd by a prodigious drain of men and materials from the army. I could wish that only a few principal passes and capital citys, should have any fortifications about them. The security of the country must depend upon our superiority in the field ; if our force is divided and appointed to the defence of particular places, the enemy will be masters of the field, and the country loose their confidence in the army : and notwithstanding the Garrisons at particular places may delay the enemys operations a little, these advantages are far overballanc'd by the pannick their loss generally strikes upon the country, and the advantage they give to the enemy to hold the circumjacent country in subjection.

" There is one strong reason why the fortifications should not be multiplied upon the Delaware ; there is not a sufficiency of cannon to put in the works, without taking from the fortifications, or the naval department ; and they cannot be spair'd from these without weakening what I esteem the principal security.

" Upon the whole I would trust the security of the River to the Cheveau de Frizes, protected and defended by fort Mifflin, the shiping, and fire rafts. The channel is so narrow, and the difficulty of removing the Cheveau de Frize so great, that there is very little danger of the enemys opening themselves a passage.

" In drawing up my opinion, its bulk is swell'd much beyond the size I intended, and the fear of enlarging the plan has induc'd me to omit many observations that were necessary as explitives to several propositions.

" NATH. GREENE.
" HIS EXCELLENCY GENERAL WASHINGTON."

A DEFINITIVE PROJECT UPON THE DEFENCE OF PHILADELPHIA IN THE PRESENT STATE OF AFFAIRS, BY DU COUDRAY.

" In the account which I have given the Honorable Congress of the state in which fort Mifflin, Redbank, and billing's port, were, the first of August, I think I have Demonstrated, that in the actual situation of things, Litle Dependance should be had on this fort, to Defend both the places, where the River is crossed by the chevaux de frize ; and that the gallies, fire-ships, and floating batteries, were the only means in which any Confidence could be placed.

" At present, here is question to Determine the best scene of position, and the best use of the Defensive expediens, pursuent to the Litle Defense that the forts furnish them.

" The two floating Batteries are at present, behind the Iland which is opposite to Billing's port. I aprove of their position in this place, because these Iland being very low and narrow, these batteries will be able to produce above it, a formidable fire against the fregates, which may present themselves, to attack the Line of the chevaux de frize, opposite to Billing's port. these batteries consisting, the one of nine, and the other, of ten pieces of 18, which appeared to me very good, and in a very good Condition in every Respect, can Certainly Defend this passage Long enough, if, as the commodore asserts, three fregates, at most, can present themselves, at the same time. Being well managed they may Defend themselves, even almost infaillibly untill the enemy repells them from this position; this the enemy cannot Do, neither by sending fregates in the chanel where they are, this chanel being not deep enough; nor Raising batteries upon the bank on the Right Side, which may be easily covered with water, as the Commodore asserts; But by making themselves masters of the eminence at billing's port, from whence they may burn or Remove them : it is the necessity of hindering, or at least, of Retarding the position of the enemy upon this eminence, to accomplish the forementioned Designe, which Renders absolutely necessary to Continue constructing this fort.

" If, I had been informed sooner of the strengt of the suport, which it is to Receive from the two floating batteries, to Defend the chevaux de frize, and of the small number of fregates, which can appear together in the chanel where the chevaux de frize are ; I should have Contracted the extend of this fort, at least on the River side; But the map which I Require for that purpose in my first visit, could not then be found; and I ask'd for it several times since, to no purpose. I shal profit, at least, by these new informations, of which the Commodore alone can warant the Certainty, to Diminish the number of Embrasures, and to Leave, at the forts of Miflin and Redbank, a part of the Cannon, which beling's port alone should have necessarily exhausted.

" The gallies and fire ships are at present at the mouth of Derby-creek, below, and in the same chanel, with the floating batteries; a chanel in which the Commodore affirms, as I have already said, that the fregates can not ascend. I aprove also of their position. As those gallies carry, some of them, cannon of 24 ; others, cannon of 18 ; and as, by their Construction, they present very Litle appearance to the fregates, who offer them a very Large one ; and the greatest

size of the cannon of the fregates being generaly only of
12, the gallies will be necessarily superior to them; since
according to the Commodore, they can not be attack, but
by two or three frigates at most, even in Coming out of this
chanel to Conduct the fire ships.

" But to protect their Retreat, and especially to hinder the
enemy from taking possession of the ground which Commands this position, and which, (as it is impossible to have
it covered with water, as well as the upper and Lower parts)
suplys them with the proper place to fix a battery, which
may Repell the gallies and fire ships: it would be necessary
to erect a battery there of 8 or 10 Large pieces, at least, defended by the gorge, so as to protect it, against the attack
by Land, which the enemy if they have any foresight, cannot avoid making to free themselves from the inquietude, in
which they must be Lest the gallies and fire ships may take
unawares the fregates, which may be embarrast in the channel of navigation, and which, being stoped by the chevaux
de frize, would scape with difficulty the effect of the fire
ships.

" Instead of a well supplied and protected battery, as I have
mentioned, his Excellency has seen that this which exist at
present in this place, has only one serviceable Cannon; that
the parapet of this battery, and particularly the defence of
its gorge, are in the worst situation; so that, if it be attacked
by Landing boats, it must unavoidably be overcome: unless
there be a Considerable body to Defend it.

" The time is perhaps too urgent, and the means too weak
to Repare, at present, the Capital fault that had been Com-
mited in neglecting a place so favourable, to the attack of
the fire ships, upon the enemy, which Renders it almost as
important as billing's port. thus, as soon as the enemy shall
take possession of the place occupied by these bad battery,
which must be keep only as a shew, the gallies and fire ships
will be obliged to Retreat, at least, to the place of the same
channel where the floating batteries are, and where, as the
Commodore says the fregates cannot follow them. they will
not be useless there; they will help the batteries in support-

ing the chevaux de frize, at billing's port; which will be accomplish then, with an assured superiority, untill the enemy establishes batteries, upon this eminence.

" For the want of a well made draught, which we allways have need off, and which I have not been able to suply, on account of the late arrival of the engeneers, who attend me; as well as the perpetual undetermination in which, both they and I, have Lived and continue to Live in every Respect; such are the sentimens, that the instructions received from commodore, permit me to propose relatively to the defence of the first Line of the chevaux de frize, with the gallies, fire ships, and floating batteries.

" I conclude then, that if the precautions be taken to sink only 8 or 9 new chevaux de frize, between and behind the in-tervalls of the first Line; which as the Commodore asserts, are preposterously thirty feet from one another, and Leaves cer-tainly an opening by which the small fregates may profit; this first Line will be easily defended, at least some days; even, in the bad state, in which the Land fortifications are; either through the neglect of administration; or the con-tracted understanding of the persons, who have been charged to fortify the batteries of belling's port, and Derby's Creek, which after the new Details I have just made are indispensa-bly necessary in both places.

" From the fast Line I pass now to the second, Reliyng allways, instead of a sure draught, upon the informations formerly and Lately furnished by the commodore.

" This second Line is formed according to him, by the Rows of chevaux de frize; the first of which is 920 yards Be-fore the point of fort mifflin, and supported, in one side, by hog iland, and in the other, by the bank which begins in that place, and take his Direction towards Red bank, where he joignes the Land, without allowing the passage to the fregates; tho' it allowes them to advance, enough to cross the batteries of mifflin fort.

" If this be the only passage; if only three fregates can attack it in front, by Directing their Course towards Red bank, to cross the batteries, as I have forementioned; the gallies and floating batteries, will be certainly sufficient to protect them.

" The most advantageous position, which they can be placed for that purpose, will be to continue keeping them in the channel where the enemy cannot come at them on account of the shallow water, and make them flank the chevaux de frize.

" Thirteen gallies, which present the prow only, will have with their Large Cannon of 24 or 18, as I have forementioned, sure superiority over three, and even six fregates if this Cannon be well managed.

" But hog's iland behind which the gallies should be placed to enjoy these Desirable position, is unhappily wider, and more elevated than that which is opposite to billing's port ; behind which the batteries are at present, and where I said they should be left, and the gallies should be carried, when the enemy, by making themselves master of Derby creek, might have obliged the gallies to abandon these position.

" If this elevation and breadth of hog's iland are too extensive to hinder the effect of the fire, they must be carried between fort mifflin and the buoys, so as not to hinder the playing of the battery of this fort, which, however ill-situated and constructed, as his excellency has seen, may notwithstanding be of some utility, even at the great Distance where it is ; specialy if there be time enough, to make the changes and suitables Reparations, in order to place there seven or eight Large pieces in capacity of playing and being defended.

" The fort where this battery lies is very bad, being inclosed, only on two fronts, by one palisade with bad loop holes, and very ill flancked ; but as the enemy can Land there, only with chaloupes, it may Resist Long time, even in this weak situation, with six or seven hundred men to gard it ; specialy if the army was not far off. but this must not be Depended upon ; as the enemy may make a march towards the north, and be more active in their movemens than they have been hitherto.

" The fort of billing's port, when it is finished, can alone
assure by a defense of fifteen days the time necessary for
the army to arrive to protect this second Line.

" The possession which the enemy might take of Red
bank, and which they will probably do, will not be of great
advantage to them ; Considering his great Distance to Repell
the gallies and floating batteries, from this two forementioned
positions ; specialy if the first may be occupied. Besides
as the fort constructed upon this eminence, can be put in a
State of Defence in that short time, and with a few men, by
contracting it, as I have proposed to his Excellency, it will
be an additional obstacle to stop the enemy.

" It Results from the premises,

" 1st That I persist in thinking that the most suitable place
to be Defended is billings port; on account of the narrowness of the River there; of the facility with which the
floating batteries can support the chevaux de frize, by remaining behind the opposite iland; of the necessity in
which the enemy will be to take possession of the eminence
of Derby's creek, to defend themselves against the fire ships,
which they will be allwais afraid to see arrive behind the
fregates, stoped before the chevaux de frize in the channel
of navigation ; and in short, of the necessity in which they
will be of making themselves masters of the eminence at
belling's port, to drive away the floating batteries from this
position, where the gallies may come to Reinforce them ;
when by their taking possession of Derby's creek they shall
have obliged them to abandon this post.

" 2^{ond} that it is chiefly to put this post speedily in a state
of defence, that we must employ the means, which we have,
which are too few to be divided between fort mifflin and Red
bank, without being exposed to the inconveniency of making
a bad defence in both post; instead of making a good one,
in a single place, as I have Declared in the first memorial I
have given on this object.

" 3° That matters being not in this situation, thro' the fault
of the administration alone, it is necessary to procure some
Remedy for the present weakness of the first Line, by putting

ourselves in state of protecting the second, and of giving thereby time to the army to arrive.

" I offer to continue in this Respect my care and that of the commissioned and non-commissioned officers, who attend me; but if his excellency intends that these care should not be useless, and that an invincible disgust should not succeed the most ardent zeal, it is absolutely necessary to cause change in the conduct, which has been observed hitherto, and to accellerate the slowness of the civil and military administration, to wich the Congress adressed us, to procure the means of execution.

" It is necessary, to accomplish the forementioned objects, that the honourable Congress himself order without delay.

" 1st thousand *effective* workmen every day, for billing's port, who are to work on holy days, and sundays, under the proper direction of the engeneers whom I have there.

" 2ond the necessary tools, as well as for these workmen, as for my artillery workmen, whom I shall employ to construct the batteries, and to repare the carriages intended either for this, or mifflin fort, in the actual circumstances; those that I keep at billing's port and here, for this purpose, having not yet been able, in spite of my Repeated solicitations, to obtain, this month past, neither all the tools they want, nor even clothes.

" 3° 200 others workmen every day at fort miflin and hundred at Red bank, under the same Conditions, with the former.

" Provided this Request be granted, I engage to put these three places in a state of defence in the course of this month: viz. to be Defended, Billing's port, with 400 men and 80 canoniers;—fort miffling with 600 and 500 canoniers; Red bank with 200 men and 20 canoniers.

" During the same time I shall employ the Rest of my engeneers to execute, suitably to the examination of the five places of incampement to be taken between markus' hook and Philadelphia, the project declared in the memorial adressed to the honourable congress, and communicate the day before yesterday, to his excellency, who honoured it with his approbation.

" I ask for these engeneers no other assistance, besides the horses, and a man to serve them and carry their instruments.

" As to the batteries so necessaries for the support of the gallies and fire ships which are necessary to hold at Derby creek, for reasons which have been given above, it is to be wished that means could be furnished at the same time with that of billing's port; particularly from the informations given by the Commodore, that there may be furnished from the province frigate fifteen nine pounders, and six of twelf from Captain Reed's[1] schooner; which vessels are not in a state of defense, for want of men.

" Upon this subject I make the most pressing sollicitations, and more so, if conjectures permitted his excellency to believe that the enemy will leave us time to finish billing's port, I should beg to employ for the Construction of this battery the labourers, that I have demanded to put fort mifflin and Red bank in a state to supply the present weakness of the first line of chevaux de frize, by supporting the second.

" Du Coudray.

" Philadelphia the 6 august, 1777."

MAJOR-GENERAL ANTHONY WAYNE.

" Gen[1] Wayne's Opinion of the Defences necessary for the River and Land in case the Enemy should attempt the Reduction of Phil[a].

" The Works as *Contracted* by Gen[1]. De Coudre to be compleated and supplied with six or eight pieces of artillery, and men sufficient to fight them with about 500 Troops. One Redoubt on the High Ground at Darby Creek, sufficient to contain 200 men. The fleet, fire ships & Rafts to lay abreast and across the western channel, to act in Conjunction with the Batteries so long as it is practicable or prudent to maintain them, boats to be kept in Readiness to carry off the Troops in case of a misfortune.

---

[1] Captain Thomas Read, who was the first to enjoy the title of commodore in the provincial navy of Pennsylvania. He resigned to enter the Continental service.

" If its found necessary to avacuate these posts, the Fleet and fire [ships] to Retire Immediately to Fort Island—or act in the Rear of the Enemy Occationally.

" It will be absolutely necessary to throw a Good Garrison into the old Fort under the Command of proper officers with a proportionable number of men from the Corps of Artillery to the Guns therein mounted. Red Bank being a post of Consequence, as it over looks and enfilades the old Fort and vessels, it will be proper to Enclose the two Bastions, and place therein 4 or 500 men, which with the assistance of the militia of New Jersey in the vicinity thereof (after cutting away the Banks, Dams and Bridges over the Creeks) will greatly retard, if not totally prevent the Enemy from penetrating that way.

" Whilst this is doing, the Banks, dams, Bridges and Roads on the west side of the Delaware ought to be broke up from Marcus Hook to Phil*, for which purpose a judicious and Determined officer with a sufficient number of men and tools ought to be on the spot ready to execute this business at a signal being given.

" The army should be stationed near Marcus Hook in order to oppose the Enemy should they attempt to move from under Cover of their shiping,—or in case they should proceed further up to the land, to be ready to move with them, taking advantage of such Strong Grounds and Marshes as present themselves in the way.

" As much will depend on the Mode and Manner of the Enemies Movements, the subject admits of nothing further than General heads, and as such they are presented by

" ANT^r WAYNE.

" PHILA. 7th August, 1777."

FROM JOSEPH REED.

" DEAR SIR

" I shall make no apology for troubling you with the following Hints, because I well know that the Goodness, and I may truly add the greatness of your mind would induce you to listen with Patience and even cheerfulness to the suggestions of the meanest soldier if properly presented.

" Whether Philadelphia is the present object of attack is yet a Question, and every one reasons upon it as his Fears, Hopes and Interest dictate. That the acquisition would give eclat to their arms as subduing another of the capital cities, the seat of the Congress, and in no small Degree the principal Magazine of all supplies—that it has been held forth in Europe as the next Object of their Pursuit, are as certain Truths as that one half of the summer has been lost in a fruitless Attempt by Land. Add to this that no military History can shew an Instance of a Feint or Diversion made with the Partys whole Force and especially subject to the Chances of Wind and Weather, and the Certainty of sickness and mortality arising from crowding Troops on board vessels in a hot season. When these Things are considered one would be led to decide without Hesitation that this is their Object. On the other Hand the obvious Advantages arising from a Junction with their Northern Army, the apparent if not real separation of the Northern and Southern States by the Possession of Hudson's River, and the great Accession of strength from the disaffected Counties of New York, seem to be equivalent to their Prospects of Philadelphia. However, as your army is now here and the excessive Heat of the Weather requires their having as much Rest as possible, Prudence and Judgment seem to require that the same Disposition should be made at present and the system of Defence formed as if their Designs upon the City were out of all Doubt.—The successful Defence of Philadel* will comprehend not only the Preservation of the City, but a Disappointment of the Campaign, and in this view our Exertions cannot be too great or our Preparations too early. And as much may depend upon the arrangement, I have ventured to submit to your Excell* a few sentiments which I have formed upon a view of our several Defences, Conversation with others both of the Land and River Departments.

" However the different Defences of the River as depending both on the Forts, Gallies and floating Batteries may be blended as forming one grand Plan with the Defence made

by the Army, it may be necessary to distinguish them in
Council least the Variety of Objects should confuse and dis-
tract.   Tho nothing seems to be more certain than that Failure in the Land Defence will be followed by that of the River
and so vice versa.—I will begin with that of the Army.

"From the conduct of the Enemy last Campaign and the
certain Consequences that would follow if it should succeed,
I think it very probable that if the River Defence should be
as formidable as I trust it will, Mr. Howe will depend more
upon his operations by Land than Water and if his Landing is safely effected will endeavor by a circuitous March to
get into our Rear.   It seems necessary therefore to take
such a Position as to prevent this, and yet at the same Time
so far advanced as to make his march as tedious as possible,
and thereby ensure as many Opportunities to check his Advances as the Distance of Ground and Frequency of advantageous Passes will admit—Some are of Opinion that at all
Events opposition should be made at their Landing and
there is no Doubt but the Landing of Troops in the Face of
an Enemy is one of the most dangerous Manœuvres in War
—but in our Case the Smoothness of the Water, the Flat-
ness of the Ground and the heavy Fire which the Enemy
can bring to cover their operations seem almost to exclude
any Prospect of success.   To throw up Lines for this Purpose seems also out of the Question from the Extent of
Ground on which they may land to advantage.   I have
never heard two Opinions with Respect to the Place of
Landing every one without the least Hesitation has fixed it
at Marcus Hook, or its Vicinity, tho they will have fast (?)
Land between that and Wilmington in spots.   I can hardly
suppose they will go lower, as they will have Christine
River (near as wide as the Delaware at Trenton) to encounter, and the high Grounds of Wilmington possessed by our
Troops would give us a very advantageous Position.   If the
advancing our Troops below Marcus Hook or to it, would
throw the Landing below Wilmington, it would be a very
happy Circumstance, but the Risque of their passing them
and landing seems too great, and the Consequences of it

would be fatal if the Enemy should by that means get between Philadelphia and our army: I have sometimes thought of a middle course viz. To take a strong Position such as that between Ridly and Crum Creeks to make a shew of Troops as far down as that they could make an Appearance to the Enemy, to deter their Landing but not farther than to be able to retire without Confusion to the East side of Chester Creek and so up to the Main Post if it should be necessary.

" Some have thought of the Enemy's landing on the Jersey shore and in the survey now making for your Excellency agreeable to what I mentioned at Head Quarters, that shore will be included, but no Person acquainted with that Ground will countenance an Idea of their Landing there with a view of marching up. The number of Creeks, Marshes and Causeways must deter them, besides that if all these Obstacles are surmounted the Delaware is still between them and their Object—The Landing between Chester and Philadelphia, or at Chester, seems to be very improbable. As to the first it is all Marsh or bank'd Meadow except in one or two Places from which they must come thro such Ground. It is extremely unhealthy and may be laid under Water for several Miles. At Chester there are but 3 or 4 wharves and they are accessible for landing Troops only at High Water and near it, so that a Landing there must be tedious and difficult. All these Circumstances seem to decide clearly that no Landing will be made nearer the City than Marcus Hook.—If the Militia should be called out, and have no Tents, which seems but too likely, they will probably be placed in Chester. In this case it will, I imagine, be necessary that some Troops should be advanced beyond them as they will hardly have Confidence enough to oppose the first advances of the Enemy—and a precipitate hasty Retreat or Flight would have a very bad Effect on the other Part of the Army.

" The Position between Crum and Ridly Creek will be very advantageous on one account—there will be but one Flank to guard, the River and Marsh effectually securing

the other—and tho it will not be so convenient to Fort
Island as the High Grounds near Darby, yet if the Post is
maintained at the mouth of Darby Creek, the Communication with the whole of the River Defence will I believe be
found full as easy from the one as the other.   I would also
beg Leave to suggest another Reason for preparing the Post
between the two Creeks to Darby—that if any Accident
should happen at the latter to make it necessary to retire
over Schuylkill, the Distance is so small that the Troops
would probably croud upon one another in Confusion at
the Passage of the River—whereas if they should be obliged
to retire from the other, the high Ground at Darby would
be very advantageous to check the advances of the Enemy,
while the Van of our Army were crossing, and if necessary
in this Case a Part must be sacrificed for the Safety of the
whole—rather than the Enemy should avail himself of our
Bridges.   Here I would remark to your Excell' that I think
if another Bridge of Boats could be thrown over Schuylkill
at the lower Ferry, it would greatly Facilitate the Communication of the Army with the City—and in Case of Retreat
I fear our Bridge would be found very insufficient for the
Troops, Artillery and Baggage.

"I have heard some Persons mention that in Case our
Army should be obliged to retire either on Account of a
superiority of numbers or any Disaster, they might do it on
the west side of Schuylkill and so cross the River above
the Falls—but the Country is exceedingly hilly, the Banks
of the River on both sides very steep, and if there should
be any heavy Rains, the Fords would not be passable—so
that I am perswaded if our Army should be obliged to give
Ground, there is no Rout so easy and advantageous as that
across the Schuylkill near the City, provided the Means of
crossing the River are seasonably attended to.

"With respect to the river defense it may be properly
divided into three parts.

"First. The Fire Vessels; secondly, the Gallies and floating Batteries; thirdly, the Posts & Forts at Darby Creek
Mouth, at Billings Port, at Fort Island & Red Bank.

" As to the First. The effect is very great when successful, but it is very uncertain; in almost every siege of mari-
time Places they have been attempted and generally failed.
Such desperate Courage is required, so many Circumstances
of Wind & Tide must concur as to make every thinking
Person cautious how he depends too much upon them.
But as great preparation is made in this Way, & the Persons concerned are very sanguine, perhaps it will be best to
run a Risque of some of the Vessels to cover them while
the attempt is made. But to ensure as far as possible the
success, I humbly apprehend it would be best for those who
are to execute it to have the sole management and Direction both as to Time & Place. It is so detached a Business
from the other, that I think it may safely be left to themselves; it is much to be feared that if they receive Orders
from the Land Officers they will not act with the same Confidence; as in Case of Failure they will have Shelter from
the Claims & Censure of the publick. There are some Vessels which move well, that I understand can be spared for
the Purpose of assisting in this Enterprize & that without
weakning the Capital Defence too much. The Effect will
be so great, if the Fire takes Place, as would seem very
well to warrant exposing them to some Danger in order to
give the Operation a fair Tryal.

" As to the Gallies & floating Batteries, they are so unwieldy & move so slow that Prudence will not warrant their
being placed but in that spot where the great Defence is to
be made, viz, at the Chevaux de frize. There are, I believe,
some Difficulties with Respect to Rank & Command. It is
much to be wished they were removed before the Enemy
approaches.

" The utility of all the shipping of every species will depend so much upon their being protected from the Shore
that I am persuaded this Circumstance will claim much of
your Excell⁷ˢ Attention.

" First. As to the Fort at the Mouth of Darby Creek.
This Work it seems was constructed for the purpose of shel-
tring such Vessels as should have occasion to retire thro'

the shallow channel which runs on the west side of the River between the main Land & an Island. It was done on the Importunity of the Captains of the Vessels, & they seem to place great Confidence in it. In this view, rather than from any Advantage they can perceive, I find many Gentlemen acquiesce in retaining it; but all agree that it ought to be made more respectable than it is at present. I do not pretend to any knowledge in the Science of Engineering, so that I do not presume to trouble your Excellency with any Opinion as to the mode of construction, or what Alterations should be made so as to give it value.

"Secondly. As to Billings Port. A Fatality has attended it from the Beginning, so that perhaps it would have been better to have been left in a State of Nature than to have it in the Condition it is, or probably will be, if the Enemy should advance. However, it is a Post. Obstructions in the River have been sunk—To abandon it totally would be losing the Benefit of what has been done, would discourage the Captains & Seamen who are to defend the River & have been taught to depend upon some Protection from it. The Enemy would probably take a Possession to swell the List of Conquests & might perhaps annoy, tho' I think not materially the Gallies & Vessels defending the upper Cheveaux de frize. Upon these Accounts, I fear the abandoning it would have bad Effects. But it would be equally against my Judgment to weaken the Army by putting a large Garrison of Continental Troops in it. For should the Enemy resolve not to pass it by, it seems too accessible in the Rear to promise much success in the Defence of it. I would therefore suggest the finishing it upon a smaller scale than has been proposed, to mount a few Guns put in such a Number of Artillery Men as would be wanted to work them—a small Detachment of Continental Troops, say 2 or 300, under a good Officer—add to these so many Jersey Militia as would completely man the Work—at the same Time they might be provided at the Water Side with the Means of Retreat whenever the Enemy's approach on the Land Side should indicate its being no longer tenable. This seems to be a mean, between abandoning & risquing too much in its Defence. If the Enemy resolve to approach by Water, this Post must be taken, or it will embarrass them; they must land a considerable Force under many unpleasant Circumstances, the Remainder in the mean Time laying on board the Fleet, or divided on different sides of the River which must be dangerous. If, on the other Hand, the great Push is made on the Land, & the Water operations are to be subservient to it, nothing is lost but the Service of those Artillery Men & that Detachment. The Militia are upon their own Guard & probably would not compose a Part of the Army in Pennsylvania, if they were not at Billingsport. The Pennsylvania Militia would serve with more alacrity & effect on this side the River than the other, tho' they are now really defending their own City.

" As to Red bank. I have never heard any other Reason assigned for making it a Post than to keep it out of the Hands of the Enemy who might otherwise annoy the Garrison at Fort Island. But when it is considered that Red bank is 1900 yards from Fort Island, that tho' it is higher it is not a very commanding situation; that it is yet unfinished; that if the Enemy are resolved to have it, it is accessible on the land; that it will weaken our Force still farther to garrison it; that some other Post must be stripp'd to provide Guns for it; I say, all these Things considered, it should seem very questionable whether it is worth retaining in the mode proposed by some Gentlemen.

" As to Fort Island. I cannot but say I feel a particular Pleasure in learning that the Idea of abandoning it, breaking up the Platforms & removing the Guns is exploded. I do not know but some Improvements may be made there, some Gentlemen are very clear in the Necessity of them. From all the Conversation I have had with the officers on the River, I am perswaded much will depend upon the Defence made at this Fort. It is secured fully in the Rear—it has Barracks for the accommodation of the Troops—Magazines for the safety of the ammunition—commands the obstructions in the River, and while defended, it will have intercourse with the city for all kinds of supplies. If it should be necessary the surrounding Land can all be laid under Water. In short, I scarcely know a Circumstance attending it which an officer would wish to have altered or added, unless it be to raise it higher above the water. I cannot but therefore repeat it to your Excell[y] that in my poor Opinion the Preservation of the City on that side will intirely depend upon the good management of this Post & a correspondent Behavior in the Gallies. Nor does it appear to me that a very great Number of Men will be required for its Defence. It cannot be stormed but from Boats landing in mud up to the waists of the men, or from keys which are few and easily defended. I should think it might hold out till it was battered down by shipping, an Event not much to be feared, as this Post will not be exposed till Billings Port is relinquished. The Garrison retiring from thence will make a handsome Reinforcement to that of Fort Island if they do not bring any Pannick with them.

"Before I conclude I would observe to your Excellency that I believe some Hint from you to Congress or the Executive Council of the State will be necessary, in order to effect a timely Removal of the great Quantity of Stock from the River side, and the necessary Preparations made to overflow the Land adjoining the Rivers Delaware and Schuylkill if necessary—or it may happen here as elsewhere that these essential steps may be deferr'd till it is too late.

"Thus I have ventured to throw together a few indigested Thoughts. I shall be happy if they are of any Use to your Excell[y]—if they are not, I am sure you will excuse it as they proceed from the same sincere Attachment to your Person and Fame which your Friendship and Favor must necessarily create in a Mind of any Sensibility. I am
"Dear Sir,
"most truly & affectionately
"yours
"J. REED.

"PHILAD. Aug[t] 7. 1777."

FROM BRIGADIER-GENERAL KNOX.

" It is the opinion of the subscriber that the Battery on Fort Island ought to have an additional work thrown up upon its left, and Garrison'd with 12 pieces heavy cannon, 150 cannoniers, and half as many assistants, with 500 Infantry.

" Red Bank is to be contracted so as to have 5 or 6 cannon on the land side, and as many heavy towards the river; to prevent any ships coming up the channel leading to it, in order to flank the Gallies which may be station'd for the defence of the Cheveaux de Frize near the Fort.

" Billingsport to be finish'd as at present contracted, or if possible more so; so as to hold 300 men exclusive of 150 cannoniers and 75 assistants, to work 12 pieces heavy cannon which ought to be in this work.

" The Gallies to lye opposite to it at the break of the low Island, in order to assist the fire of Billingsport: these Gallies would be for this purpose preferable to the floating Batteries, as they can be most easily remov'd in case of an accident to Billingsport.

" If much depends on the fire ships an inclosed Battery ought to be constructed on some advantageous piece of ground near Derbys Creek, and something higher up the river than where the present defective Battery is; this in order to prevent any of the enemy's ships mooring at the mouth of the western channel; so to hinder the fire ships sent round into the main ship channel. The western channel is thought to be most commodious for the free operation of the fire ships either in the Channel leading to Billingsport or further down the river; the Gallies ought also to lye in the western channel if their retreat is perfectly secure; as the Commodore says; as well in order to protect the fire ships, as to annoy any of the enemy's Frigates which may be opposed to Billingsport; but the two floating Batteries which from their unwieldiness, cannot be easily mov'd together with the Frigates and Xebecques, ought to lye behind the second row of Chevaux de Frize, upon a line with Fort Island.

" If there should be time enough, a strong enclos'd work ought to be thrown up on fort Island, capable of containing 4 or 500 men ; an advantage may be taken of part of the stone work already erected,. and which in its present state would be infinitely detremental to any body of men who may seek shelter from it.

" These sentiments are respectfully submitted by Sir Y^r most obt Hble Servt

" HENRY KNOX

" *Brig^r Genl Artillery.*

" CAMP SANDY RUN, 9th Augt. 1777."

WASHINGTON TO THE PRESIDENT OF CONGRESS.

" HEADQUARTERS, CAMP, NEAR GERMAN TOWN,

" Aug [9], 1777.

" SIR :

" The disappearance of the enemy's fleet for so many days rendering it rather improbable, that they will again return, I have thought it adviseable to remove the army back to Coryell's where it will be near enough to succor Philadelphia, should the enemy contrary to appearances still make that the object of their next operations, and will be so much the more conveniently situated to proceed to the Northward, should the event of the present ambiguous and perplexing situation of things call them that way. I was the more inclined to this step, as the nearness of the army to the city, beside other disadvantages, afforded a temptation both to officers and men to indulge themselves in licenses inconsistent with discipline and order, and consequently of a very injurious tendency.[1]

" But before my departure, I esteem it my duty to communicate to Congress the result of my examination into

[1] " You will take every possible care in your power, as well in your march as during your stay at that place [Maidenhead], to restrain every species of licentiousness in the soldiery, and to prevent them doing the least injury to the inhabitants or their property, as nothing can be more disserviseable to our cause, or more unworthy of the characters we profess—to say nothing of the injustice of the measure."— *Washington to Colonel Morgan,* August 9, 1777.

the nature of the River defence proper to be adopted according to the means in our possession, to prevent the success of any attempt upon Philadelphia by water.—I therefore beg leave to lay before Congress what appears to me most eligible, considering all circumstances, and comparing my own observations, with the different opinions of the Gentlemen, whom I consulted on the occasion.

" It is generally a well founded maxim, that we ought to endeavor to reduce our defence as much as possible to a certainty, by collecting our strength and making all our preparations at one point, rather than to risk its being weak and ineffectual every where, by dividing our attention and force to different objects. In doing this, we may disable ourselves from acting with sufficient vigor any where, and a misfortune in one place may pave the way for a similar one in another. In our circumstances, we have neither men, cannon, nor any thing else to spare, and perhaps cannot with propriety hazard them on objects which being attended with the greatest success we can promise ourselves, can be productive of only partial and indicisive advantages, and which may possibly fail of the end proposed, may have some serious ill-consequences, and must at all events have some disadvantages.

" It is then to be considered, where our defence can be most effectually made,—whether at Billingsport, or at Fort Island.

" It appears to me, that the last deserves greatly the preference. Billingsport has but one row of Chevaux de frize, Fort Island has three; and in addition to them, a boom and another Chevaux de frize, ready to be sunk in the channel, on the approach of the enemy; of course the obstructions in this respect are four times as great at the one as at the other. The Gallies and floating batteries, that could be brought for the defence of the chevaux de frize at Billingsport, would be unable to maintain their station, when once the enemy were in possession of the commanding ground on the Jersey side, to which they would be entirely exposed, and notwithstanding the works raising there, even supposing them complete, the strongest advocates for making our defence in this place do not pretend, that that event can be protracted more than fifteen or twenty days at most, at the end of which time, we should be obliged with the loss of our cannon at least to abandon the defence, and leave it in the power of the enemy to remove or destroy the chevaux de frize at pleasure. Nor is it by any means certain that a single row of chevaux de frize would be an impenetrable barrier to the enemy's ships. Experiments have been made that lead to a contrary supposition, and if they should hazard one, which it might be well worth their while to do, with some of their less valuable ships, under favor of a leading breeze and tide, and should succeed in it,—the consequence might be the loss of our gallies and floating batteries, which I apprehend might be intercepted, and with the assistance of their gallies and small armed vessels, taken and this would greatly weaken the opposition we might otherwise give at Fort Island, and tend powerfully to render it abortive. But if they should not attempt this, contenting themselves with safer though slower operations, I have already observed, that it is agreed, on all hands, in fifteen or twenty days they would be able to possess themselves of infallible means of frustrating our opposition there, by the capture of our works; and if we add to this, that it might very possibly happen in less time,—if from no other cause, —yet from the garrison being intimidated, by a consciousness of its own inferiority and inability to support itself against a so much superior force of numbers,—which might occasion a conduct destructive to itself—there will remain no sufficient reasons to justify the making this the principal point of defence.

" At Fort Island the boom and chevaux de frize are an ample security against any forcible impression of the enemy's ships which it would be imprudent in them to attempt. On the Jersey side the situation of the ground is such, that the gallies, floating batteries and forts employed in the defence of the obstructions would have little to fear from any batteries erected there. Red-bank seems, by its elevation to be the only advantageous spot for annoying them; but as it is computed to be above 1900 yards from Fort Island, the distance is rather too great to allow any battery raised there to act with so much effect as to be able to silence our fire. On this side, the ground by dykes and sluices may be laid under water to so considerable an extent as to leave no danger of our River force being annoyed from thence; for which purpose suitable precautions ought, at once, to be made, against it may be necessary to carry them into effect.

" But, though a battery upon Red-bank, would not in my apprehension, be able to prevent the efficacy of our defence or give any material disturbance to Fort Island, in particular, yet it might serve to make the situation of some of our gallies rather uneasy; and this perhaps makes it worth while to pre-occupy it in order to keep it out of the enemy's hands erecting a small, but strong work there capable of containing about two hundred men, with six or eight pieces of light cannon, and a proportionable quantity of stores. As the approaches to it are difficult on account of the adjacent creeks, and a communication can be kept open between it and our army, by which means the garrison might receive succors from time to time, though we could not expect to make it impregnable, yet we should have a prospect of holding it much longer than we could the work at Billingsport.

" In the position, which from my present view of it, I should think it best for our army to take, the left wing of it would be nearly opposite to Red-bank, and therefore in a condition to relieve and support it; whereas Billingsport being more remote from the probable position of the army, and detached from any other work, could not easily derive any assistance from without and must rely wholly upon its own strength.

" Either at Billingsport or at Fort Island, I believe there is not much to be apprehended from the fire of the enemy's ships unaided by land batteries; For as by the information of those who ought to be acquainted with the fact, not more than three ships can act abreast at a time at either place, and as the gallies, not requiring the same depth of water, can extend themselves at pleasure, and besides carry a superior weight of metal to that which frigates commonly have, a much superior fire, could be opposed to them than any they could bring and from the difference of size and make between the frigates and gallies, to much better effect than theirs. The comparative extent of the River at Billingsport and at Fort Island has been assigned as a motive of preference to the former, the river being narrower there than at the latter, and supposed to admit of fewer ships operating at a time; but as it is asserted by the gentlemen in the River department, that the sand banks and shallowness of the River in most places near Fort Island, compensate for the width of it and make it impossible for more than three ships to act together at a time, this reason of preferring the position at Billingsport seems to have no foundation. And if we consider, that our whole force of gallies and floating batteries, would be collected at Fort Island, assisted by the fort itself and that it would not be safe to trust them all out for the defence of Billingsport, for fear of the disaster already suggested, it seems evident enough that this is the place where our defence may be most successfully made.

" One of the most weighty considerations with me is, that our Army as before intimated, could more conveniently co-operate with the defence by water here than at Billingsport. The ground on this side is better situated here than at the other place, and the Army being so much nearer the city, it is so much the less likely, that the enemy should be able, by a circuitous route to fall into the rear of it and separate it from the city, which is a circumstance that ought carefully to be attended to.

" Some Gentlemen are of opinion that our principal dependence ought to be upon Fort Island and its appendages; but at the same time, that we should make a part of our defence at Billingsport proposing for that purpose that the works there should be continued on the new contracted scale to be garrisoned by four or five hundred men. The reasons for this are—that it would serve to delay the enemy

and give our army time to come up, should it be at any distance and that it would prevent those disagreeable impressions which never fail to accompany the abandoning works
that have been once raised and plans that have been once in
execution; especially when the persons concerned in the
defence of them repose a degree of confidence in them;—
which is said to be the case in the present instance. But
these reasons may perhaps not be so conclusive as 'tis
imagined; for 'tis a question whether, if our army was so
remote as to make such a delay necessary, the enemy would
embarrass themselves with removing the water obstructions
in the first place, but would not rather debark and make
a rapid march by land; possessing themselves of the city
and of those positions which would make the surrender of
the gallies, &c., in some sort a natural consequence; and it
is worthy of consideration, whether the abandoning the
works begun at this time, which will probably allow some
leisure for any disagreeable impressions it might make to
be effaced, will not be less injurious than the abandoning
them hereafter when they have cost more expence, time and
labor, and in the critical moment of an attack, when every
misfortune, and the loss of the most inconsiderable post is
too apt to have a much worse influence on the mind than
the real importance of it will justify. Add to this the possibility that the garrison dismayed at the approach of numbers so superior to their own, might not answer the end
expected from them, and might even be lost by their timidity—the certainty of losing the cannon after the time
limited for the defence and thereby weakening that of the
upper position—the chance of losing the gallies and floating
batteries, requisite for covering the chevaux de frize, by a
hazardous and successful attempt to break through them,
and the garrison with them, which would fall of course upon
such an event,—It is however, submitted to Congress to
ballance the advantages and disadvantages and determine
accordingly. I would only beg leave to give it clearly as
my opinion, that our principal dependence ought to be upon
Fort Island and the obstructions there, and that Billingsport

ought not by any means to be defended, more than as a secondary object.

" And to that end, I would recommend that the works on Fort Island, which on their present construction are by no means calculated for the defence of the Chevaux de frize be immediately altered and adapted to that purpose, taking care, at the same time, to make them defensible with a small number of men against any sudden attempt to land in boats and carry them by assault.—But whatever scheme is pursued, I could wish the greatest diligence and despatch may be used in bringing it to maturity; for though the danger which lately threatened seems to have subsided, there is no knowing how soon it may return and certainly it will be prudent to do every thing in our power to be prepared for it, as we can lose nothing by being so, and may lose a great deal by neglecting to improve the interval of leisure they have given us should it be their intention to revisit this quarter. As the means to this—it will be necessary to furnish Mr. Coudray to whom the Superintendency of those works is intrusted, with a competent number of workmen, tools, and what other things he may want to enable him to carry them on with propriety, ease and expedition.

" On the whole I am of opinion that the obstructions in the River, with the help of gallies, floating batteries, and with tolerable industry to put the land works in a proper state, will be extremely formidable to the enemy and authorise a reasonable expectation of their being effectual. The fire ships also will contribute to this end, for though there are many obstacles that render their success precarious, and a happy concurrence of·circumstances is necessary towards it, any of which failing may disappoint the project, and there is therefore no room to be sanguine, yet there is some probability of its succeeding and they will be at least an embarrassment and terror to the enemy, and will oblige them to use precautions inconvenient to them and serviceable to us.

" As an accurate knowledge of the country is essential to

a good defence and as the enemy's approach may be sudden and we may be called to act, without having time, when it happens, to examine it sufficiently if it is not done beforehand, it would answer a valuable purpose to have it immediately carefully reconnoitred, and sketches taken of all the landing places, great roads and bye-paths, Incamping grounds, heights, rivers, creeks, morasses, and every thing that it can be of any importance to know.

" Marcus Hook seems to be the most advanced place at which it is conjectured the enemy will land, the survey should therefore comprehend all the country between that & Phil^a.

" Mr. Du Coudray has offered his services with his Engineers to do this business, if authorized by Congress, only requiring that they be supplied with horses and a hand or two. If Congress approve of it, I shall be glad they may be desired to enter upon it, without loss of time. I have the honor, &c.

" G? WASHINGTON."

FROM DU COUDRAY.

"PHILADELPHIA, 10 August, 1777.

" SIR,

" I have received with the most Respectful gratitude, the new proofs of esteem and kindness, with which, your Excellency has honoured me, in making Colonel Hamilton communicate to me the Letter, which you have addressed to the Congress, with regard to the defence of the aproaches of the enemy to philadelphia.

" The manner in which your Excellency has discussed the different opinions about the fortifications of the River, places in the most evident Light the sentiment which you preferably adopt.

" It is beyond all Dispute, that the situation of fort iland is more advantageous, than that of billing's port, by the difficulty which the enemy shal have of aproaching it; by the Resources which the ground affords of erecting there a better fortification; and by the facility of conveying assistance. The chief Reason which induced me to prefer Billingsport, was the narrowness of the river in this place,

which is in Reality two third less than at fort iland, and
upon that account, seems to Reduce the enemy to a necessity of bringing to action, at the same time, a far less number of vessels to Destroy the means of Defending the
chevaux de frize. But the informations given your excellency, having demonstrated, as you say in your Letter, to
the Congress, that notwithstanding the breadth of the river
at fort iland, the enemy can present there but three fregates
at a time; it is certain that preferable aplication must be
given to defend that part of the river; if there be time
enough, to put this fort in a condition of Resisting the
forces which the enemy, by the means of small vessels and
chaloupes, might conduct there a number sufficient to nail
up the cannon, and destroy the single palissade badly
flanked, badly [?], which constitutes actually its only Defence on three of its four fronts.

"The immediate assistance which your excellency Demands, of Congress for this object, and the Reasons which
you Lay before them to show the importance of a Ready
Complayance, cannot fail of changing immediately the
critical situation in which matters are in this Respect, and
in which the most unavoidably Remain a far longer time
than at billing's port, if the means employed be similar.

"Tho' your excellency has Declared nothing Definitive
to me on this subject, when I left you before yesterday, the
idea however which I had of your opinion, has induced me
yesterday to go to fort iland with four engeneers, where we
passt the whole day in examining, combining and drawing
all its particulars circumstances, as well as those of the environs, which have any Relation to it. The aproach of the
night, and the absolute cessation from all work in this
country during sundays, even in the most urgent momens,
obliged us to deffer the continuation of this work till tomorrow, when I hope we will finish it. I believe we shal
be employed tuesday and wenesday in drawing these particulars in such a manner as to put them in a Condition of
being presented to your excellency; which I intend to do
thursday or friday at farthest. I shall deliver at the same

time the Result of the examination of the cannons, and the carriages which are at present fit to be employed, or may be rendered so in the course of this month; the end of which I think ought to be Declared of the time when all these works are to be finished, both at fort island and Red bank, which your excellency think proper to be put in a state of Defense.

" I hope also that the same period will be sufficient to execute the minute examination which I proposed to your excellency, to make from markus' hook to philadelphia; a project which you have honoured of your aprobation, and sollicitations to Congress.

" I shal think myself happy if the execution of these different objects should afford me, as well all the officers who accompany me, an occasion of engaging with the enemy, and of carrying with us proofs of that esteem, which we came so far to seek for; and the certainty of which will at the same time constitute our consolation and glory.[1]

" I am with greatest Respect
" Sir
" of your excellency
" the most obedient servant
" Du Coudray."

---

[1] " That A. met Ld B. & Gen. Howe at the entrance of the Delaware, that he informed them of the state of the river, and the chain, the chevaux de frize, &c.; that they on that inquired into the state of Chesapeake, and the possibility of landing at the head of Elk. It was urged to them that it would be better to land below the impediments, as they would by that means save the sea voyage, and be almost as near Philadelphia. To this was answered, that the taking of the city was not the principal object, but as it afterwards appeared that all the magazines were then at York Town or Carlisle, and the taking of them would effectively crush Gen. Washington, and therefore they pursued their intention of going up the Chesapeak, as the demolition of the magazines was to be more easily effected by so doing. After having landed at the Head of Elk with this view, the Gen'l gained secret intelligence that Gen. W. had promised his officers to risk a battle, and preparations were accordingly made to tempt him to keep his promise, which ended in the affair of Brandywine. That led on to the taking of Philadelphia, the danger the army incurred at German Town, and the laying aside all in-

WASHINGTON TO THE PRESIDENT OF CONGRESS.

"HEAD QUARTERS, CAMP AT CROSS ROADS,
"15 August, 1777.

" SIR,

" Mr. Du Coudray has laid before me a plan of the river, by which it appears that for a considerable space between the two sand banks on the east side of Fort Island there is from four to 4½ fathoms depth of water. According to this representation there would be room for three frigates to lie between those banks, in such a position as to enfilade the works at Fort Island, and make it difficult to maintain them. There are but two ways of remedying this inconvenience; one by having a sufficient number of chevaux de frize sunk at the entrance between the two banks, and the other by having the left flank of Fort Island fortification supported by a good battery, capable of resisting the cannon of the ship, & obliging them to quit their station. The first is evidently preferable because the efficacy of it will be more certain. A few chevaux de frize properly placed might effectually bar all access to the ships; but there is a possibility that any battery we can construct might be overpowered by the fire of the shipping. And as we have few cannon and Fort Island is itself a marshy spot incapable of affording earth for the batteries necessary to be raised upon it, which must be brought from the opposite shore, it would not be prudent to multiply works there more than cannot be avoided. It would also be a great advantage gained, to secure the island from annoyance, except in one point and that in front from only three ships at a time, which would be effected by stopping up the passage between the two banks with chevaux de frize. I should therefore think it of importance to have this measure immediately adopted and carried into execution.

" With great respect &c.
" G? WASHINGTON."

tentions upon the magazines, which has never been renewed during the whole winter, or before the opening of the campaign in the Spring, tho' those magazines subsisted the whole army of the enemy."—*Earl of Carlisle; note of a conversation.* Stevens's " Fac-similes," Vol. I. folio 82.

COUNCIL OF WAR.

" At a Council of General Officers, held at Neshamini Camp, in Bucks County the 21st day of August 1777.

" Present

" His Excellency, the Commander in Chief,

" Major Generals Greene   Brigad^{rs} Muhlenburgh
        " Lord Stirling   Weedon
        " Stephen   Woodford
        " Marquis Fayette   Scot

" Brigadiers Genl Maxwell   Conway
        " Knox
        " Wayne

" The Commander in Chief informed the Council that the British Fleet left the capes of Delaware on the 31st of July and have not been seen, from any information he has obtained, since the 7th Instant, when they were off Sinapixon and steering to the Southward, and propounded the following Questions for the opinion of the Council.

" *First Question.* What is the most probable place of their destination, whether Eastward or Southward & to what part ?

" *Answer.* The Southward, & that Charles Town, from a view of all circumstances, is the most probable object of their attention.

" *Second.* If it should be thought, from a consideration of all circumstances, that the Fleet is gone far to the Southward, will it be adviseable for this Army, taking into view, the length of distance & unhealthiness of that climate at this season, to March that way ?—or will there be a probability of their arriving there in Time, should it be attempted, to give any effectual opposition to the Enemy, or to prevent them accomplishing their purposes ?

" *Answer.* It will not be adviseable for the Army to march to the Southwards, as they could not possibly arrive at Charles Town in time to afford any succour.

" *Third.* If It should not be thought adviseable in such case for the Army to march to the Southward, How shall it be employed? Shall it remain where it now is, or move towards Hudsons River to act as the situation of affairs shall seem to require?

"*Answer*. The Army should move immediately towards the North River.

"Peter Muhlenberg B. G.   G° Washington
"G. Weedon B. Genl.   Nath^L Greene M. G.
"W^M Woodford Brigd Gen^L Stirling M. G.
                            "Adam Stephen, M. G.
"Ch^s Scott B. G.   The Mrquis de Lafayette M. G.
                            "W^M Maxwell B. G.
"T. Conway B. G.   H. Knox B. G. Artillery
                            "Anty. Wayne B. G"[1]

MEMOIR UPON THE DEFENCE OF THE TWO PASSAGES OF THE
RIVER,—VIZ., BILLINGSPORT AND FORT ISLAND.

"The soundings made yesterday by the navy board having confirmed those which I made last week with Mr. Donaldson, who have sunk the chevaux de frize, it is demonstrated in the most incontestible manner that Fort Mifflin, instead of having to act against three frigates only, as his Excellency General Washington had been assured, and as this General has informed the Congress in the letter in which he discusses the preference that ought to be given to one of these forts; it is incontestible, I say, that as Fort Mifflin, being exposed to the fire of about 15 frigates, is thereby in a situation of being demolished in a few hours, if it be attacked in the condition in which it is at present; viz., surrounded by a single palissade, or with a wall without a terrass, which can only defend it against a coup-de-main, and cannot by any means resist the cannon.

"It is not less evident that the ground being almost upon a level with the water, it is only with vast expences and a considerable time that by a rampart, and other convenient alterations, this fort can be put in a situation of resisting so many vessels, the effect of which would be so much the

[1] See my "Writings of Washington," Vol. VI. p. 47.

more dangerous to it, as being upon a level with the river, and on its banks, the balls which could not arrive on account of the distance of some frigates, would get there by rebounding.

" I join, however, to this memorial two projects suggested upon this head by Augustus le Brun, one of the Engineers who have accompanied me from France. These projects suppose that for reasons which particularly regard the State of Pennsylvania, or the plan of his excellency General Washington for the defense of the Delaware, it would be absolutely necessary to put this fort in a condition of sustaining some time the attacks of the enemy.

" That of these projects, which is the plainer and affords only a very imperfect defense, could not be executed without employing the earth brought from the dikes which surrounds the Isle and putting it under water; this would render it a very unwholesome place of abode.

" The second project, which affords a very complete and well conceived defense, requires that beside this earth more perhaps should be fetched from the other side of the river.

" But the execution of even the plainest of these projects, could only be accomplished for the next campaign; unless means which would be very expensive to this country were employed.

" This, however, would not dispense (as it is certainly necessary in the present State of the fort) from hindering the enemy by chevaux de frize to place themselves in the two chenals where the soundings lately performed, shew that they can place so many frigates.

" But to support these chevaux de frize it would be necessary to have on the opposite bank a battery of 12 or 15 pieces at least, of eighteen or twenty four pounders on account of the great distance, to which they would fire; and that their battery might not be taken, it should be fortified on the land side, or in other words, a new fort should be constructed, which would also be intended with a great expence in Artillery, ammunition and construction,

although the ground I have examined with the Deputies is
very favourable.

" If we count the expence of this fort which should [be]
built quite new; that of red bank being by far too much
above the position of the chevaux de frize; and that of
Bush Island being only a child's plaything; if to this expence be added that of the chevaux de frize, which are to
be sunk either in the channel where there are yet none or
in that channel where there are some already, but which are
separated 40 feet the one from another; if in short we add
to all those expences these of the most necessary alterations
to be made in fort Mifflin, it will appear evident, as I have
declared in the first memorial which I laid before the Congress in the beginning of June, when they consulted me on
this head, that there can be no thoughts of defending this
passage of the river, unless, as I have forementioned some
reasons regarding particularly the State of Pennsylvania, or
the future operations of the army should absolutely require
to enable this fort to resist for some time the attacks of the
ennemy.

" If these reasons do not exist, it is evident that we must
confine ourselves to the defense of that passage alone of
Billingsport, where the river is more than two thirds narrower than at fort Mifflin; where the ennemy can present
no more than three frigates at a time; where the frigates
can do very little harm to the battery which protects the
chevaux de frize, because this battery, being very high, is
safe from the rebounding of the balls and commands the
frigates; where the galleys and fire ships are more capable
of acting with more profit and facility than at fort Mifflin;
and where in short the work is far advanced, and propor-
tioned to the small quantity of artillery which is at present
in a state of serving.

" If the Government intend to unite all their efforts in
finishing this fort, I would propose to hire instead of militia
men, workmen by the day, which after an exact calculation
of all expences, will cost incomparably less, I believe, will
work a great deal more, give far less trouble to those who

conduct the works, and not consume such an immense quantity of tools of all kinds.

"Du Coudray.

"Philadelphia, 29 August, 1777."

DU COUDRAY TO WASHINGTON.

"Sir,

"According to the desire of the board of War I have the honour to send to your excellency a memorial which I have written yesterday upon the request of the Navy board, on the two passages of the river, after the verification that this board caused to be made of the soundings performed by me in the last week before fort Mifflin, and the result where of I had the honour to give an account verbally to your Excellency, conformable to the letter which I had directed before to Colonel Hamilton, one of your aid de camps, who ought to have received that letter since his departure from hence.

"I am waiting for an answer to the letter which I had the honour to direct to your Excellency three days ago by Colonel Pinckney with regard to the nine militia men whom General Armstrong took away from the Engineers employed about the map from Walmington to Philadelphia, which remain interrupted since the taking away of these militia men who are not yet replaced. I am with great respect.

"Sir,

"of your Excellency

"the most obedient and

"respectful servant

"Du Coudray.

"Philad. 30 Aug. 1777."

DU COUDRAY TO CONGRESS.

"Philadelphia 7 7bre 1777

"Sir,

"When the enemy's Fleet threatened the Delaware, General Gates, and General Mifflin did me the honour to invite me to reconnoitre the country with them, to determine the place where it was probable the landing of their Troops would be made, and the principal situations which might be taken successively to stop their March to Philadelphia.

"The Result of this recconnoitring having been addressed to Congress, and afterwards communicated to General Washington, was thought by his Excellency worthy of his Attention, and recommendation to Congress, to employ my service, and that of my Engenieurs, to survey these different positions in the most minute detail, and determine on the best manner of fortifying them; whilst, in the mean time, we determined by an accurate examination of the river, round fort Mifflin, if it was possible to defend this post as his Excellency desired, and as he had reason to think could be effected, from the assurances given him that the Enemy could only bring three frigates to act against it.

"I have addressed to the Board of War and to the Supreme Council of Pennsylvania, the result of the soundings of the river near Fort Mifflin, which I have made and which have been confirmed by those taken by the Navy Board; both which shew the necessity of defending only the passage of Billingsport, as I proposed in June, upon the first view of this spot, and upon considering the small number of Artillery that could be furnished.

"I have been waiting these twelve days to know the measures that the Board of War, and Supreme Council would take upon this subject, but whatever it may be, it is evident that from the part which the ennemy have taken of making a descent in Cesepeak bay, the object the least pressing is the defense of the Delaware.

"This being supposed, it is clear that the greatest attention ought to be directed to defend as well as possible, the Route which the Enemy have determined upon, by their landing in Chesapeak.

"It is certain that fixing on this spot to land, instead of Mark's hook (which General Gates, Mifflin, and myself thought they would chuse) will encrease considerably the Posts, which in proportion as they advance in the Country, they will be oblig'd to establish to keep up a Communication with their fleet. But the greatest disadvantage attending this, gives not however an entire certainty against the success of their march to Philadelphia, which I always judged and declared, since my arrival here, to be the true object of their Campaign.

" To ensure, as much as possible, the success of this Campaign, it is necessary not to be merely contented with securing the Position of Wilmington, where his Excellency has very wisely thought proper to collect his first Efforts.

" However strong this position may be supposed by nature, or may be rendered by Art; it appears to me, after what I have heard, that it will be possible for the enemy to pass it on the flank, or perhaps force it; considering especially the small number of Artillery belonging to his Excellency's army.

" It appears to me then prudent for Congress to think of providing beforehand for their army, another fortyfied Position, which may secure the army in case they are obliged to abandon the first, and where they may collect new force against an enemy, whom the first success may render more audacious; more especially as Schuylkill is the only considerable river that impedes their March to Philadelphia; and that this River offers at Grays-ferry a Passage which no officer can (I should think) propose to defend.

" For this purpose, I offer again my service and that of my officers; in hopes that there will result from it an opportunity of our being in action, which the delay of Congress in pronouncing definitively upon our existence in the service of the United States, always removes at a distance, and which probably we might wait for in vain at the forts on the Delaware; at least before our return in France, should this take place. If the Congress consent to the proposition which I make, to prepare a fortified Camp between Wilmington and Philadelphia, I beg them 1° to communicate this proposition to his Excellency General Washington.

" 2° To give me, as a principal cooperator, General Mifflin, who knows perfectly well this country; who has a very great ascendant over the Inhabitants, by whom the works would be executed and whose great activity and penetration I have had occasion to observe.

" 3ᵈ To bring forward, as soon as possible, the remainder of the fifty two pieces brought in the Amphitrite, of which twelve alone are in the northern army, ten, within these few weeks, at the army of his Excellency General Washington; the rest in Springfield, and, at other Places on the east side of Hudson's River.

" These thirty remaining pieces of the said fifty two, will be so much the more necessary, as artillery is the foundation of all defensive war; and that of these thirty pieces, there are twenty one which being of a greater length than the others, and even any pieces in the army, are for that reason better for defending the intrenchments.

" Besides this there will be an occasion to try, if these pieces, which weigh only one thousand one hundred weight, that is to say, much less than the lightest loaded baggage-wagon, are so difficult to be transported, as some have endeavoured to persuade his Excellency; and if their service is so useless that they ought to be cast over again, in the middle of a campaign in order to make from each of them three six pounders, which at most could only weigh three hundred weight each, and would be of a service as little durable as safe; supposing even that the founders at Boston, or Philadelphia, were capable of executing this casting without hazarding not only the loss of the fashion of these pieces, but also the loss of the metal, so difficult to replace in this country; this a disinterested, and intelligent person will not believe, who has seen the pieces cast by these different founders, and particularly the cannon and Howitzers, which were sent to camp the other day.

" The Proposition which I have the honour to present to the Congress as a mark of my zeal for the service of the United States of America, appears to me worthy of all their attention; considering the important consequence which would follow, if the army failing of support in its retreat (a case which may possibly happen) should be obliged to abandon Philadelphia.

" I cannot avoid embracing this Opportunity of recalling the attention of Congress to another proposal, which appears to me of equal importance, and what I had about a fortnight since, the honour of making to the Board of War, who, I suppose have communicated it to Congress, it is to cast in some of the forges most contiguous to the City of New York twelve Iron Mortars with the necessary number of shells in order to drive the enemy from that Place, or, at least, to prevent its being a safe harbour, for their vessels. The success of such a measure appears to me almost infallible, if the Geographical accounts which I have received of the situation of that place may be depended upon.

" I am

" Sir

" with great respect

" Your humble servant

" DU COUDRAY.

" HON JOHN HANCOCK, ESQ

" Presd' of Congress."

COUNCIL OF WAR.

" At a Council of War held at the Camp near Potts Grove the 23ᵈ day of Septemʳ 1777.

" Present

" His Excellency the Commander

Major Generals	Brigadiers General
" Sullivan	Knox
" Green	Weedon
" Lord Stirling	Nash
" Stephen	Scott
" Armstrong	Conway
	" Potter

" Besides the above Major Genˡ St. Clair and John Cadwalader Esquire were also present.

" His Excellency informed the General Officers that the Reason of his calling them together was to acquaint them that the Enemy had, the preceding Night crossed the

Schuylkill by several Fords about twelve Miles below and by the best accounts were proceeding towards Philadelphia. He also informed them that the Troops under Generals Smallwood & Wayne had not yet rejoined the Army and that a Brigade of Continental Troops under the command of General McDougall might be expected in a few days from Peekskill and about one thousand Militia from Jersey under Gen¹ Dickinson in the same time. He therefore desired the opinion of the Council whether it would be most advisable to advance upon the Enemy with our present Force or wait till the Reinforcements and detachments above mentioned should come in?

"Previous to taking the Voices upon the foregoing Question His Excellency begged leave to inform the Council of the present State of the Army and the Reasons which had induced him to make the late movements which (tho' well known to most of them) were not so fully to Major Gen¹ Armstrong and Brig. Gen¹ Potter, who had been detached from the main Body of the Army. This being agreed to, His Excellency proceeded to inform the Council

"That when the Army left Germantown upon the 15ᵗʰ instant it was with a determination to meet the Enemy and give them Battle whenever a convenient opportunity should be found—that they advanced the same day to the Sign of the Buck and the day following to the Warren Tavern upon the Lancaster Road. On the 17ᵗʰ in the morning intelligence was brought that the Enemy were advancing upon which the Army were paraded and a disposition made to receive them, the pickets had exchanged a few shott when a violent Storm of Rain which continued all the day and the following night prevented all further operations. Upon an examination of the Arms and Ammunition on the 18ᵗʰ it was found that the former were much impaired and all the latter that was in Cartouch Boxes was intirely ruined, wherefore it was judged expedient to withdraw the Army to some place of security untill the Arms could be repaired and the Ammunition recruited. Before this could be fully effected advice was received that the Enemy had quitted their former position near the White Horse Tavern and were marching down the Road leading to the Swedes Ford, but the Army not being in a condition to attack them owing to the want of Ammunition, it was judged most prudent to cross the River at Parkers Ford and take post in the Rear of the Fat Land Ford opposite to the Enemy. In this position the Armies continued for two days when on the 20th instant that of the Enemy appeared to be in motion, and from our own observation and the accounts of our reconnoitring parties were marching rapidly up the Reading Road this induced us to move up likewise to hinder them from crossing above us and by getting between us and Reading take an opportunity of destroying a large collection of Military Stores deposited there. On the night of the 20th the Army decamped and marched up to the Trap and on the 21st to within four miles of Potts Grove, the Enemy's Van then being at French Creek upon the West Side of Schuylkill. In the night of the 22d advice was received that the Enemy had crossed Schuylkill at Gordons Ford below us, but the account was again contradicted, but in the morning of the 23d certain accounts came to hand that they really had crossed in large numbers and were Moving towards Philad*. His Excellency further informed the Council that the Troops were in no condition to make a forced march as many of them were barefooted and all excessively harrassed with their great Fatigue. The Question being then put—The Council were unanimously of opinion

" That, from the present state of the Army it would not be adviseable to advance upon the Enemy, but remain upon this Ground or in the neighbourhood till the detachments and expected Reinforcements come up."

COUNCIL OF WAR.

" At a Council of War held at Head Q^{rs} at Pennibeckers Mill the 28th day of Septr 1777.

" Present

" His Excellency, the Commander in Chief.

"Majors Gen¹	Brigad⁺ Gen¹ˢ
" Sullivan	McDougal
" Greene	Maxwell
" Lᵈ Stirling	Smallwood
" Stephens	Knox
" Armstrong	Wayne
	" Muhlenberg
	" Nash
	" Weedon
	" Scott
	" Conway
	" Potter
	" Irvine

" Besides these, John Cadwalader & Joseph Read [Reed], Esqʳ were present.

" His Excellency informed the Board, that the main body of the Enemy, by the last accounts he had obtained, lay near German Town and that part had marched into the city of Philadelphia whether to remain there or not he could not learn. That their whole force from the best accounts he could get, and from a comparative view & estimate, amounts to about 8000 men.

" That a detachment of Continental Troops from Peekskill, under the command of Brigadʳ Gen¹ McDougal, consisting of about 900 men had joined the Army. That Gen¹ Smallwood, with the Militia of Maryland, amounting to about 1100—had also arrived, and that Brigadʳ Foreman with about 600—Jersey Militia, would be near the Army today on the Skippack Road. That of Continental Troops, at this time in Camp, exclusive of the Detachment under Gen¹ McDougal and that under Gen¹ Wayne at the Trap, there were returned present fit for duty 5472, to which is to be added the light Corps, lately under Gen¹ Maxwell supposed to amount to 450—Men, and the Militia of the State of Pennsylvania under the command of Major Gen¹ Armstrong. That upon the whole, the Army would consist of about 8000 Continental Troops rank & file and 3000 Militia.

" His Excellency further informed the Board that a Body of Militia was coming from Virginia & that part had arrived at Lancaster.—That he understood from Report, that the number of 'em amounted to near 2000 men, but, that from good authority, he was advised they were badly armed and many of them without any at all.

" His Excellency also informed the Board that on the 24ᵗʰ Inst he dispatched an Express to Genˡ Putnam with a letter dated the day before ordering a Detachment to be sent immediately from Peekskill to reinforce the Army under his Command, which Detachment in addition to the Corps then on the march under Genˡ McDougal, should make the whole force directed from that post amount to 2500 Effective Rank & file.

" Under these circumstances he had called a Council of War to consult & resolve on the most adviseable measures to be pursued but more especially to learn from them, whether with this Force it was prudent to make a general & vigorous attack upon the Enemy or to wait further Reinforcements upon which he prayed their opinions.

" The Board having taken into consideration the whole circumstances and the Question propounded, are of opinion that an immediate attack should not be made; But they advise, that the Army should move to some grounds proper for an Encampment within about 12 miles of the Enemy, and there wait for a further Reinforcement, or be in readiness to take advantage of any favourable opportunity that may offer for making an attack.

" Alexander McDougal

" Jⁿᵒ Sullivan

" H. Knox B. G. Artillery   Nathˡ. Greene

" F. Nash B. G.

" P. Muhlenberg B. G.   Stirling

" T. Conway B. G.   Adam Stephen B. G.

" John Armstrong

" The subscribers being of opinion our Force was sufficient to attack with, but being overruled concur with the
above

" W. Smallwood   Jas. Potter
" An^t Wayne   James Irvine
                        " Ch^s Scott "

BRIGADIER-GENERAL FORMAN TO GENERAL WASHINGTON.

" Red Bank Fort, 26 October, 1777.

" Sir :

" Your Excel^ia fav^r of the 22^d Directed to me at the Salt
Works unfortunately went to the Salt Works by the lower
road at the same Time I came to Freehold by the upper, by
which means your Excel^ys orders ware not handed me until
Friday afternoon—previous to which I had rec^d an Express
giveing an Acct. of The Defeat of ye troops your Excel^y mentioned to have Crossed to attack the Forts and their retreat.
—Nevertheless being fully Impressed with the Importance
This Fort is to us and Equally so to the British Army, I made
no Doubt but a second Attempt woold shortly be made.—
I therefore gave Directions for the Troops y^t Could be
possably spared from y^t station, vizt one hundred, to Hold
themselves in readiness to march Next Day, vizt. Saturday—
& Early in the morning Come forward my self to, if possable,
give a spurr to the Burlington Militia & put them in motion—
But am sorry to Inform your Excel^y y^t Neither our Late suck-
sesses or the Danger of haveing their Country ravaged gives
y^t spring to Their sprits y^t is Necessary to bring them out—
I have however in the Most Express manner ordered The
Colo^ls to Exert Themselves and am in hopes y^t a few Days
will produce Two or Three hundred men.—

" The Lower Militia under Genl Newcomb have not as yet
produced a single Man—As being Elder in command Then
Newcomb I have taken the Liberty this Day to Issue orders
for Their Immediate Assembling, and will from Time to
Time do every thing in my power to assemble Them.

" I got to this post before Noon This day and rec^d Information from the Commodore that his Boats on Guard last Night near the mouth of Schoolkill Heard a Constant rumbling of Wagons coming from Philadᵃ Ward and Crossing over to Province Island from Ten o'clock untill Near Day Break.— Colᵒ Green informs me yᵗ he saw a Large Body of men passing the Ferry; at one Time they could Discover yᵗ Those who had Crossed wore Diferent Uniformes, some red, some Blue—& yᵗ a very Considerable body ware Waiting on the Crossway and in the Woods on Philadᵃ side to Cross. The Day was too Dark to make any Nice Discoveries.—When I Got Down There ware plainly to be discovered a Large Number of Wagons on the Crossway—but it was become too Hazy to Discover whither they Crossed to the Island or returned— at four o'clock I was informed yᵗ a Body of British Troops had landed at Billingsport last Evening in thirty five Boats —I think from the Accᵗˢ its tolerably well Ascertained yᵗ There are some Troops There, but the Time of their Landing and Number of boats appear rather a loose Accᵗ not to be depended on. The Garrison at Red Bank has been lately so Exceedingly Fatigued and in its size small yᵗ They have not been able to keep any party on the Shoor.—The Movements of Last Night & to Day amongst the Enemy has occasioned the Officir Commanding at Fort Miflin to Imagine They mean to Attack yᵗ fort & has This day Drawn a reinforcement of seventy men from Colᵒ Green and wished to have Drawn 100 more.

" I make no Doubt but the Genᵗˢ request to Colᵒ Green was judicious at it respects fort Mifflin. But at The same Time am fully Convinced yᵗ Colᵒ Green woold in Case of an Attack Absolutely stand in need not only of Them men but a greater Number to Defend it. As soon as any of my Troops arrive, I will send as many of Them into the Forts as will Compleatly mann it.

" By these means the fort will be in as good state of Defence as before The late Attack should they make a second Attempt to carry it by Assault, but should they Attempt to take the Fort by regular Approaches they will be so many men Lost.

"The Gen^t who have been on this Station for some Time may be better able to Judge of the Enemies movements of last Night and This day than I can.—it may be y^t the[y] Immediately mean to attack Fort Mifflin or Red Bank or Boath. But I should rather be of opinion (from the Acc^t. of their Wagons moving at night), that they ware moveing There stores and Baggage from Philad^a a Cross Province Island & to Chester. Tomorow morning will perhaps Determine. I have the honor &c

"DAVID FORMAN."

LIEUTENANT-COLONEL SMITH TO WASHINGTON.

"FORT MIFFLIN, 26 Octr 1777

"SIR :

"I rec^d your Excell^{ys} Order to remain in the Garrison & shall obey it. When I wrote I expected there would not have been that Occasion for my being here which I now see there will. Baron d'Arendt's ill State of Health will oblige him to retire to Red Bank for three or four days perhaps more. Whether Coll. Green or I are to Command I know not. I presume I am to have the Command untill an express Order from your Excell^y to the Contrary, even should he be an Elder Officer. for if an Elder Officer (for Instance Coll. Green of Red Bank) was to throw in his Reg^t. to our Assistance, would not d'Arendt Command. I believe so if he would, then I certainly after him have the Command by your Excell^{ys} Order. Coll. Green says his Commission will be dated ye 23^d Decr last. mine ought & I expect will be dated the 10th as all the Officers from Maryland have their Commissions from that Date. 'tis true the Commissioners first appointed me Major. the Lieu^t Coll^o who they had appointed, did not Serve. the Assembly disapproved of many of their Appointments, alterd Some among the Rest made me a Lieu^t Coll. these are my Reasons for thinking that my Commission will bear that date. if your Excell^y

thinks them good Coll. Green will be Satisfied to Serve under me.

" A Reinforcement of 100 or 200 Men would not be too much to resist a Spirited Attack of 2000 Men. with 100 Infantry & 20 or 30 good Artillery, we might do. Our Artillery are & will be very ill-serv'd. the few Artillery of Militia are Constantly taring [?] to be discharg'd. their Times will be out in Ten or 15 days. I am Clearly of Opinion if we had a Commodore who would do his Duty, it would be impossible for the Enemy ever to get Possession of this fort. without we are properly guarded the Enemy may be with us before we can form. the Channell which they are to cross is so narrow, in the Night they may bring their Boats & Embark opposite to us without our seeing them. the Baron has just rec^d an Answer to a Request he made for the Galleys, to be sent early & begging that 6 might be sent, three to guard above Reed's House who would rake all that part of the Island, and three below Hog Island & the Battery. with this Guard (if they would do their duty) all Sir Williams Army could not take the fort. his answer the Baron inclosd to you. The enemy are very busy making some work near the ferry Wharf opposite to our Wharf. for what I cannot Conceive, unless 'tis to cover their landing, or to fortify the Island against our attack & by that Means to keep open their Communication by Tinnicum. they have all this Day been Carrying fascines & waggons, & in the Evening Earth to fill up the Breaches in the Causeway.

" Fifty Blankets as many p^r of Shoes, 4 Coats 1 Vest 4 p^r Breeches & two Great Coats (all farmers) were all I rec^d this day for my poor ragged fellows, now chiefly without Breeches, who are oblig'd to turn out before day, & perhaps may Soon be oblig'd to be so all Night. the last reinforcement are equally unfurnish'd. This Garrison ought to be well-cloth'd or we destroy their Constitutions. I Hope your Excell^y will give Order. My Officers & Men think they ought to be reliev'd but could they be cloth'd I could make them Content. I have the Honor &c.

" SAM SMITH."

CONTINENTAL NAVY BOARD TO WASHINGTON.

"CONTINENTAL NAVY BOARD
"BORDEN TOWN, 26 October, 1777

"SIR :

" As soon as we had the Honour of receiving your Letter
of yesterday, we ordered exact Returns to be immediately
made of every Man on Board the Frigates Washington &
Effingham ; these Returns we have enclosed for your In-
spection.

" We have the fullest Conviction of the Necessity there is
to exert every Power for the Defence of the Pass near Fort
Mifflin, & happy should we be, could we furnish Men in the
least likely to be of service there.   But as these Frigates
have been only officer'd & no attempt ever made to man
them, we have few or no Seamen, on board.   The men we
have are, for the most part, militia left sick at Burlington
& Bristol, & being found on the Recovery were taken on
Board merely to assist in getting the ships up to this Place.
With these Hands such as they are, & the Assistance of a
few on Board private Vessels that have taken shelter here,
we have put the Frigates in as good a Posture of Defence
as we could, against small armed Boats ; not apprehending
Danger from any larger Force by Water, on account of the
Difficulties of the Channel.

" Your Excellency's Desires shall always be a Law to us,
& if you think the Men in the enclosed Returns will be of
more service in our Fleet, they shall be immediately ordered down.   Every thing may be got ready for scuttling
the Frigates in Case of impending Danger, but we apprehend that Business may be safely deferred 'till the Enemy
have got up to the City with their Shipping.

" We have removed the chief of our Stores to Easton,
particularly our Canvass, of which we have a considerable
Quantity ; agreeable to Orders we saw from your Excellency some Time ago.

" There are a number of Shallop men, & a few Sailors on
Board the Vessels here which, if you think proper to un-

man our Frigates, we will endeavor to Enlist for a temporary service. But as there are but few of these, & fewer still we fear will be induced by any means to leave their vessels destitute, we apprehend little can be expected from such an Expedient.

"One thing your Excellency may depend upon, that whatever method you may point out in our Line, for the public service; our Abilities shall be exerted to the uttermost to fulfill your Desires. We have the Honour &c

"FRA⁸ HOPKINSON
"JOHN WHARTON."[1]

LIEUTENANT-COLONEL COMSTOCK TO WASHINGTON.

"RED BANK, Oct°. 27ᵗʰ 1777
"SIR :

"By order of Co¹ Greene I again put Pen to Paper, and inform your Excellency; that Yesterday he received your Favour of the 24ᵗʰ instant by Express; in which your Excellency was pleased to express your warmest approbation of the conduct of the whole Garrison on the 22ᵈ, accompan'd with your 'particular Thanks.'

"The whole Garrison entertain a grateful Sence of the Honour done them; and hope their future Conduct may be such as will render essential Service to their Country, and continue 'em in your Excellency's Good Opinion.

"The Number of Arms taken from the Hessians the late Action were about 300. The poorest of our Arms were yesterday exchanged for the same Number of those taken. The spare Arms in the Garrison are this day ordered away agreeable to your Excellency's directions; and the Wounded Prisoners delivered to the care of Mʳ Clymer, Commissary of Prisoners; and all judg'd fit to remove will be immeately sent to Allin Town.

[1] A letter from Commodore Hazelwood, of this date, is printed in Sparks's "Correspondence of the Revolution," Vol. II. p. 18. Washington wrote to the Navy Board on the 27th.—"Writings of Washington," Vol. VI. p. 145.

" Col. Greene directs me to acquaint your Excellency that Yesterday a Party of the Enemy landed from their Fleet with Cannon at Billing's Fort; at Night Co¹ Greene sent a Patrol that way to observe their movements, who took a Prisoner near the Enemy's Lines, & brot him in. The Prisoner says he is a Marine & that a Number of Highland Granadiers & Marines (in all 300 Men) with 10 Days' Provisions and 2 Eighteen Pounders were in Billing's Fort strengthening the works, and at present Commanded by the Capᵗ of the Eagle.—he likewise says it is given out that part of the Army at Philadelphia are to take post there.

"I am directed to inform your Excellency; that by a Person who last Night went from hence into Philadelphia and return'd, and by several ways of inteligence we are inform'd that Yesterday, and last Night, the Enemy imploy'd near 200 Waggons in carrying Brush and Plank across the Schoolkill toward Fort Mifflin, & that they have repaired the lower Bridge across that River. The Persons imploy'd in this work say it is preparitory to Attack on Fort Mifflin.

" Co¹ Greene begs your Excellency would send him a Reinforcement of 200 Continental Troops, the Militia he cannot depend upon, as no one has yet made his appearance here when there has been the least appearance [of] an attack.

" We have rec'd some Powder of the Fleet and imploy'd this rainy Day in making Cartriges; and this moment some Waggon lo'ded with Cartriges for us and Fort Miflin —now we have a fine supply. I have the Honʳ &c

" ADAM COMSTOCK,

" *Lᵗ Coᵗ*" [1]

---

[1] A return dated October 27 showed that five hundred and thirty-four men fit for duty were at Red Bank, as follows: Colonel Greene's regiment, two hundred and forty-four; Colonel Israel Angell's, two hundred and twenty-seven; and Captain David Cook's company of artillery, sixty-three.

WASHINGTON TO LIEUTENANT-COLONEL CHRISTOPHER GREENE.

"HEAD QUARTERS, Oct. 28ᵗʰ 1777

" SIR :

" Colonel Arendt writes me, that the state of his health will make it absolutely necessary for him, to withdraw himself awhile from the Garrison. I am apprehensive, that during his absence, there may arise some difficulty about the command between you and Lᵗ Col : Smith ; as it is uncertain which of your Commissions is oldest, and cannot now be easily determined. The good of the service however requires, that disputes of such a nature should be waved, and as Lᵗ Col : Smith had originally the command of the post, has been longer in it, and may be supposed to have more thoroughly considered every circumstance of its defence, than one who has been less time there ; these are arguments, with me, in the present uncertainty, respecting rank, that it should be waved in his favour.—I have no doubt that they will have their full weight with you when duly considered, and that you will readily avoid any difference about punctilios, when the advancement of the service, in the least degree, may seem to require it. Relying upon this, I flatter myself you will chearfully acquiesce in Colonel Smith's command, in the absence of the Baron, and that there will be the most perfect harmony subsisting between you. I am &c.[1]

" Gᵒ WASHINGTON."

WASHINGTON TO BRIGADIER-GENERAL FOREMAN.

"HEAD Qᵣˢ, 28ᵗʰ Octoʳ, 1777

" Dᴿ Sᴿ

" I wrote you last evening with respect to reinforceing Red Bank & Fort Mifflin. My anxiety from the importance of these places is so great, that I cannot help urging you again to throw in without loss of time, what assistance the Commanding officers and yourself may think necessary, and such as you may be able to afford them. I inform'd you

[1] In manuscript of Lieutenant-Colonel Hamilton.

that the reinforcement order'd from hence was detain'd by the weather, a continuance of which, still prevents the march of it, and may retard their passage, when they put off; for which reason, I wish your immediate consultation with the officers, that you may know what reinforcements are necessary by them, if possible without loss of time.

"I am &c.

"G° WASHINGTON.

"P.S.—If you mention the comeing down of a reinforcement, it may reach the Enemy's Ears, and they endeavour to intercept it, for which reason I wish it may be kept as secret as may be."

WASHINGTON'S INSTRUCTIONS TO GENERAL VARNUM.

"HEAD QUARTERS, 28th Octr 1777.

"SIR:

"You are immediately, or as soon as the weather will permit, to proceed to Woodberry with the Brigade under your command. Your most convenient rout will be from this to Bristol, thence to Mt. Holly, across the Delaware, thence to Haddonfield and thence to the place of your destination. You will be circumspect on your march, and use every precaution to prevent your party being surprised or intercepted. The design of sending you to Woodberry is to aid and give greater security to the Garrisons at Red Bank and Fort Mifflin; for which purpose you will co-operate with them in every necessary measure. You will probably find General Foreman at the head of a body of Jersey Militia, in the neighbourhood of Red Bank; as he is there for the same end that you will be, a co-operation between you and him will be also requisite.

"I cannot delineate particularly the line of conduct you are to observe.—I leave it to your own discretion, to be adapted to circumstances.—The general idea, I would throw out is, that you are in conjunction with the Jersey militia to give the Garrisons and fleet all the assistance and relief in your power. As the men in them must be greatly harrassed by labour and watching, and in need of rest and refreshment, I would have you send detachments from time to time to relieve and replace an equal number from the garrisons; who are during the interval to remain and act with you.—You are also occasionally to reinforce them with additional numbers, as they may stand in need of it.—In case of an attack upon or investiture of Red-bank, you are to act upon the rear or flanks of the enemy; not to throw your troops into the Fort, except such reinforcements from them as may really be wanted in defence of the works.

" Woodberry I have pitched upon as a general station, from its nearness to the forts, and the greater facility there will, on that account, be, to answer in common the ends proposed.—In case of the approach of the enemy towards you, you are to take such a situation as shall seem to you most eligible.

" I hope it is unnecessary to caution you to be, in every circumstance upon your guard against surprises. At Woodberry you will be between two creeks—if you can draw any security from this, by breaking down bridges or otherwise, so as to render the march of the enemy in their approach more circuitous, or to lessen the number of approaches, it will be an advantage worth improving. I am, &c.

" G° WASHINGTON."[1]

WASHINGTON TO LIEUTENANT-COLONEL SAMUEL SMITH.

" HEAD QUARTERS, 28 October, 1777

" SIR :

" I am fav^d with yours of the 26th. As there seems to be a doubt of the priority of the date of your or L^t.-Colonel Green's Comm^n I have, in a letter of this date, desired him to wave the matter in dispute for the present, and act under your command, as you have been in the Fort from the Beginning and must be better acquainted with the nature of the defences than a stranger.

" I have ordered a very handsome detachment for the

[1] Body of instructions is in Lieutenant-Colonel Hamilton's writing.

reinforcement of Forts Mifflin and Mercer and the Gallies
—they have been ready since yesterday, but the weather has
been such, that they could not march. When they arrive,
the duty will not be so severe, and if the men that you carried down at first can possibly be spared they shall be relieved. I will send them down necessaries out of the first
that arrive from Lancaster. You seem to have mistaken
the Commodore's meaning. From his letter I understand
that he will always assist you whenever it is in his power.
He tells you that in rough weather his Gallies and armed
Boats cannot live and therefore guards you against expect-
ing much assistance from them at such times. I beg you
of all things, not to suffer any Jealousies between the land
and sea service to take place. Consider that your mutual
security depends upon acting perfectly in concert. I have
wrote to Col° Green to afford you every possible assistance
from Red Bank till the reinforcement gets down. I have
the greatest hopes that this Storm of Rain and Wind at N. E.
will overflow all the enemy's lower works upon province
Island, and ruin the new Roads they have been making. I
recommend every attention to you and I hope a glorious
success will reward your exertions. I am &c

" G° WASHINGTON.

" P.S.—Keep the Banks of province Island constantly cut
and you will embarrass the Enemy excessively. Do not
mention anything of the expectation of a reinforcement lest
the Enemy take means to intercept them." [1]

WASHINGTON TO COMMODORE HAZELWOOD.

"HEAD QUARTERS, 28 October, 1777
" SIR :

" In consequence of your representation of the Weakness of your Fleet, I have order'd a return of Sailors in
the Army to be made to me, & find they amount to more
than 100, which will March with a Detachment for the
Forts, as soon as the Weather will permit.

[1] In manuscript of Lieutenant-Colonel Tench Tilghman.

" This Re-enforcement, I expect, will amply supply your wants, & enable you to give every assistance to the Forts that can be reasonably expected from you, & as their Strength will be greatly augmented, it is my most earnest desire, that every mode may be adopted, by which your force may be brought to co-opperate against the designs & approaches of the Enemy, & that a mutual confidence & perfect understanding may chearfully take place.

" The Ammunition you have & will receive is to be considered sent for the use of the whole, & distributed accordingly.

" As there is a greater possibility that the reduction of the Forts might be effected by surprize than any other means, you will see the necessity of giving them every Aid by your Gondolas & Guard Boats as may effectually prevent any mischance of this kind. I am &c.

" G⁰ WASHINGTON."

BRIGADIER-GENERAL FORMAN TO WASHINGTON.[1]
" SIR :

" Your Exc^{lys} fav^r of the 27th was handed to me This afternoon, previous to my rec^t of it I had given orders to several of the Militia officers of This part of the Country to Assemble their men—and have used my endeavours with Genl Newcomb to obtain a return of The men it is said he has assembled That They might be put on some Duty either in the Garrisons or on some out guards—But the Genl absolutely refuses to render me any Acc^t of himself or his men —y^t I am not able to Inform your Excel^y whether Genl [Silas] Newcomb really has or has not any men Assembled.

" The Excessive rainy weather has prevented the Troops from Monmouth and Burlington Coming forward as fast as I could have wished—They are however some of Them This

---

[1] In connection with these letters should be read a series from Major John Clark, Jr., to Washington, published by this Society in the first volume of its Bulletin, 1845–1847. Major Clark was under orders to obtain intelligence of the enemy's movements in and about the city, and acquitted himself in a highly satisfactory manner.

day advanced as far as haddon field, and will in The Morning be down when I will Immediately incorporate them with the Two Garrisons—They will not be equal to there wants, yet they will be a feeling reinforcement.—had it not been for the Excessive rains for some Days past I should have had more men Collected Then woold have been Necessary to man Red Bank and Fort Mifflin; and yet Think I Could be able to Collect a respectable body of Militia was I able to overcome the Obstinacy of, or to Displace, Gen¹ Newcomb.

" from the best information I can Collect he has at no time given any assistance either to The Garrisons or the fleet—particularly in The late Attack on red Bank he neither harrassed The Enemy in their Advance, During the Assault or in Their retreat.

" he Thinks himself only Accountable to The Gov͏ͬ [Livingston] and Major Gen¹ Dickinson—I should be glad of your Excel͏ͬˢ directions respecting my treatment of him.[1]

" On Sunday Last a number of Marines and Highlanders Landed at Billings Port—and have been Imployed in Throwing up a five gun Battery on the water side below the Bank, as we suppose to prevent our Gally men geting the Guns and provisions out of the Two Ship of war yͭ were blown up the Day of the attack on the Chevaux de frize. The Deserters and prisoners Differ in their Acc͏ͭˢ of Their Numbers—some of Them say Three or four hundred, others say not more then 150.

" The Late rain and Winds have Occasioned an Uncommon High Tide, all the Meadowes are under Water, and I am sorry to inform your Excel͏ˡʸ yͭ we have much reason to fear Fort Miflin will receive Very Considerable Dammage.

---

[1] " General Newcomb's conduct is such as might naturally be expected from a Gentleman who was made a General, because your Excellency did not think him fit for a Collonel. . . . If he makes any more Difficulties of that kind, I doubt not, by his present down-hill character with the present house, he will run a great risque of being superceded, which I may venture to say would prove no Loss to his Country."—*Governor Livingston to Washington*, November 5, 1777. For Washington's opinion of Newcomb's uselessness, see my " Writings of Washington," Vol. VI. pp. 157, 169.

" One of the Enemies Bridges of Boats over the Schuylkill has broak loose in the Deluge and Drifted off—A very
Considerable part of it is allready brought under red Bank,
and at sun down when I left The Fort the row Gallymen
ware going after the remainder.

" At Two o'Clock This day a Number of the British
Troops (by Estimation 1000) ware seen Crossing the Mouth
of Schuylkill to province Island & for a Considerable Time
stood paradred on The hill round y⁰ Pest House—(the only
Dry ground in yᵗ Nabourhood,) a small mist prevented our
observing where They afterwards went to—The Troops yᵗ
I mentioned to have Crossed on Sunday, we have heard
nothing of since—but Think it highly probable They returned.

" from the spirits of the Garrison at red Bank, the reinforcements your Exceˡʸ mentions sending and the Militia yᵗ
I flatter myself I shall raise, I hope we shall be able to give
a good Accᵗ of The Enemy should They make a Second
Attempt on this post—all though This post is of great Importance to Them—I cannot believe They will Dare to send
a Very Considerable body of Men to invest it—Least They
Lay Their grand Army too open to an Attac from your
Exceˡʸ.

" We have the pleasure to hear yᵗ your Excelʸ has reᶜᵈ The
Articles of Capitulation of Genˡ Burgoin's Army. I beg
most Heartily to Congratulate your Excelʸ on pleasing
appearance of our affairs. I have &c

" DAVID FORMAN.

" Mᴿ LADDS NEAR RED BANK
  " 29 October, 1777."

LORD STIRLING TO WASHINGTON.

" READING, October 29 1777

" DEAR SIR

" After leaveing Potsgrove I could not meet with any
place where I could Conveniently put up 'till I came to this
place, and I find myself so much better for the Rest I had
here that I intend to set out for Camp again as soon as I
find the Roads are passable with a Carriage. On Saturday

last I sent off to Camp an Officer with 64 men fit for Duty, there remain in this place 244 wounded, 63 sick, & 57 Convalessents—in a very few days near 100 more of them may be sent to Camp   I am &c

" STIRLING.

"Poor Smith, D. A. G. is dead of his wound.   Lieut. Baylor recovering fast.   Major Clow very Ill.   Lieut. Randolph better.

"P.S.—I take the Liberty of enclosing a Memorandum of a few thoughts which have occurred to me, for your Excellency's peruseal.

[Enclosure.]

" The Enemy probably will detach another Body of Men to Attack Red Bank with heavier Cannon, & by a Cannonade in breach endeavour to render an Assault more practicable & more successfull.   I say it is probable, because I believe they are now Convinced that it is their only Chance of Opening the Communication between their fleet and Army at Philadelphia; and that without it, they cannot long exist there.   We should therefore do everything in our power to retard & render difficult their Operations on that side; by Collecting the Militia & setting them at work in destroying all the Bridges, Causeways, & Roads between Cooper's ferry & that fort, & in harrassing them whenever they do approach, & whenever it is discovered that they are about to make an Attempt that way, I would send a respectable Body of Continental Troops to Counteract their operations.

" If this should not soon appear to be their Intentions, they must mean to retire from Philadelphia to the other side of Schuylkill, or to give this Army Battle—the first should be prevented, and the latter in our present scituation avoided, if possible; I would therefore be for passing the whole Army (except 1000 men) over the Schuylkill and takeing post somewhere near Radnor Meeting House, where we should be equally distant from all the fords on Schuylkill below the Valley forge, & by Vigilantly watching them on such timely Notice of their Motions as would put it in our power to attack them on their March with the greatest Advantages. Our Station on that side the Schuylkill would put it in our power Effectually to Cutt off their Communication by land between their fleet & Army, and would reduce Gen[l] Howe to force a march under every disadvantage. The 1000 men left on this side the River would under a Vigilant Officer be Sufficient to prevent their small parties from Ravaging the Country & gaining intelligence; our whole Army in their present Scituation can do no more."

BRIGADIER-GENERAL JAMES POTTER TO WASHINGTON.

"DARBEY, Oct[r] 30th 1777, 3 oClock.

" SIR :

" I have been Round all the ferreys, and taking a vew of Carpenters Island the enemy sent over to the Island a large Reinforcement yesterday, all the Meddows are under watter and the breeches we maid are all opned there Bridge is carreyed off by the flud, a part of it is on this side of the River which I have Just Hard of at this place, and I will go Immedatly and destroy it. I will do every thing in my power to prevent there Gating a Bridge across again, and live in hopes that your excelancey will send over some Cannon and men to command the ferreys. I am of opinion that if the communication between the enemy and there shiping was cut off the wold be son oblidged to move there Quarters, this night I will cut places in the Banks that has not been opened yet, and I am In hops it will be Imposable for them to get aney provision by Rodalphs ferrey. in Hast I am &c

"JA[s] POTTER."

CAPTAIN LEE TO WASHINGTON.

" SIR

" I wrote your Excellency yesterday, since which I have been active in acquainting myself with the disposition & connexion of the enemy on this side the Schuylkill.

" They have a body of men (not five hundred in number) on Carpenters island; the possession of this post secures a

constant & ready supply of provision. It is brought up by
water, from the fleet off Chester, deposited under cover of
the ships against the chiveaux de frise, & then conducted
thro' Carpenters island to the new lower ferry, & so on to
Philad*. If this communication is not interrupted, supplies
of provisions will be as abundant, as if the fleet lay off the
wharf of the city.

" There is a beef trade carried on between the inhabitants, & the enemy at a place called Grubs Landing, about
six miles below Chester. This illicit correspondence came
to my knowledge but yesterday. I have detached a party
of dragoons to disturb them ; & make no doubt my endeavours to interrupt this connexion, will be effectual. I
have &c.

" Hen^y Lee.

" Oct. 31, 1777.

" N.B.—At present, the communication between the fleet
& Carpenters island is totally cut off by the inundation of
the Schuylkill. The fleet are engaged daily in bringing up
provision to the mouth of Darby Creek, which will be con-
veyed to Carpenters Island as soon as the roads will admit."

WASHINGTON TO BRIGADIER-GENERAL VARNUM.

" Head Quarters, 31 October, 1777

" Sir :

" The loss of our heavy Cannon on the North River, and
the possibility however remote of our losing those which are
in the Forts on the Delaware, in which case we should be
totally divested of these necessary opponents to the Enemys
Fleet, make it adviseable to remove from Red Bank and Fort
Mifflin all the large Calibers that can possibly be spared from
the necessary defence of those posts—to some Place of safety
where they may be kept in Reserve. Fort Mifflin has had
an acquisition of Cannon, taken from the Wreck of the
Augusta,[1] by which this will probably have a superfluous
number. The Approaching Frosts will effectually stop the

---

[1] See Lee to Washington, November 3, *post*.

Blasts of our Furnaces, which is a further cogent Reason for making a store of heavy Cannon in case of accidents to our Forts. I mentioned in my Letter to General Forman that the Crews on board the Galleys should not expose themselves to the fire of the Battery which he thinks the Enemy have raised for the purpose of interrupting them—but if a Plan which I have suggested to him can be carried into execution, the difficulty will be removed and a farther acquisition made of the valuable Article in question.[1] I am &c

" G° Washington."

WASHINGTON TO BRIGADIER-GENERAL POTTER.

" Head Quarters, 31 October, 1777

" Sir

" As soon as the Schuylkill is fordable, I shall send over a large body of Militia to you, for the purpose of executing some particular matters. The principal are, to endeavour to break up the Road by which the enemy have a communication with their shipping over the Islands, if it is practicable, and to remove the running Stones from the Mills in the neighbourhood of Chester and Wilmington. This last, I would have you undertake immediately with your present force, as I have information that the Enemy are about making a detachment to Wilmington, probably with an intent to take post there, and secure the use of the Mills. To execute this matter at once, you should impress a sufficient number of Waggons for the purpose, without letting any person know what they are for, and send them under good Officers with sufficient parties to the following Mills—Lloyd's about two Miles on this side of Chester. Shaw's, about one Mile back of Chester. Robinson's, on Naaman's Creek, and the Brandywine Mills. If there are any others that I have not mentioned, contiguous to the River, they are also to be dismounted. Many of the Mills have spare runners, they must also be removed. The stones should be marked with Tar and Grease, or in some other manner, that it may [be] known to what Mills they belong, that they may be returned

---

[1] In manuscript of Lieutenant-Colonel John Laurens.

and made use of in future. And they should be moved to such distance that the Enemy cannot recover them. If there is any Flour in the Mills, it should be removed, if possible, after the stones are secured. I am inform'd that there is a considerable quantity in Shaw's, particularly, which there is reason to believe is intended for the Enemy. It is very convenient to the Navigation of Chester Creek and should therefore be first taken care of. I beg you may instantly set about this Work for the reason before mentioned. That no previous alarm may be given, let a certain day and a certain hour be fixed upon for the execution of the whole at one time, and even the officers who are to do the Business should not know their destination till just before they set out, lest it should take wind.

"I have yours of yesterday afternoon, and am glad to hear that the flood has done so much damage to the meadows—endeavour by all means to keep the breaches open. When the party that I mentioned in the former part of my letter gets down, I hope you will be able to break up the dykes effectually. I am &c.

"G° WASHINGTON.

"P.S.—I have desired Capt. [Henry] Lee of the light Horse to give you any assistance that you may want." [1]

WASHINGTON TO LIEUTENANT-COLONEL SMITH.

"HEAD QUARTERS, 1 November, 1777

"SIR:

"I have this moment received your favor of yesterday, & hope General Varnum with the Detachment from this Army, have by this time arriv'd to your support, & that your little Garrison will, with the greatest confidence & Vigor, exert itself to baffle every attempt of the Enemy to reduce it. When I last saw Genl Foreman I authorized him to collect all the Cloathing, such as Shoes, Stockings, Shirts, Breeches, &c^a, which he possibly could; & by this Opportunity I have requested him to let you have as many of them as he can

---

[1] In manuscript of Lieutenant-Colonel Tench Tilghman.

spare for your men, who, I make no doubt must be greatly in want of them. You will therefore apply to him.

" From the Idea I at present bear of the Island on which your fort stands, I am of opinion, that, if the upper End of it was laid under water it would very much retard any operations of the Enemy against you—but whether this is practible, or whether opening the Banks to effect it would not be productive of Inconvenience to the Fort, I leave to you and the Officers with you to determine, & only mean to propose it for your consideration. I am &c

" G⁰ WASHINGTON." [1]

WASHINGTON TO COMMODORE HAZELWOOD.

"WHITPIN, MORRIS'S, 2 November, 1777

" SIR :

" Upon maturely considering the nature of the Fortress on Mud Island incomplete in such works as would secure it against Storm, and investigation what mode of defence is best adapted to its deficiency in this respect—it appears absolutely necessary to keep the Enemy at bay as much as possible and confine them to distant Combat—this can only be effected by the co-operation of the Fleet under your command, or such part of it as may appear to you proper to be detached for the purpose. Nothing but the Fire of your Vessels and Galleys can prevent the Enemys making a descent upon the Island, if they are determined to effect it by such a Sacrifice as the importance of the object to them certainly deserves. I would advise therefore in case of the Enemy's attempting to throw a number of men over in boats, not to suffer the attention of the Fleet to be intirely call'd off by any concerted attempt which may be made on the Chevaux-de-frise at the same time—but to order a sufficient number of Galleys to meet their boats and keep up a well directed fire, or board them, as circumstances may require —in a word every measure should be taken which your

---

[1] A letter of this date to the President of Congress is printed in my "Writings of Washington," Vol. VI. p. 156. Also letters to Brigadier-General Varnum and Governor Livingston, pp. 168 and 169.

skill in naval manœuvres can dictate to prevent them from getting footing on the island. A fire of Red-hot balls thrown with judgement from a few Vessels, and the Solidity of the work itself will be a sufficient security in the meantime to the Chevaux-de-frise. If the Enemy can be foiled in this stratagem of causing a diversion to your fleet, by cannon-ading from their ships, and making preparations to clear the Chevaux-de-frise, there will be but one way left them, which is to attempt a Landing by night. How necessary the Guardianship of the Galleys will be in such Case, must be obvious. If a sudden Assault from superior numbers, taking the advantage of weak parts, would be dreadful by day, when someth⁵ of the Enemys designs is to be discovered, how fatal might it be in the confusion of darkness when the Guns of the Fort could not be brought to bear.

" Galleys stationed between the Fort and province Island at night are the only Security which the Garrison could have in such case against a sudden Descent from the Enemy, cover'd perhaps by false Attacks and Demonstration from the Shipping.

" You are the best Judge of the most proper Situation for the Galleys. However, if there is no cogent Reason for keeping the whole of them on the Jersey Side, it appears to me that station⁵ them or part of them where they will be within distance for giving immediate Support to the Garrison on Mud Island would be turning their Service to the best account.[1]

" I am &c

" G⁰ WASHINGTON."

MAJOR FLEURY'S JOURNAL,[2] AND LETTER TO COLONEL HAMILTON.

"*Novem.* 2ᵈ. About 2 O'Clock in the morning we hear a great noise of oars near the Shore of Province Island, and the Mouth of Schuylkil—a great number of Troops as far as we could judge by their voices, and the noise fil'd off

[1] In manuscript of Lieutenant-Colonel John Laurens.
[2] At Fort Mifflin.

upon the Bank towards the Pest-house—at 5 oClock every-thing was quiet again.

" 3. For two days past we had suspected that the Enemys Vessels made different turns in the course of the night to the Augusta's wreck—either to carry off the Cannon which the Galleys had neglected throwing into the water, or taking possession of, or to tow off the Hulk—but they had a more important object which they have been permitted to execute without interruption — and this morning's daylight dis-cover'd to us their two nights' labour—they are raising a battery of heavy Cannon upon the hulk which is aground on the sand bank, the Galleys do not disturb them in their work, which, if they finish it, will do great injury to our Fort—where you know there is no Shelter for the Troops—it is important to drive them from that particular spot of the River, and thirteen Galleys with two floating Batteries may do it if they please.

" As we are in want here of Joist, Pickets, Palisades, and even Earth, and as it is impossible to fortify a place with water unless one has means to stop it—I went yesterday with 20 men to endeavour to get wood on the Jersey Shore, but I could get only a few Pickets, of which I shall make palisades, if I am permitted to use them according to my Ideas.

" When His Excellency approved my Zeal and my re-maining at Fort Mifflin in quality of Engineer, he did not give me an order to act in that capacity, and I can only advise without being heard. While Baron Arendt was present he understands the Military Art, and my Opinions in point of fortification were his—but he is absent, and you know there are persons who know a great deal without having ever learnt—and whose obstinacy is equal to their Insufficiency. However I do not complain of any one, I confine myself only to observing that my Zeal for your Cause cannot be useful unless I am permitted to display it, in a branch which I have studied, on a spot with which I am well acquainted, by my own Remarks, and those of many other Engineers skilful and accurate men.

" Honour commands me to do everything in my power.   I hope to do my Duty in whatever way I am made use of—and to die in the breach if necessary—but I will observe only that I thought myself employ'd in a different capacity from that of a Grenadier." [1]

LORD STIRLING TO WASHINGTON.

" READING Nov 3ᵈ 1777

" DEAR SIR :

" Your Excellency's letter of the first Instant, I received yesterday, and am happy to find that any part of my thoughts on the measures necessary to be taken Coincided so nearly with those you had already pursued: and I am in hopes they will be amply Sufficient to render abortive any measures the Enemy may attempt on the side of Red Bank. The objection to the other measure is indeed a very Capital one, and the Communication is Certainly better kept up from the present position : But it is my duty to inform your Excellency no freshet whatever does totally Cut off the Communication between the two Sides of Schuylkill, for at this place there are two rope ferry's with excellent large Scows which can carry near an hundred men at a time, and move so quick that a Column of Troops would pass at each of them as soon as at the best ford at any time; there is also a good ferry at Potts Grove; I mention this least they should be wanted on some future Occasion.   I believe General Howe is in a very awkward Scituation, he cannot attempt another attack on Red Bank without detaching a larger body than he can spare from his Army, nor will he this season be able to advance a Battery on province nearer to fort Miflin, in short he cannot cooperate with the Navy in attacking the forts or raizeing the Cheva. de frize ; unless it be by some desperate attempt to storm fort Miflin in Boats —but desperation he is almost drove to. . . . .

" STIRLING."

[1] Translated by Lieutenant-Colonel John Laurens.

BRIGADIER-GENERAL POTTER TO WASHINGTON.

" SIR :

" The enemy brings provision in Boats in the night along the side of the Shore, and up the Schulkill about a mile above the lowest ferrey, on Saterday evining last there went down 30 Boats I think the came up Last night in the Time of the flud they maid a voige.

" You may be asured that the Enemy are Bulding three floting Battereys one at Ougdons [?] ferrey and two about a mile above, the lowest ferrey   the two letter ones we can see Clearly one seems allmost finished the other the Began to Nale the plank on last Saterday, if these Battereys are once finished, and they have persession of Carpenters Island, our fourts and Galleys must unavetable fall into there Hands. I can see no way of saving our fourts and Galleys but by Immedatly Taking there fourt, and Battreys on carpenters Island, which I think can be dun with good Troops with no crait Loss if that was dun we coud use there Battrey at the pest Hous against themselves and by that Means Defiat there intencions—I hope a great part of the mill Stones were Removed yesterday as I had sent out for that purpose 150 men—the enemy are in hopes of gating up there shiping and has brought up there Bagage as far as Chester.   I wold Refare your Excelancey to Mess⁸ Lytle Hunter and Mountgomrey for a more full Account of these Metters— they have Been with me in meaking Discovereys.   I am &c
" JA⁸ POTTER.

" M ͬ WILLINGS
" Nov ͬ 3, 1777

" P.S.—I mount a gaurd of 100 men at the middle ferrey and at Grayes, 30, near Boons dam 50 with a proper num- ber of Officers.

" My men have severe duty to do.

" I have Been Reinforged my Strenth is about 950 men with Arms and wanting arms 300 Exclusive of Officers."

BRIGADIER-GENERAL VARNUM TO WASHINGTON.

"Woodberry, 3ᵈ Novʳ 1777

" Sir :

" We arrived at this Place yesterday. I have taken a
View of the Forts, and think them in a good State of Defence.
The Want of Confidence between the Commodore and Colᵒ
Smith is very great. I shall do every Thing in my Power
to cause that mutual Support between the Land and Water
Forces, which appears very essential for the Security of Fort
Mifflin. I am not yet fully acquainted with the Ground, so
as to give your Excellency that satisfaction wᶜʰ I coud wish.
Have ordered Four Capᵗˢ, Eight Subs, Twelve Serjeants,
Twelve Corporils and Two Hundred Privates into Fort
Mifflin. I shall give that Post a still greater Support, by
relieving the Invalids. The Enemy are in Possession of
Billing's Port : Some of their Shipping lay above that Place,
about Two Miles below Fort Mifflin. In this Situation it is
impossible for the Commodore to drag for the Cannon &c.
as mentioned in your Orders of the 31ˢᵗ ultᵒ. There are no
more Cannon in the Forts than are really necessary. There
are no Militia of Consequence in Force here. General Newcomb has perhaps between one and two Hundred, General
Foreman is not upon the Ground. I am &c.[1]

"J. M. Varnum."

LIEUTENANT-COLONEL SMITH TO WASHINGTON.

"Fort Mifflin, Novembʳ 3ʳᵈ 1777

" Sir :

" I have this Insᵗ the honor to receve your Excellency's
Letter of the 1ˢᵗ. Genˡ Vernum has arriv'd and will send
me 200 men this morning. Genˡ Foreman has some
Cloathing of small consequence, which I am to have this
day. We by order of Genˡ Vernum begin this day to take
the Inhabitants Cloaths. I fear it will be a very poor Resource—this Garrison must be well cloathed or they will

---

[1] A postscript omitted, as of no consequence.

perish. I always keep the part of the Island you mention under water, and hope now to be able to maintain the Fort.

" The Industrious enemy turn their Misfortunes to advantage, these two nights they have been employed in raising the wreck of the 64 Gun Ship, and have this morning shewn a floating Battery almost compleat. I presume to morrow they will open it, unless Gen¹ Vernon [Varnum] takes Billingsport from them. I think *that* one of the most effectual strokes that can be struck in our favor, and have recommended it to him, if he takes it, they then will have no alternative but storming this Island which they appear to be much afraid of. I have the honor &c

" Sam Smith."

CAPTAIN LEE TO WASHINGTON.

" N° 3ᵈ 77

" Sir :

" I mentioned to your Excellency in my last letʳ, an intercourse subsisting between the inhabitants & fleet near Grub's landing. Having received a confirmation of this intelligence I pushed down with twelve dragoons & reached the place early yesterday morning. At Robinsons mill on Namur Creek I fell in with a foraging party; on the appearance of my dragoons the enemy ran without giving one fire. A Captain of the Queen's Rangers, a factor from Baltimore County & seven mariners & soldiers were made prisoners. The Captain I indulged with his parole, till the 10 insᵗ, on or before which day, he will wait on your Excellency to be farther disposed off. The transports have all moved up from New-castle to Chester. They are generally loaded with the wounded & baggage; so that their being ordered up, predicts another attempt on the fort, which they suppose will be effectual. Major Cuyler, Sir Wᵐ Howe's first Aid de Camp sailed in a packet the day before yesterday for London—his business is to press Administration for strong & early reinforcements.

" Among the mariners taken yesterday is a mate belonging to the Union transport, he informs, that Lord Howe had sent orders to the Captains of the transports to send up each, four or more of their seamen. What he can want with them is not certainly known. I conjecture they are designed to mann the floating batteries now building in the Schuylkill. It is a certainty from the intelligence received from various characters, that the enemy design shortly to make a push on fort Mifflin. Their only possible mode, by which they can promise themselves success, is their floating batteries. In this they may be totally blasted; if we take possession of Carpenters island. From this post throwing up strong works, we most assuredly can put a stop to their favourite scheme, & what is of great consequence, co-operate with the gallies in preventing those supplies of provision which go up by water every night to Philad^a. Your Excell^y may rely on it, that thirty or more boats, with muffled oars, pass our fort & gallies every night to the city. The ships blown up the other day were the Augusta, & Merlin sloop of 18 guns. The Augusta took fire from her own cannonading, one L^t, chaplain & forty privates perished in the explosion. The Merlin being fast on ground was set fire to, by order.

"There is brisk trade carried on at New-castle. I have detached a party of dragoons to that place, with directions to visit the several landings on the river, to disperse the late resolutions of Congress[1] among the inhabitants, & to assure the people, that they will be strictly carried into execution. I set out myself this moment with a desire to burn some of the enemy's small craft which lay at Grubs landing, under cover of an eight gun schooner. Your Excellency's &c

"HEN^y LEE."

MAJOR FLEURY'S JOURNAL.

"3^d night—a considerable number of the Enemys boats pass'd and repass'd in the course of the night, near the Shore of Province Island—it appears that this Communication between their Fleet and Philadelphia is established, and what will surprise you perhaps, is that it is a sure one, there being no Interruption on our part—we cannot cannonade

[1] *Journals of Congress*, October 8, 1777.

them from the Fort, the shade of Trees prevents our being informed of their passage otherwise than by the noise of oars, and firing at sounds would be wasting pretious Ammunition.

"4. The work of the Enemy upon the Augusta's Hulk is interrupted by the difficulties which they must have met with in raising a Battery on it—I believe however that they will make a further Trial, if they know their own Interest.

"The Enemy's Land-batteries are likewise silent."[1]

WASHINGTON TO COLONEL CHRISTOPHER GREENE.[2]

"WHITE MARSH, 4 November, 1777

"SIR:

"I am led to believe from the conversation I have had with Lt Col^o Green, that you have made Fort Mercer impregnable against an assault; and that nothing is to be feared but from regular approaches and shells—to guard against the first, it would be found necessary to have some out works, which time may, possibly, allow you to raise—to secure the garrison against the second, some Bomb proofs should be constructed.—The first you can easily do, but how far the other is practicable I know not, for want of competent knowledge of the place—its extent—&c^a—I would suggest to you however, by way of quære, whether caverns could not be cut out of the Bank below the work, and supported (the Earth) by Pillars, would not be the quickest, and most effectual method.—If this should be found to answer, all your Men, in case of a Bombardment, might be concealed in them, except such as should be found necessary for Guards.

"It is unnecessary, I am persuaded, to suggest to you the propriety of keeping a sufficn^t quantity of salt provision and Bread or Flour in the Fort in case of an Investiture—as also Wood for Fires and Cooking.   I am &c^3

"G^o WASHINGTON."

[1] Translated by Lieutenant-Colonel John Laurens.
[2] At Red Bank.   [3] In manuscript of Washington.

WASHINGTON TO BRIGADIER-GENERAL VARNUM.

"WHITE MARSH, 4 November, 1777

" DEAR SIR

" The Inclosed I had written to Col° Greene before your
favour of yesterday reached my hands.—I am happy in receiving so favourable a report, as your Letter contains,
of the situation of the Forts—I most devoutly wish that
the exertions of yourself & Officers may be crownd with
the success that so good a cause, and such labours deserve.

" My Letters to Comodore Hazlewood, & Col° Green, go
unopened under this cover, that you may read—seal, &
deliver them.—If the measure proposed in the Letter to
Col° Green can be carried into execution no time should be
lost.—I thank you for your endeavours to restore confidence
between the Com' & Smith. I find something of the same
kind existing between Smith & Mons' Fleury, who I consider as a very valuable officer. How strange it is that Men
engaged in the same Important Service, should be eternally
bickering, instead of giving mutual aid! Offic'* cannot act
upon proper principles who suffer trifles to interpose to
create distrust & jealousy.—All our actions should be regu-
lated by one uniform Plan—& that Plan should have one
object only in view, to wit, the good of the Service. Where
this is the case, although there may be a deversity of opinion, there can be no real obstruction.—I hope all these little
rubs will be done away by your prudent Managem'. I
am &c

" G° WASHINGTON.

" P.S.—What force have the Enemy at Billingsport? Is
there a moral certainty (with your force) of driving them
from thence? If there is, I have no objection to the attempt; but wish circumstances to be well consider'd before
any resolution is come to."[1]

[1] All but the postscript is in the manuscript of Washington.

WASHINGTON TO LIEUTENANT-COLONEL SAMUEL SMITH.

"HEAD QUARTERS, November 4, 1777

" SIR :

" I have received your Letter dated yesterday, giving an account of the reinforcement which you expect from Gen¹ Varnum and the supplies of clothing from Gen¹ Forman. It gives me pain to learn that the latter are likely to be so inadequate to your wants, but hope that by taking proper measures, the Contributions of the Inhabitants will not prove so poor a Resource as you seem to fear.

" Inclosed is a Letter to Majʳ Fleury, whom I order'd to fort Mifflin to serve in quality of Engineer, as he is a Young Man of Talents and has made this branch of Military Science his particular Study, I place a confidence in him. You will therefore make the best Arrangement for enabling him to carry such Plans into Execution as come within his Department. His Authority at the same time that it is subordinate to yours must be sufficient for putting into practice what his knowledge of Fortification points out as necessary for defending the post.—and his Department, tho' inferior being of a distinct and separate nature, requires that his orders should be in a great degree discretionary— and that he shᵈ be suffered to exercise his Judgement. Persuaded that you will concur with him in every measure which the good of the service may require, I remain &c.¹

" Gᵒ WASHINGTON."

WASHINGTON TO COMMODORE HAZELWOOD.

" HEAD QUARTERS, WHITEMARSH, 4 November, 1777

" SIR :

" Gen¹ Potter and Capᵗ Lee, who are posted upon the West side of Schuylkill to interrupt the Enemy's communication across the Islands, both assure me that they undoubtedly pass by Night with Boats between province and

¹ In manuscript of Lieutenant-Colonel John Laurens.

Mud Island and into Schuylkill. If this passage is not stopped in some measure, it is in vain to think of hindering them from getting supplies from their shipping as long as the River remains free of Ice. I will not undertake to point out to you the mode of doing this, but in my opinion the most probable is, to keep small Boats rowing guard between the south end of Mud Island and the pennsylvania shore, and a Galley or two under the north end of Mud Island, when the weather will permit. If the guard Boats make a signal, the Gallies may get ready to intercept the Convoy. The Enemy will not chuse to fire in the dark, because there will be a greater chance of damaging their own craft, than hurting our armed Vessels, as being greater in number. I beg you will immediately fall upon this or any other Scheme, which to you may seem more effectual to put a stop to this intercourse. I am &c.[1]

"G⁰ WASHINGTON."

LIEUTENANT-COLONEL SMITH TO WASHINGTON.

"FORT MIFFLIN, 4ᵗʰ November, 1777

" SIR :

" I wrote your Excellency yesterday—am happy to find I was mistaken. The enemy have not constructed a Battery on their work as I then expected. I was deceiv'd by the water being much lower than usual, which left a greater part of the wreck naked. General Varnum's reinforcement arriv'd yesterday. Last night about 8 o'clock we were alarm'd with the rowing of Boats between this and Province Island. We at first conceived they intended an attack, but found they passed us with the Ebb, they came out of Schuylkill and passed along the Shore of Province Island to their Shiping, with the flood they return'd up again to Schuylkill. We informed the Gallies that lay near us. Unless some method is taken to prevent that communication, they will without much risk supply themselves with everything wanting from their ships. I have the honor &c

"SAM. SMITH."

---

[1] In manuscript of Lieutenant-Colonel Tench Tilghman.

BRIGADIER-GENERAL POTTER TO WASHINGTON..

" SIR

" I'm a sorey to Inform your excelancey that the Officer I send to the Brandwine Mills has not obay'd my orders Instead of Taking the stons away he has taken the Spinnels Rines and Ironnale heads. I was preparing to send a party to move the Runners But as it is Hard to get waggans and as I am Informed that the Taking these Artecals answers the same end as Removeing the stons, I wait to know your Plesure in this matter. I gave writen orders to the officer. I will Trey him for disobedance I am oppresed with Bad Officers. I wold Rather be a shew boy [?] then what I am, if it wold sarve my Countrey as well. I am &c.

" JA⁸ POTTER.

" CAMP, Novr 5th 1777.

" P.S.—Col: Crafords men are uneasey and wanting to go home. I will not detain them. I think I have men sufficient for all I can do in this place, as the enemy has got that new way of carreying their provision."

WASHINGTON TO BRIGADIER-GENERAL POTTER.

" HEAD QUARTERS, 5 November, 1777

" SIR :

" I have received your Letter of this morning : and am sorry to find that your orders respecting the Mills have not been carried into execution.—it is my desire that the Officer employed in this business should be put under Arrest and tried for disobedience of orders—the parts of the machinery which he has removed may be very easily replaced, whereas had he followed the directions given him, the end in view would have been effectually answer'd.

" Colonel Crawford's party was order'd to join you only for the particular purpose of distressing the Enemy by cutting their Banks ; if this service can be done without them or is found impracticable altogether, I have no motive for detaining them. I am &c

" G° WASHINGTON.

" As the Corps under your Command will probably be an object for the Enemy, you cannot be too vigilant nor guard yourself by too many precautions against surprize. I mention this in consequence of hints given me of their Intentions—and hope therefore it will have its proper effect." [1]

BRIGADIER-GENERAL VARNUM TO WASHINGTON.

" WOODBERRY, 6th Nov[r], 1777

" SIR :

" Great Manto Creek is situated two Miles and an half from Redbank, where it empties into the Delaware. On the west side of this Creek is the Promontory Billingsport, fortified, and garrisoned by three hundred Men, made up of the seventy first Regiment, and of Marines, according to the best Information I have been able to obtain. On the east side of the Creek upwards of a Mile from Billingsport, is a small Eminence on w[ch] the Evening before last, we erected a small Fascine Battery, intending to play upon the Shipping, the morning following, with one Eighteen, and one Twelve Pounder. The Eighteen was overset on the way, and could not be got to the Battery 'till two o'Clock in the afternoon. The Twelve in the intermediate Time, was ply'd with great Advantage upon the Sommersett, a ship of sixty four Guns. The Roebuck and a Frigate were soon driven from their Stations, and the Sommersett fell down to the Distance of a Mile and a Quarter from the Battery, where she touched upon the Beach, and was obliged patiently to take our Fire. In this situation, the Commodore sent down four Gallies, which began their Fire at the Distance of more than two Miles. They advanced however 'till the Sommersett & Roebuck, with a Galley began to discharge their Bow Guns upon them, when they immediately retreated. The Flood Tide making, floated the Sommersett; but, as there was no Wind, she could not get far from us, by w[ch] means she suffered extremely from our Eighteen & twelve Pounders. She hoisted Signals of Distress; the Commo-

---

[1] In manuscript of Lieutenant-Colonel John Laurens.

dore came down with a great naval Force, and began a tre-
mendous Fire, out of Gun Shot, he advanced firing 'till
some of his Shot reached the Ships.   He expended an immense Quantity of ammunition, &, I am pretty certain, hit
the large ship once, in her stern; soon after he retired.
The Battery discharged, from both Guns, more than one
hundred and twenty Pounds; two Thirds of wch at least took
place : And as almost every Shot was directed at the sixty
four, she must be greatly shattered.   Captⁿ Lee who commanded the Guns, behaved perfectly well.   Had the Gallies
behaved tolerably well, the Sommersett must beyond a
Doubt have fallen into our Hands [1]—Could we be furnished with sufficient Ammunition for a Twenty four and
an Eighteen Pounder, without drawing from the Forts, I
am confident we should oblige the Shipping to keep down
the River as low as Billingsport.   By wch means they cou'd
not attempt raising the Chievaux de Frise.   We should be
provided with proper Harness & Horses for these Pieces,
to move them to any part of the Shore at Pleasure.   I am
apprehensive we might do much by throwing up a Battery
about one Third of a Mile below Billings Port, from which,
& the Battery before mentioned, we could easily cross fire
upon every Intch of Channel Way opposite the Mouth of
Manto Creek, and oblige the Shipping to move farther
down, liable to be disen[?]ed from our lower Battery; or
farther up, when they would probably stick upon the
Chievaux de Frize, and be in danger from Fort Mifflin and
the Fire Craft.   The great Injury their Shipping would
receive might probably draw them out from Billings Port
to attack us—their present numbers we could beat, & by
that means possess ourselves of their works, should they
considerably reinforce, wch I immagine they might occasionally do from their Shipping, we might loose our Cannon,
by being obliged to retreat.   Billingsport is the key of the

---

[1] During this engagement Washington was at the Chew house, in Germantown, and, looking from the top, " could discover nothing more than
thick clouds of smoak, and the masts of two vessels, the weather being
very hazy."

Delaware, as the Ship Channel is within Musket shot of it.
I can perceive but one Objection to a Manouvre of this kind;
and indeed that is an important one; Should the Enemy
attack Red Bank in the mean Time, by landing below
Timber Creek, which they might do, we could not afford
that Garrison timely aid. The Remainder of General
McDougall's Division, could they be spared, would form a
Counter ballance to that Difficulty.—Colᵒ Smith is continually complaining of the Remissness of the Fleet. I
have conversed freely with the Commodore upon the Subject
of Defence, wᶜh he ought to afford. He has pointed out to
me the Plans where he has ordered his Guard Boats and
some of his Gallies stationed by night. His Plan, if
spiritedly executed, would sufficiently aid Fort Mifflin,
and Prevent the Enemy from making a Lodgment in its
rear. The Commodore says he cannot prevent the Enemies
Boats from passing up and down the River, as they are
covered by their Batteries upon Province Island and at the
Mouth of Schuylkill. In short, the Commodore appears to
be a very good kind of a Man; but his extreme good Nature
gives too great a Licence to those under his Command, who
would obey only from severity, if any such he has, to[1] their
Duty. From the Conduct of the Fleet yesterday, your
Excellency will be able to know my sentiments respecting
their Prowess. I shall religiously avoid any personal Disputes myself, where I cannot be of service by them, to the public; I shall continue however, to create, if possible, greater
Harmony between the Fleet and Garrisons.—As the Garrisons have necessarily many sick, we are in great Want of
some Gentlemen from the Hospital Department, to establish
a Plan for their Reception, with Medicine and other Articles to make them comfortable. Indeed they suffer on that
account.

" I should have mentioned, when speaking of Fort Mifflin,
that the Enemy were busy, yesterday, in erecting a Fortification upon Province Island, in such a Position as to play

---

[1] A word that is illegible.

obliquely upon the Palisadoes.   This Circumstance convinces me that they do not intend a very sudden Attack upon the Fort.   Should they destroy the Palisadoes, the Defence of the Island will then greatly depend upon the Gallies; altho' it will be difficult to approach to the Rear of the Work, as the Enemy must pass upon a Meadow w°h is very miry.   They cannot surmount that Difficulty by laying Fascines, unless the Gallies quit the Passage between Red Bank and Mud Island intirely.   In fine, I must beg Liberty to repeat that Billingsport is of far more Importance than all the Forts and Gallies put together.   This seems also to be the concurring sentiment of the Gentlemen here universally.

"I have not seen Gen¹ Foreman, nor can I learn where he is.¹   There are about sixty of his Militia at Red bank. Gen¹ Newcomb is still here, & his Troops may amount to two Hundred.   I cannot tell their number exactly, and believe he cannot.   They are badly provided, and can be of little Service in any serious Operation.

"I hope your Excellency will excuse the Prolixity of this, & believe me sincerely yours

"J. M. VARNUM.

"P.S.—12 oClock.   This Moment your Excellency's of the 4ᵗʰ Instant comes to Hand.   In your letter to Col° Smith you mention Clothing.   Since my arrival, have vested three Officers from Fort Mifflin with full Powers of gathering Clothing.   Have sent them to Salem among the Tory Quakers, directing them to procure the Articles necessary for the Garrison, giving their Receipts, specifying the Quantities and Qualities.   I should not have presumed upon such a measure, but from the urgent Necessity ; & being persuaded it was agreeable to what your Excellency had ordered in Pennsylvania."

¹ "General Foreman has to my great concern, & contrary to my warmest sollicitations, resigned his Commission, upon some misunderstanding with the Assembly."—*Governor Livingston to Washington,* November 9, 1777.

WASHINGTON TO BRIGADIER-GENERAL VARNUM.

"HEAD QUARTERS, 7 November, 1777

" SIR :

" From various accounts I am convinced that the Enemy are upon the point of making a grand effort upon Fort Mifflin. A person in confidence of one of their principal artificers thinks it will be today or tomorrow. No time is therefore to be lost in making that Garrison as respectable as your numbers will admit, for should the attack commence before they are reinforced, it may probably be out of your power to throw them in. I think you had for the present better draw all the continental Troops into or near Forts Mercer and Mifflin, and let what Militia are collected lay without, for I am of opinion that they will rather dismay than assist the continental Troops if shut up in the Forts. Acquaint the Commodore that my informant says there are three floating Batteries and some fire rafts prepared which are to fall down upon his Fleet at the same time that the Island is attacked, and desire him to keep a look-out and make the necessary preparations to receive them. As Fort Mercer cannot be attacked without considerable previous notice, I would have you spare as many men to Fort Mifflin as you possibly can ; for if accounts are to be depended upon that is undoubtedly the post the Enemy have their designs upon. I am very anxious to hear what was the occasion of the heavy firing of Musketry on the Evening of the 5th. It seemed to us to be at Fort Mifflin. I am &c [1]

" G[o] WASHINGTON."

BRIGADIER-GENERAL FORMAN TO WASHINGTON.

"PRINCE TOWN, 7th Nov[r] 1777

" SIR

" Your Exce[lys] fav[r] of the 31[t] I rec[d] the 1st Nov[r], and the same Morning I rec[d] an answer from the Council of Safety to a Letter I had wrote to Gov[r] Livingston Respecting the Conduct of Brig[r] Gen[l] Newcomb.—The Council of Safety

---

[1] In manuscript of Lieutenant-Colonel Tench Tilghman.

in their Letter to me enclosed one for Gen[l] Newcomb which
they assured me contain'd their orders to him to make me
returns of his Brigade and receive my orders—I Immediately sent a Horseman to Gen[l] Newcomb with the Letter,
but rec[d] no kind of answer from him.—I then wrote a Note
requesting him to furnish a Number of men to mount Certain Guards as were Necessary to insure early inteligence
of the Enemies movements should they make a second Decent on this Shoar as to prevent a Communication with the
Enemy, and sent Lieu[t] Colo[l] Laurence with it to Gen[l] Newcomb.

" At the Colo[ls] return I rec[d] a Verbal Answer y[t] the
Counsil of safety had no right to give him any Directions.
Neither woold he furnish me with one Man or receive any
orders from me—That He had called the Militia together
without any order and woold if he pleased Dismiss them
the Next Day and requested he might not be troubled with
any further Applications from Gen[l] Forman.

" The Militia from y[t] Quarter was then Comeing in, in
Considerable Numbers—it struck me very fully y[t] by pur-
sueing any rough measures towards Gen[l] Newcomb, the
Militia might make a pretence of our Dispute to refuse to
Assemble & y[t] it was not Improbable to Conclude Gen[l]
Newcomb woold even Dismiss those y[t] ware allready As-
sembled—I thought it very Imprudent to risque either of
these events at y[t] critical time—on Considering y[t] part of y[r]
Excel[ys] Letter of the 31[t] wherein your Excel[y] recommends
my making a Pointed representation of Gen[l] Newcomb's
Conduct, I come to the Following resolution, Viz[t].

" The Troops y[t] marched from Monmouth with me ware
previously incorporated with the Garrison in red Bank fort.
Those from Burlington I ordered to mud Island as soon as
They should arrive—Conceiving I could at no Time be
better spared to make the Necessary representation in person to the Gov[r] Counsil & Assembly of Gen[l] Newcomb's
Conduct & at the same time give the Militia Time to Assemble—Gen[l] Varnum's being in the Nibourhood allso Conspired to make my Presence less Necessary—On Coming

to Trentown I found the Assembly had adjourned to prince Town—To which place I followed them on Monday—The Gov.ʳ was not then come.

" On Teusday Evening he arrived, but too Late to do any Business—Wednesday morning I waited on him Early and fully Explained Genˡ Newcomb's Conduct—a Counsil of Safety was called and a Letter wrote by the Gov.ʳ with the Advice of the Counsil to Genˡ Newcomb to give me the Command as being the Eldest officer—and No farther Notice Taken of him.

" While I was here Two Petitions ware handed into the Assembly most unjustly charging me and sundry other Genᵗ with undue practices on the Day of Election & praying the Election to be set aside—The Petition was read in the House and a Hearing ordered on Teusday next and a Notice served on me to attend.

" I immediately went to the Assembly, Informed them of my then situation and requested the hearing might be Deferred for a few Days until the militia ware assembled and put in some order—my request was Denyed.

" I informed them yᵗ it was impossable for me to do Justice to my Command at red Bank, and attend the House on Teusday—yᵗ I found myself hurt as a Genᵗ by the Illiberal Charges in the petition—yᵗ my reputation as such might suffer should I Neglect to attend—

" On the other hand my reputation as an Officer might be injured by my absence from my post for so long a Time as I Conceived my Attendance on their House would be Necessary.

" Yᵗ I knew of no way to save my reputation as a Genᵗ and at the same time to risque nothing as an officer but resigning my Commission—Which I then Delivered to Mʳ Speaker and Left the House—a few Minutes after I recᵈ a Message From the House Informing yᵗ as I had not recᵈ my Commission from Them, they could not receive it and returned it to me. I went Immediately to the Gov.ʳ from him I recᵈ it and returned it to him.

" Although I have long been Disgusted with the Indolence and want of Attention to military Matters in the Legislature of this State, I was Determined to spin out this campaign in my Slavery, untill I found a set of Men Ploting by the most unfair Means to stain my Reputation.

" for I am well perswaded they ment to take advantage of my Absence & at a Time when they conceived I woold not have been able to attend.—Gen¹ Varnums being at red Bank will I doubt not abundantly supply my absence.

" I have at pres^t no anxiety but y^t the steps I have taken may not so fully meet your Excel^ys approbation as I could wish, & y^t I flatter myself I shall have it when I have an opportunity fully to Explain to your Exce^ly my Treatment. I have the Hon^r &c

" DAVID FORMAN.

" N.B.—I This minute rec^d good Information y^t 36 sail of ships sailed from New York and Sandy Hook on the fifth of This Inst Supposed to be Gen¹ Clinton."

WASHINGTON TO MAJOR-GENERAL DICKINSON.

"HEAD QUARTERS, 8th November, 1777

" DEAR SIR :

" I have received your Letter of the 6th Inst., and thank you for the intelligence contained in it. You will farther oblige me by communicating immediately whatever new matter of public consequence may occur.

" The importance of the Post at Red-bank makes it necessary for us to employ all possible resources in rendering it so respectable by the strength of the Garrison, and the number of Troops stationed within distance to co-operate with it, as not to fear even a more formal Attack than was exhibited in the first successless effort of the Hessians. All the men in your State that can be spared should therefore be collected and march'd to join Gen¹ Varnum.

" Your present of salt-water delicacies will be the more acceptable to us, as they are so great a Rarity, and as I anticipate the pleasure they will give, I return you my thanks for them before their arrival.   I am &c.[1]

"G. WASHINGTON."

WASHINGTON TO BRIGADIER-GENERAL VARNUM.

"HEAD QUARTERS, WHITEMARSH, 8 Nov. 1777.

"SIR :

"Your fav[r] of the 6th relieved me from much anxiety as it was confidently reported that the firing upon the 5th was upon Fort Mifflin.   I am pleased to hear of the Success of your cannonade against the Shipping, and I am very certain if we had more heavy Cannon mounted upon travelling carriages to move up and down the Beach occasionally, that we should annoy and distress them exceedingly.   To possess Billingsport as well as Red Bank is certainly a most desirable object, but circumstanced as we are at present in respect to numbers it is impossible.   In a letter from Gen[l] Dickinson of the 6th he informs me that he had ordered two detachments of Militia to march from Elizabeth Town to Red Bank, one consisting of 160 men ; he does not mention the number of the other.   I have just seen a very intelligent person from Philadelphia.   He has been conversant with many people who stand high in the confidence of the British officers of the first rank.   He finds from all their discourse that a formidable attack is to be made upon Fort Mifflin very soon ; if that fails they will be obliged to change their quarters, as they find they cannot subsist in the city without they have a free communication with their shipping. I therefore repeat what I wrote yesterday that you should immediately reinforce Fort Mifflin as strongly as possible, and give the Commodore notice of the intended attack.   I approve of the Measures you have taken to procure Cloathing for the Troops, and am, Sir, &c.

"G[o] WASHINGTON.

[1] In manuscript of Lieutenant-Colonel John Laurens.   "I am preparing a Waggon Load of the Woodbridge Oisters, they are too fresh, but are Oisters, as such, hope they will be acceptable, shall send them on in a few Days to Head-Quarters, when I shall beg your Excellency's acceptance of them."—*Dickinson to Washington,* November 6, 1777.

" The inclosed for Commodore Hazelwood, Col° Green and Lt. Col° Smith are from Congress, and as they bear honorable testimony of their behaviour hitherto, I beg they may be put into their hands immediately. Perhaps it may prove a further incentive to their gallant exertions." [1]

BRIGADIER-GENERAL VARNUM TO WASHINGTON.

" WOODBERRY, 8th Nov^r, ½ past 5 p m 1777

" SIR :

" I have to acknowledge the Rec^t of your Orders of 7th Instant. The Intelligence you are pleased to communicate, I received last Evening, by two Persons who came out of Philadelphia yesterday, & by a Spy whom I had in Billingsport yesterday, two Hours.—My Acc^{ts} give these additional Circumstances, That the Garrison at Billingsport consist of two Hundred of the seventy first Battalion,[2] & two Hundred Marines. That they were, this Day, to be reinforced by two Hessian Regiments. That there were four Row Gallies & two floating Batteries in Schuylkil; That an attack was to be made upon Fort Mifflin by the way of Schuylkill; That they were to attack Red bank at the same Time, landing just below Timber Creek (a fine beach, and no Obstruction between that and Fort Mercer); that the Troops from Billingsport were to move across Manto Creek, at a Signal given from Philadelphia, & act in Conjunction with Those from Philadelphia, against Fort Mercer;—That they were to attack this Day Morning at four, if possible; If not, the first Time they should be Ready—Last Evening, at Ten, Sky Rockets were seen on Province Island, wch determined me the Action was about to commence. I took every Precaution in my Power; just before Sunsett this Evening, There appeared to be a large Number of Men, Horses, & I tho't Fascines, passing Schuylkill to Province Island. The Ships below fired Guns, wch were supposed to be Signals. The

---

[1] In manuscript of Lieutenant-Colonel Tench Tilghman. The inclosures were the resolutions printed in *Journals of Congress*, November 4, 1777.

[2] The Scotch regiment, commanded by Simon Fraser.

Acct⁹ respecting the Enemy's Intended Movements were given in the same Manner, by two Prisoners of the second Battalion of the seventy first Regiment, whom my Scouts captured yesterday, near Billingsport.—I shall send a Detachment this Night into Fort Mifflin, tho' upon my Honor, I think that Garrison sufficiently manned.—I have the Pleasure to Inform you, that we had Guard Boats last night between Hog and Province Islands, the Rout of the Enemy's Boats, wᶜh met with, fired upon, & caused them to retreat. The Commodore will fix a chain this Night that is already prepared with dry logs to buoy it up, & anchors to fasten it down, between those Islands. Fourteen Gun Boats will lay in the Passage; the Commodore with all his Gallies will lay close to the North End of Mud Island, the Floating Batteries, & Xebecks to guard the chievaux de Frize, & oppose the shipping, should they attempt to advance. And the Continental Vessells under Capᵗ. Robinson's Command will lay at the Mouth of Schuylkill, and at the Mouth of Timber Creek. I have placed the Continental and Militia Guards, upon Timber & Manto Creeks. In a word, I am perfectly satisfied with the different arrangements, & the universal spirit, wᶜh apparently pervades the whole; & unless I am too ignorant of military Dispositions, the Great Governor of the Universe will give to your Arms Success in this Quarter, should the mercenaries attack, as we sincerely expect and wish they will; and to your Excellency, additional Laurels! Pardon me—I write upon the Run, and am thinking of many things at once.—The musketry you mention was the Ecco of Cannon in the Groves. I am &c

"J. M. Varnum."

CAPTAIN LEE TO WASHINGTON.

"No. 8ᵗʰ 77

" Sir

" Mr. Lindsay[1] is just returned from New-castle & has brought with him two Prisoners, the one Capᵗ Nicholas of the Eagle-packet, the other Capᵗ Fenwick of a sloop in

---

[1] Lieutenant William Lindsay, of Bland's regiment.

the service of Government. These two gentlemen being fatigued with their ride, will not arrive at Head-quarters 'till tomorrow.

"The transports have received orders to furnish themselves with six weeks provision, & make ready for sailing with all despatch. A french ship laden with arms & ammunition lately taken by some of the enemy's cruisers, was the other day brought into New-castle harbour. There prevails a report in the fleet, that a channel has been discovered which avoids the chiveaux-de-frise, & that, the Somersett man of war ordered up to try her success on the fort, by that route.

"One of the enemy's batteries on the Schuylkill has been launched two days past, & another is near finished. The mode now pursued by the enemy in transporting supplies, to the city, is as follows. They land their provision above Jones wharf, near a branch of Eagle-creek, they are carried from hence by water to Guien[1] dam, where they again put them in boats & readily convey them down another creek to the Schuylkill. There is no way of interrupting them in this business, but by taking possession of Carpenters Island.

"Mr. Lindsay acquaints me, that the enemy obtain large supplies of fresh provision, &c., from the inhabitants in the lower Counties; his report of this & several other matters engage me to wish for an excursion for a few days in that country.

"There is not the smallest intercourse now subsisting between the country & Navy from Wilmington to the Schuylkill. Your Excellency will please favor me by return of the dragoon with your instructions respecting this route. Enclosed is a let[r] found; supposed to be wrote by Gen. Grant. I am &c

"HEN[Y] LEE."

EXTRACT OF A LETTER FROM MAJOR FLEURY.

"I have received His Excellency's order authorizing me to exercise the functions of Engineer at Fort Mifflin. Since

---

[1] I am unable to determine what name this is intended for, as the writing is illegible. General Potter speaks of "Giers Warff."

my being placed here I think I have neglected nothing to gain the Esteem of my superiors. by my constant attention I have endeavour'd to second the Zeal, Intelligence and Activity of Colo. Smith.

"I never have undertaken any work without previously consulting the Commandant and Principal Officers, and rectifying my Ideas by theirs.

"Colonel D'Arendt entrusted me with the Command of the Reserve and Colo. Smith has continued me in it."

Journal.

"Novem. 5th 6th. The Enemy's boats continue to go up the River with the Tide every night—they seem to direct their course towards the mouth of the Schuylkill. I believe it would be possible to intercept this communication, but our Cannon would be of no service in it—& to fire by guess is throwing away Ammunition.

"The Enemy seem determined to Winter in Province Island if they can't take Fort Mifflin. They are raising a 4th work between the two bank batteries, and half way to Gayers house, where their great work is situated on an eminence. I believe it would be possible to interrupt or even to ruin their works. If His Excellency would form some Enterprise on their Rear, I believe we might make a useful diversion—as I know the Island I offer to serve as Guide to any party that shall be order'd there, in concert with Col. Smith I intend this night to reconnoitre in an arm'd boat the position of their Sentinels, and the safest Landing places, of which I shall make a Report.

"7th. The Enemy appear desirous of fortifying themselves in province Island to maintain the Communication with their Fleet at Billingsport—they are raising Redouts from 5 to 600 yds from the Bank, and the Fort on the rising ground advances rapidly towards Perfection.

"8th. The Enemy have enlarged the upper Battery opposite the Fort, we this morning discover 5 Embrasures, masked as yet with Fascines—it is probable they will all open at

once—their project seems to be, to knock down our palisades, and storm our west front between the two block
houses. To cover our palisades on this side we have
apply'd to Gen¹ Varnum to furnish us with fascines, which
we shall place on the Summit of the bank to serve instead
of Earth, which is not to be had—I don't know whether we
shall be able to procure the Fascines." [1]

CAPTAIN CRAIG TO WASHINGTON.

" FRANKFORD, 8ᵗʰ Novʳ 1777

" SIR

" By every Accᵗ from the City the enemy intend to Attackt
the Fort tomorrow. The Hessians are to stand Guard, the
Highlanders, Grannattier and Light Infantry to make the
Attackt. One of their Floating Batteries that was lanced
[launched] Yesterday is sunk to the bottom. My Guard was
rainforced Last Night. I hope I shall have it in my power
to prevent the Enemy a Comming into the Country as much
as the[y] have done. I am with much Truth &c.

" C. CRAIG."

BRIGADIER-GENERAL POTTER TO WASHINGTON.

" I Receved your excelancys favour of yesterday leat last
evining, ocasioned by my being leat on the enemys lins,
there is nothing perticquler that I see in my power to do
heare, could I Belive that my Troops were fit to storm
Brestworks I wold have actacted the Island before this time.
But Common prudance considring who I command has
forbid it—altho I flater myself I have not the worst of men.
I have sent all my Bagage six miles Back of where I am
encamped and there unloaded all my waggins and ordered
carridges to be maid for the waggons to move the stones
from the Brandewine Mills and sent off one Hundred men
for that purpose. at present the men under my command
are mutch scattred on difrent Commands as the lines I have

---

[1] Translated by Lieutenant-Colonel John Laurens.

ocqupeyed are from Vanderings on the Schuylkill to Grubs
on the Dalawer. I Keep a Piquit at Brooms Dam of one
Cap^{tn} 2 sub^s 3 sajants, 50 men one at the Brest Works of
12 men one at Grays ferrey of 30 men one at the middle
ferrey of 100 men one at the uper ferrey 25 men up by Vanderings a Reconoitring party under Major Miller. all these
parties has a shutable number of officers I have all ways
a number of other partys on difrent Command I mount a
guard in and about Camp of 100 men and Officers to command them as soon as it is in my power to collect in these
men I will order as maney as is over six Hundred privats
to join the Camp at Head Quarters agreeable to your orders.
There is one Batt^n times out yesterday and two more tomorrow and when there times is out they will go the Militia under Col. Crawford Came to me at Night and went
off in the morning. I Requested that the[y] might assist in
Moving the mill stons, Col. Crawford thought the[y] wold
not and we did not ask them, as for Breaking the Banks
there is Enuf of that sort of works dun alredey the[y] have
found out an easer way of Bringing there provision the[y]
unload at Joneses warff about 100 yarrds from Eagle Creek
and careys it up the Creek to Giers warff, thence to Mingas
Creek and into the Schulkill at Everleys the floting Batt^y
the[y] Bult at Everleys sunk in the lancing the enemy has
Carried down a Great number of fagats to the point whether
for the purpose of Defence or for to make Bridges I cant
say, when I send the Troops away I must draw back, and
work on a smaller scale. I am &c.

"Ja^s Potter.

"P.S.—James Gray, son of Mr George Gray came out
of Town yesterday who says it is Reported in town that a
Bot load of Hessens was latly sunk amounting to 60 men
ocasioned by a Cannon Ball going throo the Boat, there
was a number more drounded on Provance Island in the
flud." [1]

[1] The endorsement shows the date of the letter to have been November 8.

COUNCIL OF WAR.

" At a Council of War &c. 8th Novem. 1777
" Present

" Major Generals Sullivan   Brigadiers Maxwell
     " Greene   Knox
     " Marquis La Fayette   Wayne
     " McDougall   Weedon
                            " Woodford
                            " Scott
                            " Conway
                            " Huntington
                            " Irvin

" His Excellency having informed the Council of the Rein-forcements that were expected from Peekskill and that among them was 1600 Militia from Massachusetts under Gen¹ Warren, whose times would expire the last of Novem-ber.

" His Excellency informed the Council, that from a variety of circumstances he was of opinion that the Enemy mean a formidable attack upon Fort Mifflin very soon, and desired their opinion whether under our present circumstances as to Numbers, &c., we could afford further assistance to the Forts than has been hitherto given without endangering the Safety of this army.

" The following Question was put: Whether, in case the Enemy should make an attack upon the Forts upon Dela-ware, it would be proper with our present Force to fall down and attack the Enemy in their Lines near Philad^a?

" Ans^d in the Negative unanimously."

WASHINGTON TO FRANCIS HOPKINSON AND JOHN WHARTON.

"HEAD QUARTERS, WHITEMARSH, 9 November, 1777
" GENTLEMEN :

" I yesterday rec^d a letter from Congress informing me that they had received a Report from your Board with your opinion upon the most probable means of securing the Frigates. Whereupon they came to the following Resolu-tion on the 4th ins^t:

" ' Ordered, that a Copy of the said report be sent to Gen[l] Washington for his approbation and if he approve the same that a detachment of troops be sent to assist in the Construction and Management of the Batteries aforesaid.' [1]

" Upon the Rec[t] of this I took the opinion of the General Officers who unanimously agreed that, as we had not any men to spare to construct and defend the works recommended by you, there were no other possible means of effectually securing the Frigates but by scuttling them. You will therefore be pleased to have it done in such manner as will render the weighing of them most easy in future, and in such depth of Water as will secure them from being damaged by the floating Ice in the Winter.   All the other Vessels capable of being converted into armed ships should be scutled also.   This should be done as speedily as possible, and as secretly, for should the Enemy get notice of your intentions, I should not at all wonder at their sending up a force purposely to destroy them or bring them down. You will dispose of the men that were on Board of them as directed in my former.   I am &c [2]

" G[o] WASHINGTON."

BRIGADIER-GENERAL VARNUM TO WASHINGTON.

"WOODBERRY 9th Nov. ½ past 6 Ev., 1777
" SIR :

" Previous to the Rec[t] of your Commands of yesterday, I had sent an additional Reinforcement of a Cap[t] two Subs, three Serjeants and fifty Rank & File into Fort Mifflin.   I have been at Fort Mifflin to day; The Enemy are prepared to open a Batery of five Guns, I take them to be Eighteens or Twenty fours, this Night or to morrow Morning; In Conjunction with their two Howitzers, besides two small Batteries, w[o]h they have heretofore fired from.   They have been

---

[1] See *Journals of Congress*, November 4, 1777.
[2] In manuscript of Lieutenant-Colonel Tench Tilghman.   It will be remembered that it was on this day that Washington received from Lord Stirling the sentence from Brigadier-General Conway's letter to Gates which gave him the first definite intimation of the cabal against him.

very busy this Day in Crossing the Mouth of the Schuylkill
with Waggons, Fascines &c.—Two double Deckers more
have pass'd thro' the lower Frize. There are Eight in the
whole upon this upper Station, but all of them are below
my two Gun Battery. Thirsday last one Floating Battery
was launched in Schylkil. it sunk with its Guns wᶜh were
bro't from the Eagle; Two more upon the stocks, one to
have been launch'd this day. They are very busy in building two Bridges across Schuylkill, all their Force seems to
be in that Quarter, wᶜh is destined to the Attack of Fort
Mifflin. Their Boats are moved from Delaware; This is
Intelligence gained from a Ferryman opposite Cooper's
Ferry, who came from Philadelphia this Day—Our Guard
Boats keep the Enemy from transporting Provisions &c., the
usual Way, but they pass unmolested over Tinnicum Island,
by the Way of Derby Creek, a Rout that lays out of our
Power—They enemy will make Fort Mifflin very warm. I
shall relieve them from Time to Time to my utmost. I
think they will Open their Batteries with great Activity:
Soon after wᶜh, it is probable they will bring down their
Water Craft from Schylkill, which will make a Line of
Fire intersecting that from their Principal Battery on Province Island, at an Angle of about thirty Degrees.—The
Commodore seems determined to meet them with Spirit,
adhering to the same Dispositions, wᶜh I had the Honor of
mentioning in my Letter of Yesterday—The two Mischiefs
the Enemy will Effect by their cannonade, will be making
of Breeches in the mud walls, and knocking down the Pallisades. To remedy wᶜh, as much as possible, I am sending
numbers of Pallisades, into the Fort, & great Quantities of
Fascines.—I hope to God, our mutual Efforts here may be
pleasing to your Excellency; I am certain they arise from
Good Intentions.—I ardently wish to see Genˡ Foreman!
I cannot yet hear from him. Genˡ Newcomb has, he tells
me, about five hundred Militia here.—They are principally
without Ammunition.—They are good Men, & have many
good Officers with them. It is a Pity they cannot be properly
furnished. The Old Gentleman, like Imlach of old, is anx-

ious to do all the good he can, But, unfortunately the Motions of the Stars are not committed to Superintendence. I am like a body without a soul, for the want of light Horse. I have not been able to procure any.

" I am out of patience with the commissaries. No Provisions of any consequence in the Garrisons—I have strip'd this Post today, & sent to Fort Mifflin—I will continue sending in Supplies as fast as I can.—If these Gentlemen do not act with a little more Sincerity, I will lessen their Number.

" The Baron is really unfit to be in this Neighbourhood. He will not be fit for Duty for a long Time, if ever.—I hope he may obtain Permission to retire.—His letter is inclos'd.

" Be pleas'd to accept of my sincerest Thanks for your Excellency's repeated Informations, and the paternal Care you exercise towards this little part of your Family.

" I am, in due Submission, &c.

" J. M. VARNUM.

" N.B.—In Justice to Col⁰ Frink I must mention, he delivered your letter of yesterday, at Nine, last Evening.

" P.S.—¼ past Seven. Wᵐ Ward is bro't in by my Scouts, a Prisoner from Camilla, who was this afternoon taken. ' He come ashore with the Captain to dine at Billingsport; —He says the Ships are in Readiness to move up upon a Signal, wᶜʰ is to be given from Province Island, wᶜʰ will be an English Jack hoisted. They are to attack Red Bank, saying that if they should take fort Mifflin, red Bank would cover the Garrison. Says the Shipping have orders to move, some to New York, some to one Place, & some to another, in a Fortnight, should they not take the Forts.—Says the Ships have not more than a Third of their Complement, & are very sickly.'

" Whether their Preparations against Mifflin are real or a Feint, I cannot say; but believe the former; however shall attend to both Circumstances." [1]

---

[1] Endorsed: "This goes by Quartermaster Wheatly, who is permitted to pass all Guards, and others, unmolested."

COLONEL SMITH TO WASHINGTON.

"FORT MIFFLIN, 9ᵗʰ November, 1777

" SIR :

" About the 20ᵗʰ Instant if we are not attacked sooner, I am of Opinion we shall have put this Fort in a good posture of defence, at which time the Officers of the Virginia Regiments and my party hope your Excellency will relieve them and their men. Your Excellency will see the propriety of this request when I assure you that out of 200 Men compleatly Officer'd which my Party consisted of, there are not now in Garrison more than 4 Officers and 65 Privates. the 6ᵗʰ Virginia Regᵗ brought 120 rank and file, and this morning returned only 46 fit for duty, the first nearly in proportion, and the party from Genˡ Varnum have already sent off 4 officers and 16 privates besides Convalescents. for some time past there has not been one night without one two or three Alarms—one half of the Garrison are constantly on fatigue and guard. these reasons I hope will induce your Excellency to send the Relief they request.

" As the Business and Duty Incumbent on the Commanding Officer of this Garrison has been of a very difficult nature and attended with much fatigue, I shall be oblig'd if your Excellency will also relieve me. I shall expect to stay several days after the Relief arrives to shew the officers the Advantages and weak parts of this place. This Garrison will require 500 Rank and file during the winter besides 80 Artillery Men, they will perhaps not be so sickly as we have been, as the fatigue will be chiefly finished, and the sickly season over. A Large stock of Salted Provision ought immediately to be laid in, for in the Winter they will not always be able to cross for Provisions &c. a want of Rum has occasion'd our late very extraordinary sickness. A quantity sufficient for a Gill each man pʳ Day ought to be provided for Winter. I have the Honor &c

" SAM. SMITH."

COLONEL SMITH TO WASHINGTON.

"FORT MIFFLIN 9ᵗʰ November, 1777.

" SIR :

"I receiv'd your Excellency's favour of the 4ᵗʰ. I presume you must have mistook Major Fleury's meaning, he has since he arrived acted fully in his department of Engineer, when I proposed anything he has generally been so polite to approve it. he writes and I presume will acknowledge that his Ideas have been adopted as far as the strength of the garrison would permit.

"The enemy since I wrote you last have been fortifying their Island for an advanced post and for a pass to the City, they have strengthened the first work which they made on the height with Pickquets and Abbatées, and yesterday threw up a breast work or Redoubt, a quarter of a mile below that, I Immagine to defend some narrow part of the Creek where you might pass to repossess the Island. Within these two nights they have thrown up a long Breast work to the left of their first Bomb Battery. it is not yet opened, but we can distinguish 5 Embrasures and Ship Carriages for their Cannon. I am of opinion their Intentions now must be to knock down our pallisades on that side, destroy our Block houses & storm us. We had your Excellency's notice last night and prepared accordingly, but I conceive they will not attempt any thing until they make a breach.

"The Honble the Congress have done me too much Honor; perhaps the enemy may give us an Oppᵗʸ to merit the high approbation they are pleased to express of my conduct and the Officers under me. I have the Honor &c

"SAM SMITH."

CONTINUATION OF MAJOR FLEURY'S JOURNAL.

"9ᵗʰ at night. The Enemy appearing ready to open their batteries, we raised the bank which covers our Palisades on the west Front, against which the whole Fire of the Enemy is directed, and which will be the point of attack in case of their storming the Fort. I have some fascines making at Red-bank, but shall want a great number.

"10—The 24 and 18 pound shot from the Batteries No. 16 and 17 broke some of our Palisades this morning, but this does not make us uneasy—they save us the trouble of cutting them to the height of a man—which we should do, as the fire of loop-holes [is] in itself not very dangerous, and our loop-holes in particular are so badly contrived as to leave two-thirds of the Glacis unrak'd.

"It is probable that the Enemy will undertake to carry this place by storm, and I should not fear them if we could fix the floating Chain described in the Figure; it would cover the Front which is likely to be attacked, and by delivering us from our uneasiness for this side, would enable us to post the men destined for its defence, at the Wall of Masonry which is ten feet high and is not out of the reach of an Escalade, notwithstanding the Ditches, Pits and Stakes &c^a with which we have endeavour'd to surround it.

"The Commodore, Master of the *incomparable* Chain in question, proposes to stretch it by means of Buoys, between our Island and Province Island. I believe this obstacle to the communication between the Enemy's Fleet and Army will be of little consequence, and if he would spare us the Chain, the Enemy would pay dear for their Hardiness if they dared attack us. Colonel Smith wrote this morning to ask this favour, but I am afraid that public Interest will suffer by private misunderstandings. I am interrupted by the Bombs and Balls which fall thick.

"10 at noon. The Firing increases but not the effect—our barracks alone suffer.

"At 2 o'clock. The Direction of the fire is changed—our Palisades suffer—a dozen of them are broke down—one of our Cannon is damaged near the Muzzle—I am afraid it will not fire streight.

"11 at night. The Enemy keep up a firing of Cannon every half hour—Genl Varnum promised us Fascines and Palisades, but they are not arrived—and they are absolutely necessary.

" The Commodore has promised the Chain—Our Garrison
diminishes, our soldiers are overwhelmed with Fatigue—
they spend nights in watching and Labour without doing
much on account of their weakness." [1]

WASHINGTON TO BRIGADIER-GENERAL VARNUM.

"HEAD QUARTERS, 10ᵗʰ November, 1777

" Dᴿ SIR :

" I am pleased to find by yours of the 8ᵗʰ that proper dispositions were formed for the reception of the Enemy at
Forts Mercer & Mifflin and that the Garrisons were so full
of confidence. We already hear a firing which we suppose
a prelude to something more serious. I sincerely wish you
success; but let the event be fortunate or otherwise, pray
let me have the speediest intelligence. I am &c

" Gᵒ WASHINGTON.

" P.S.—Your Detachments are on their march from
Fishkill to join you."

CONTINENTAL NAVY BOARD TO WASHINGTON.

"CONTINENTAL NAVY BOARD

" BORDEN TOWN 10ᵗʰ Novʳ. 1777

" SIR :

" In Answer to your Letter of yesterday, we would inform your Excellency that when we first fixt the Navy
Board at this Place & got our Frigates up, we had formed a
Plan for defending them by a small Battery; of which
among many other Things we gave Notice to the Marine
Committee of Congress. We had no Answer to our Letter
from that Committee till the Day before yesterday, when
they sent us the Resolve of Congress referred to in your
Letter. In the mean Time, however, we had the Honour
of a Correspondence with your Excellency on this Subject;
in which you fully declared your Judgment of the Matter
and explicitly told us what you would have done. We
have the satisfaction of assuring your Excellency that your
Orders were immediately complied with, & as punctually

[1] In manuscript of Lieutenant-Colonel John Laurens.

executed as our Situation would admit of. The Frigates have been long since sunk, and now lie fast aground in a Place where they can receive no Damage from the Ice & cannot possibly be got off by the Enemy unless they knew the particular Parts where they have been bored, & of which we have a secret Gage that will enable us to raise them with Ease when a suitable Time shall offer. We gave you our Words that your Desire should be complied with & we have fulfill'd our Engagement so far as respected the Frigates; the men indeed have not been discharged owing to the following Accident: In sinking one of the Ships she unfortunately lay against a steep Bank, which on the Tide's falling, caused her to heal outwards from the Shoar. As this is an uneasy Situation & may injure the Ship we have been obliged to retain all the Hands & even hire more to get her up-right again. We have not yet been able to Effect this Purpose, but hope to do it in a few Days with the Purchases & Powers we are preparing to apply. All other Vessels great & small (one only excepted) we have with great Labour crouded up Crosswick's Creek, where most of them lye aground at high water, nor can any be got down but by means of an extraordinary Tide, or Fresh, nor then, but with the utmost Skill & Patience. Not trusting wholly to this, however, our Determination is to sink a Vessel at the Mouth of the Creek, which must effectually secure them from the Enemy. The Ship excepted above, is a large Vessel belonging to M^r. Robert Morris, having on Board a valuable Cargoe of Tobacco, part Continental & part his private Property. This ship cannot possibly be got up the Creek with her Cargoe, we are therefore unloading her into Shallops & when empty shall get her also up the Creek, or sink her, which ever may be most suitable. We request your Excellency would be perfectly easy as to the Shipping at this Place. The Enemy may possibly send up & burn them,—this we cannot help— but you may depend upon it none of them shall fall into their Hands, so as to become an Annoyance to your military Operations.

"It gives us great Concern to think your Excellency

should for a Moment suppose us capable of neglecting your earnest Instructions after having so solemnly assured you we would strictly obey them. We confess, however, the Resolve of Congress in Consequence of our former Representation, gave you sufficient Reason to suppose we had applied to that Body, instead of following your Advice. But the mystery will unfold when you consider that our Application to Congress was prior to the Letters we received from you on this Subject. We did indeed write to Congress a second Time, enclosing a Copy of your Instructions to us, and declaring our Determination of complying with them. But Congress, anxious, as we suppose to save the Frigates, & not so apprehensive of Danger from the Enemy, framed their Resolve parellel to our first Scheme; which on further Consideration appears to be ineffectual.

"We shall be happy in hearing from your Excellency that the above Representation is satisfactory; & that our Conduct in this Affair meets with your Approbation. If anything is amiss, or you would wish anything further to be done in our Department, you may depend on our earnest Endeavours to comply with your Desire.

"We request your Excellency would be so good as to forward the enclosed Packet to York Town by the first Opportunity. We have therein informed Congress of what we have done & our Reasons for so doing.

"With the utmost Esteem & sincere Prayers for your Health & Success, we have the Honor to be &c.

"FRAˢ HOPKINSON.
"JOHN WHARTON."

BRIGADIER-GENERAL VARNUM TO WASHINGTON.

"WOODBERRY, 7 o'clock Ev. 10ᵗʰ Novʳ 1777

" SIR :

" The Enemy this Morning opened against us with five Batteries. At two this afternoon, no Man was killed or wounded. The Cannonade and Bombardment have continued feebly since that Hour. I suppose the Rain has prevented their being more brisk—They have thrown some

Shot among our Shipping : Theirs remain below us. They have made but little Impression upon the Works or Pallisades.—I have just desired Col°. Smith to put his Men into their Barracks, thinking that it is better to have a few killed or wounded, than to have the whole suffer, expos'd to the Inclemency of the weather, upon mear Mud.

"I have reason to expect the Attack will be more severe tomorrow as Cannon have been observed to pass over Schylkill this Day—Happy might it be for Troops to attack Province Island upon the rear of the Batteries— Should Heaven continue the Rain, so as to overflow the Meadows, we shall attack it upon this Side.

"It would be serviceable either to furnish the Militia here, with Ammunition, or discharge them. The important Moments are swiftly rolling on, in w°h they can assist us. It is with your Excellency only to supply them.

"Fort Mifflin will soon be in want of Cartridges for their Cannon. The supplies are very inadequate to the present Siege. I am &c.

"J. M. VARNUM."

COLONEL SMITH TO WASHINGTON.

"FORT MIFFLIN, 10th November, 1777

"SIR :

"This morning the Enemy open'd their Battery in the Rear of our Nor' West Block House, about 500 Yards distance from it of 6 Pieces of Cannon 18 to 32 Pounders, and one Eight inch howitz, one other eight inch Howitz opposite the right of our Battery. they were so fortunate to strike one of our 18 Pounders in the two Gun Battery on the Muzzle, by which she is rendered useless; their Shott from that Battery rakes the Pallisades fronting the Meadow, and cuts down 4 or 5 at a time, they have laid open a great part of that side, and chiefly destroyed that range of Barrocks, they also keep up an incessant fire from the Hospital, they have dismounted 3 of our Block house Guns, and much injured the Block houses and the other Range of

Barrocks. We cover our Men under the Wall, and have the good fortune as yet to escape unhurt, in 5 or 6 Days (unless the Seige can be rais'd) the fort will be laid open, and every thing destroyed, if they continue to cannonade and Bombard us as they have done, of which I haven't the smallest Doubt. Our Men already half Jaded to Death with constant fatigue, will be unfit for service.

"Gen¹ Varnum has promis'd to prepare for us new Pallisades, if so, we will replace at night what is destroy'd in the day, and endeavour to keep the Fort as long as it is in our power. As the principal object I presume of your Excellency is to hinder the enemy from raising the Chevaux de frize this winter, I am of Opinion it could be done nearly as well from the other Shore as from this fort, was our Cannon there. Gen¹ Varnum inform'd you of the two Gun Battery he erected, with which the enemy might be hindered from raising the Obstructions with the Assistance of the fleet and 2 Guns that may be placed on Bush Island. My Opinion & the Opinion of the Officers in this Garrison is, that unless the Seige can be rais'd the enemy must in a short time reduce this place. We are determined to defend it to the last extremity, but we are of Opinion that it wou'd be for the common good to destroy the whole of the works and take the Guns to the Jersey Shore, where they'll serve to guard the River, and in case we could get Possession of Billingsport to mount on it, had we that post it would secure the River Effectually. The Galleys will be much annoyed from the enemies Batteries, and when the Shiping comes up, we shall have the whole of their fire. A Saylor taken this morning says they are prepar'd to come up and act in concert with their Batteries.

"Our present Situation strikes us in the light I have described, shou'd circumstances alter our Sentiments I shall give you the earliest notice. I have the Honor &c

"SAM SMITH.

"P.S.—The enemies Boats still pass up and down the river. I presume with provision."

WASHINGTON TO BRIGADIER-GENERAL VARNUM.

"HEAD QUARTERS, 11 November, 1777

" DEAR SIR :

" Your Favors of the 9th & 10th Instant I have duly received.
I think we may reasonably Hope, that, from the good disposition of the Troops in your Quarter, & the Zeal & activity
of the officers and men, join'd to the present very advanced
& cold Season, which must greatly retard if not prevent the
Operations of the Enemy; Matters may Terminate with
you agreeable to our Expectations, this must have the greatest Influence upon the Conduct of Gen¹ Howe & force him
to adopt disadvantageous or disgraceful Measures.

" Gen¹ Knox informs me that he has sent down a person
to get an exact return of the Ammunition which you now
have, & of what may be want'd, & that he has sent down
17 Waggons loaded with Ball, which you will receive about
this time.—A Waggon with 20,000 Musket Cartridges will
be immediately despatch'd to be deliver'd to the Militia (if
you see fit) by your order only.—It is greatly to be wish'd
that all firing could be prevented except where there is a
real Necessity & the distance such as might promise a good
effect.

" I have wrote to Gen¹ Potter ordering him to take every
Step by which he can assist you & distress the Enemy on
Province Island—he may alarm them & draw off their Attention from Fort Mifflin if nothing more.—You are acquainted with the reasons why a greater Force is not sent
to annoy them in that quarter. I am &c

" G⁰ WASHINGTON."

BRIGADIER-GENERAL POTTER TO WASHINGTON.

"Novr 11th 1777

" SIR

" I have just Received Intelagance of 38 sail of the enemey
fleet coming up the River the latters was wrote five oclock
yesterday evining altho the[y] are dated as of this day.
the fiering yesterday was from the enemys Battereys on

province Island near the River Banks I Believe the[y] have dun little damige if any I Riceved your excelanceys of the 10ᵗʰ of Novʳ. as for my doing any thing that can be of us[e] to the fourt—I can't conseve how I can do it. I am &c.

"Jaˢ Potter."

BRIGADIER-GENERAL POTTER TO WASHINGTON.

" Sir

" Yesterday I sent Col. Rankan and Capt. Livis to give me an account of the fiering. Rankan is Returned, and says that about eight o'cLock there was an Attact maid on Rid Bank which continued one hour and a half. about 11 oClock the Attact Began and continued upwards of one hour, and about 3 oClock the[y] attactᵉᵈ again and Continued about 3 Quarters of an hour about one quarter after 3 oClock the[y] Began again and Continued about one hour and a half and after the small Arms seased, the cannaiding Continued about 3 minits, and all seased. Col. Rankan is confidant that the fourt is ours yet and says he will wiger his hors against a gill of Whisque. I hope your Excelancey will have Glorious Accounts from Rid Bank. I am &c

"Jaˢ Potter.

" Novʳ 11ᵗʰ 1777 ten o'clock."

JONATHAN RUMFORD TO BRIGADIER-GENERAL POTTER.

"Wilmington 9ᵇᵉʳ 11ᵗʰ 77

"Dᴿ General

" This will acquaint you with the loss of a 64 Gun Ship— Wednesday last, shee was drawn up with springs to her cables to fire on forte Miflin, alias mud Island, but as Heven would have it, the Springs broke or by some means gave way. The Ship ran a Shore n'r [M]anto Crick. Our People Errected a small Batery on Billings Port & soone sunk the Ship—there is now three Ships more going up one of which a 64. I am &c.

"Jonᴬ Rumford."

MAJOR EVANS TO BRIGADIER-GENERAL POTTER.

" WILMINGTON, Nov' 11ᵗʰ 1777

" DEAR SIR :

" Having Just arived at this place I had account of thirty Eight large ships lying at or near reedy Island yesterday with a number of troops on board some say 3 some 4 & 5 thousand, the ships are all now standing up the River by this place now five of the Clock, therefore thought it my indispensible duty to give you the earliest intelligence that you might provide yourself accordingly. I am &c.

" GEO : EVANS, Major M."

JONATHAN RUMFORD TO BRIGADIER-GENERAL POTTER.

" WILMINGTON Nov 11ᵗʰ 1777

" DR. GENERAL

" I am acquainted by Capᵗ Hugh Mongomery who is Just come from the River Shore that hee Counted thirty Eight Sales of Vessels Cheifly ships & that hee heard from Mʳ Whitehead Jones these had Ten Solders landed & came to his House who acquainted him That there was a fleete now in the Delawar with Several Thousand Brittish Soldears on Borde. The Ships are Now Passing by I therefore send you this Inteligance & am &c.

" JONᵗ RUMFORD."

BRIGADIER-GENERAL VARNUM TO WASHINGTON.

" WOODBERRY 11ᵗʰ November, 1777

" SIR

" Capᵗ [Samuel] Treat of the Artillery and one Man besides was killed this Morning. The Enemy have battered down a great Part of the Stone Wall. The Pallisades and Barracks are prodigiously shattered. The Enemy fire with Twenty four & thirty two Pounders. Upon these, and other Considerations, Colᵒ Smith is of Opinion that the Fort must be evacuated. A storm would not be dreaded; But it appears impossible for the Garrison to withstand point blank

shot. I am now going to consult the Baron & Col° Greene.
I expect we shall cause an evacuation this Night. I
am &c.

"J. M. VARNUM.

"N.B.—The Evacuation may enable us to take Billingsport."

BRIGADIER-GENERAL VARNUM TO WASHINGTON.

"WOODBERRY, 11ᵗʰ Novʳ 12 o'Clock P.M. 1777

" SIR :

"I am this Moment returned from Fort Mifflin—Every
Defence is almost destroyed. Poor Col° Smith is on this
Shore, slightly wounded.—I have ordered the Cannon, least
in use, to be brought off. Lᵗ Col° [Giles] Russell of Col°
[John] Durkee's Battalion commands. I have ordered the
Garrison to defend at all Events 'till your Pleasure can be
known. Nothing shall be wanting to support them, which
we can give—They cannot hold out more than two Days.—
Col° Smith urges an Evacuation still ; at least, to continue
a small Garrison only, wᶜʰ might be bro't off occasionally, I
cannot acceed to the Measure, as long as we have lost but
few Men.—The Enemy have pass'd seven Boats this Evining
between the Fort and Province Island.—The Cannonade is
renewed; If as great Injury should take Place to morrow
as to Day, we may be obliged to relinquish the Place.—I
wish to know your will—The Fort shall be held, at all
events, 'till then.

" Your Commands of this Day, just come to Hand. I am
much obliged.

" At Red Bank, an Eighteen Pounder burst—one man
killed and several wounded; at the two Gun Battery, a
Sergᵗ killed and one wounded.

" The Baron ought to know whether he shall go farther
than this, as he is extremely unwell. I am &c

"J. M. VARNUM."

COLONEL SMITH TO BRIGADIER-GENERAL VARNUM.

" SIR

" I am clearly of your opinion to keep the fort to the last extremity, which in my opinion may as well be done with 100 as 500 men.   By tomorrow night every thing will be levelled—our block houses next the enemy are almost destroyed—the N. West Block has but one piece of cannon fit for service—one side of it is entirely fallen down—they have begun on that next Read's House & dismounted two pieces—the Pallisades next the meadow are levelled; the small battery in front of the gate torn up—the [a word that is illegible] battery torn up also.   The wall is broke thro' in different places.   In fine should they storm us I think we must fall.   However, as it is your opinion I will keep the garrison tho' I lose mine and my soldiers lives.   I hope the night may prove sufficiently favorable to get out some of our cannon; and then should we fall, you may still defend the River.   I am now without 18 cartouches—must beg you will send me 300 which will serve me to-morrow—it must be done in the night.   I would advise the garrison to be with-drawn except about 50 men, who could just keep up the same fire that is done now, and might escape in case of a storm—This would be my advice.   'Tis true I fight for glory, but at the same time must study the general good.   I am &c

" SAM SMITH.

" FORT MIFFLIN, 11 Nov. 1777.

" N.B.—Reflect if they make the attack that their cannon will be placed against our Block house, in which case no man can stay in them.   I expect to see the whole of the N. W. Block house fall every minute.   If you should be of my opinion send boats in the first place to get over the cannon, and before day take off the men leaving as I mentioned." [1]

[1] " General Dickenson, to whose Discretion it was left to take the Command of our Militia now under General Newcomb, or to continue on his present station as he should conceive most for the Publick Interest, has preferred the latter, on account of a Plan he has formed to make a Descent on Staten Island, which he says is a favorite scheme of his ; and

WASHINGTON TO FRANCIS HOPKINSON AND JOHN WHARTON.[1]

"HEAD QUARTERS, 12 November, 1777

" GENTLEMEN :

" I have your fav^r of the 10th and am only sorry that I did not sooner know my request of sinking the Frigates had been complied with. The delay of the Resolve of Congress, from the time you first applied for their advice, was what led me into a mistake, and I am obliged to you for the genteel manner in which you excuse me. I am perfectly satisfied with the measures which you have taken to secure the shipping and desire when you have no further occasion for Men that they may be disposed of as directed in my former letters. I am &c [2]

" G^o WASHINGTON."

BRIGADIER-GENERAL POTTER TO WASHINGTON.

" I received your Excelanceys favour of yesterday at 10 o'Clock last night. I was out Reconnitring, the Shiping are com up. the number of soldiers I cant assurtain.

" As to the marching of the Militia the[y] were all at Head Quarters before I Rec^d your Letter. as for my Harrassing the Enemy the sitation of the pleace is such that I can do Little, and my numbers so Trifling, that I cant prevent there coming over the Bridge, they are alarmed on the Island, and have strenthened that place with men and works and cannon there will be mutch more dificqualty in Redusing it than would have been eight days ago,

" I am sorey that Genl [John] Armstrong is under a mistake

from which he expects to derive considerable Advantage to the Cause. From the frequent Complaints I have had of General Newcomb's Inactivity and utter want of all Discipline, I have sent for him to this place to account for his conduct to General Forman ; & hope his friends here will embrace that opportunity to persuade him to resign a Post, which most of them seem now convinced he is incapable of discharging either with Honour to himself, or Advantage to the State."—*Governor William Livingston to Washington*, November 11, 1777.

[1] Some letters of this date are printed in my " Writings of Washington," Vol. VI. pp. 187, 188.

[2] In manuscript of Lieutenant-Colonel Tench Tilghman.

in Regard of my givin Interruption to the enemy in Bulding there Bridge, I drove there gaurd three times down to the warf, but my men were oblidged to Run back again the ground on the other side commands that on this side and they soon drive us off with there cannon—If it is agreeable to your Excelancey I could wish some other officer was to take the command here.

"I will do all in my power to get a Communication with Ridbank But cant vew it in such an easy light as some Gentlemen do.

"I am your Excelanceys &c

"Jaˢ Potter.

"Novʳ 12ᵗʰ 1777."

BRIGADIER-GENERAL POTTER TO WASHINGTON.

" Sɪʀ

"I am sorey to Inform your excelancey that Last night in the night the enemy got two Briggs and one sloop up past the Island on the side nixt the Island, and this day they were unloading them at the Lowast ferrey in Schulkill, there has been a verey hevey fiering this day at the fourt from the Battereys on the Islands the fourt seldom Returned the fier the Galleys went lower down the River [   ] and fired on the ships.

"I hope I will Receve Accounts tomorrow from Red bank this Evining I have Received the within closed from a gentleman that was in the City several days he assures me that I will get Intiligance from two good whigs in the City—I have just Received a letter from George Reed, Esqʳ of the Dalawer State Informing me that there Militia hav Destroyed 6 Vessels in Duck Creek with provisions going to the enemys shiping and Taken a number of the Treaders he can give no Account of the numbers of soldiers that were in the fleet that came up—sum says there did not appear to be meney on Board. I am &c

"Jaˢ Potter.

"Novʳ 12ᵗʰ 1777   9 oClock

"P.S.—We have Taken five Prisners this day and will send them to your Excelancey tomorrow."

MAJOR FLEURY TO WASHINGTON.

" Excellencey

" in my quality of engineer in chief at fort mifflin I think that my duty obliges me to informe you of the present situation of the fort.

" the Fire of the enemy has been successfull enough to spoile our three Block houses, and dismount the canon of all, except two.   the great lockes [logs ?] of which we had covered them are not strong enough to preserve the inside of the block houses, and we have none others to mend them.

" some of our Palissades at the nordside are broken, but we can mend them every night.

" in all the fort is certainly yet in state to be defended, but the garrison is so dispirited that if the enemy will attempt to storm us, I am afraid that they will succeed.   they are so exhausted, by watch, cold, Rain & fatigue, that their Courage is very Low, and in the Last allarme one half was unfit for duty.

" I have informed Gen¹ Varnam of the situation of the fort, and how small was the garrison considering how large is our enclosure.

" I think it necessary for my honour to put under your eyes the same observation, to not be thought guilty in case of bad event.   I am excellency &c

" Fleury.

"10 o'Clock   12 9ᵇᵉʳ 1777"

BRIGADIER-GENERAL VARNUM TO WASHINGTON.

" Woodberry, 12ᵗʰ Novʳ Sunset 1777

" Sir.

" The Garrison holds out; tho' the Enemy continue to batter with great Success upon the Works, but few Men are killed and wounded.   The Troops are extremely fatigued. I shall send one Hundred fresh Troops this Night, & all that I have tomorrow Night, if the Fort should remain defensible.   The most fatigued will be taken from the Garrison.—

Col⁰ Smith will be unable to return to his Command for
some Time; It is a misfortune, but, Col⁰ Russell will command with Spirit, & Col⁰ Durkee will go in tomorrow Morning, should Col⁰ Russell be much fatigued. Inclosed you
have Major Fleury's opinion.[1] I am anxious to hear from
you. Have no particular Intelligence save that Forty sail
of Vessells with Troops, on Saturday last, entered the Dele-
ware.—Should the Enemy continue their Cannonade the
Island will be lost: however, the Garrison will continue 'till
your Excellency shall order otherwise. I am &c.

"J. M. VARNUM."

COLONEL SMITH TO WASHINGTON.

"WOODBERRY, 12 Novr 1777

" SIR :

" I yesterday unfortunately rec^d a Contusion on my Hip
& left Arm, both which give me much pain. I imprudently
went into my Barracks to answer a Letter from Gen. Varnum
& a Ball came through the Chimney & struck me on the Hip
so forcibly that I remained senseless for some time. however
I am happy to find myself much less hurted than I at first
imagin'd & Hope in 5 or 6 days to be again fit for duty.
Coll. Russell now commands in fort Mifflin. The troops
there are worn out with fatigue, watchings & cold. All the
Guns in the Block Houses are render'd unfit for service &
the Houses almost destroy'd. the Pallisades were renew'd
last Night & this Day destroy'd again. the other Guns on
my two Gun Battery render'd unfit for service. An 18 p^r
next to the right of the Battery dismounted, the New Well
very much injur'd, the whole of the Garrisons Heap of
Ruins. this Night Gen. Varnum intends removing some
of the heavy Cannon. We shall perhaps be able to keep
the fort three days, in which Time it will be levell'd to the
Ground. Yesterday Capt [Samuel] Treat was kill'd by a
Ball which came through the Grand Battery & this Day his

---

[1] This opinion is not different in detail from that submitted to Washington, p. 120, *ante.*

Lieut. [John] George wounded, so that there are now but 2
Artillery Officers in Garrison. if they attempt a storm, I
fear the Garrison must fall. Such weather as this the Gallies
can give no Assistance. I Have advis'd the Garrison to be
withdrawn, except the Artillery & ab^t 50 Men who could
keep up the same fire that the whole can. But to be prepar'd & in Case the Enemy attempt a Storm they might set
fire to every part & withdraw. Gen. Varnum waits your
Order. I have the Honor &c.

" SAM SMITH."

WASHINGTON TO BRIGADIER-GENERAL VARNUM.

" HEAD QUARTERS, 13 November, 1777

" SIR :

" I wrote you two Letters yesterday; the first contained
positive orders to maintain the Fort on Mud Island at all
events, the second in consequence of subsequent advices from
you gave discretionary powers to evacuate the post, and a
copy of it was sent to guard against miscarriage; I refer you
to its contents and repeat that I would have a Show of defence kept up as long as possible by such a number of men as
you shall judge necessary. The importance of delaying the
farther progress of the Enemy and preventing their making
a lodgement on the Island is too obvious to need my insist-
ing upon it. In addition to the perseverance of the Garrison, I think an Enterprise of a more active nature might
be carried into execution in concert with a detachment from
the Fleet. I mean a Descent upon Province Island for the
purpose of spiking the Enemy's Cannon and levelling their
Batteries—which would considerably embarrass the Enemy
and gain us a great deal of time. This is proposed however
only by way of consulting you upon the subject: you will
be best able, being on the spot, to judge of the practicability
of such a Scheme. Voluntiers and pick'd Men would be
most likely to do this Service effectually: and as a Stimulus
to their Courage and Exertions I promise ample Rewards
in case of Success. I would have Fort Mercer strengthen'd
as much as Circumstances will allow—it may be put in such

a condition as to require a greater Sacrifice than the Enemy can afford to make in attempting it. I am &c

"G⁰ WASHINGTON.

"P.S.—Present my Compliments to Col⁰ Smith. The Contents of his Letter are fully answer'd by this to you." [1]

MAJOR FLEURY'S JOURNAL.

"Nov. 13ᵗʰ at night.—The Enemy have kept up a firing part of the night—their shells greatly disturb our workmen, and as the moon rises opposite to us, her light discovers to the Enemy where we are. As long as my Workmen would remain with me, I employed them in covering the two western Blockhouses with Joist within and without and filling the interstices with rammed Earth. I have closed the breaches made in our Palisades, with Planks, Centry-boxes, Rafters, and strengthen'd the whole with earth—General Varnum has sent me neither Ax, Fascine, Gabion nor Palisade, altho he promised me all these Articles, I suppose it has not been in his power—it is impossible however with watry mud alone to make works capable of resisting the Enemys 32 Pounders.

"14ᵗʰ Day light discovers to us a floating battery of the Enemy, placed a little above their grand battery, and near the Shore; it seems to be a Bomb-battery.

"Fort Mifflin is certainly capable of defence if the means be furnished—if they supply us from Red-bank with Tools, Fascines, Palisades, &ca all which they may do in abundance—the Fire of the Enemy will never take the Fort, it may kill us men but this is the Fortune of War. and all their bullets will never render them masters of the Island, if we have courage enough to remain on it—but they are removing our Cannon from the grand battery under pretext that it is necessary to raise a battery on the Jersey side to keep the Enemys shipping at a distance—but what signifies it, whether their Fleet be at the point of Hog Island or a quarter of a mile lower—will they not by taking this

[1] In manuscript of Lieutenant-Colonel John Laurens.

Fort have the Channel of province Island open, for their small Sloops and other light vessels—will they not drive the Gallies from the River—Fort Mifflin is the important Object, it must be maintained and furnish'd with means of defence. Men, Earth and Fascines to cover them—Our new Garrison consists of 450 Men—what can they do in a circumference of works so extensive as ours—being weak everywhere, they could make a defence nowhere and the Fort would be carried—The apparent Project of the Enemy is to debark on the Island; either to risque a Storm, or to establish a battery on the old ferry wharf, or nearer if they can—what means have we of hindering them—with a Garrison so feeble, can I make any advantageous Sallies—can I dislodge the Enemy—if I raise a battery against them will it not serve against ourselves in case of attack—for without a sufficient number to defend it, it must be given up—our grand Battery has 19 Embrasures and 8 cannon, two of which are dismounted—we must have Artificers to make Wheels—Fascines and Palisades for breaches. Genl Varnum supplies us scantily—We must have men to defend the Ruins of the Fort—our Ruins will serve us as breastworks, we will defend the Ground inch by inch, and the Enemy shall pay dearly for every step—but we want a commanding Officer, ours is absent and forms projects for our defence at a distance.

"P.S.—As the Light becomes clearer, I perceive the Enemys floating battery, not to be a mortar battery but that it contains two 32 Pounders—we are going to raise a Counter battery of two eighteen Pounders taken out of our River battery—which will now have no more than 7 Guns, the Wheels of two of which have been disabled by the Enemy's Cannon. We are so much neglected that we have been 7 days without wood, and at present have only cartridges of eighteen pounders for a Piece of 32 which does considerable michief to the Enemy.

"14th at 7 oClock. The Enemy keep up a great Fire from their Floating Battery and the shore.

"I repeat it, our Commanding Officer issues orders from

Woodberry—if he were nearer he would be a better judge of our Situation.

"Our blockhouses are in a pitiful condition, but with fascines I hope to cover two pieces in each lower story which will be sufficient to flank us. I say again the Enemys fire will not take our fort. if they attempt a storm we shall still have a little parapet to oppose to them, but we must have men to defend it.

"Novem̄ 14th at noon.

"We have silenced the Enemy's floating Battery, I know not whether we have dismounted her Cannon, or whether her present Station exposes her too much, but the firing from her has ceased. I suspect that she is destined to land men on this Island.

"Their grand battery is in little better condition than our block-houses—We have open'd an embrasure at the Corner of the Battery, and two pieces here joined to two others on the left which we have reinstated, throw the Enemy into disorder.

"I repeat it—their fire will kill us men, because we have no cover, but it will never take the Fort, if we have sufficient courage to keep our ground—but a stronger Garrison is indispensibly necessary, we are not secured against Storm, if the Enemy attempt it—I fear they will succeed—in penetrating a Circumference of 1200 Paces defended only by 450 men and half ruined Palisades—A boat which this day deserted from the Fleet, will have given the Enemy sufficient intimation of our weakness—they will probably attack us or attempt a Lodgment on the Island which we cannot prevent with our present strength.

"Tonight an Attempt is to be made on the floating battery of the Enemy."[1]

BRIGADIER-GENERAL VARNUM TO WASHINGTON.

"WOODBERRY, ¼ p^t 4 Mor.
"14 Nov. 1777

" SIR

"One Hour since, all was pretty well in Fort. Three killed yesterday, and seven wounded. Our greatest misfor-

---

[1] In manuscript of Lieutenant-Colonel John Laurens.

tune has been, that so high, we could get nothing across the River. However it is now calm, & the time improving. I have sent all the fresh Troops into the Fort & shall, in every Respect pursue your Orders signified 12ᵗʰ, 5 oClock P.M. The Garrison may continue for some Time. Possibly we shall keep the Island. To day we shall open upon their Shipping with three Guns from the lower Battery. I am &c.

'" J. M. VARNUM."

BRIGADIER-GENERAL VARNUM TO WASHINGTON.

" WOODBERRY, ½ past 3 P.M. 14ᵗʰ Novʳ 1777

" SIR :

" Your Favor of yesterday is received. Major [Simeon] Thayer has the Command at Fort Mifflin at Present. Inclos'd you have his Sentiments. I have continued nearly four hundred Rank & File in the Garrison. All Colᵒ Smith's Troops are brought to the Main to get a little Rest. I have no more Troops fit for Duty. I am very happy that a tolerable Prospect of holding the Post appears—Last Evening my whole Company of Artillery went into the Fort. Capt. [James] Lee commands. He is brave and good.—It is very unhappy that the Wind has been so great ; However, we shall be now [better] able to send supplies, than for several Days. —An Attempt upon Province Island is desirable, but impossible for us, who have no Troops, but fatigued ones, & those in less Force than the Enemy's upon that Place. As your Orders appear discretionary, in some measure, we shall risque many things in attempting to keep the River.—I think we may hold the Island till such Time as you can send us five Hundred Troops to make a second Relief.—If that cannot be done, we will endeavour to hold it.

" The large Howitz we want very much. I am &c.

" J. M. VARNUM.

" N.B.—I am now going with Colᵒ Smith to Fort Mifflin, & shall be able, in the Morning, to give you a particular accᵗ."

MAJOR THAYER TO BRIGADIER-GENERAL VARNUM.

"FORT MIFFLIN, Nov. 14, 1777
"SIR

"By this I would give you to understand that the canonade we have here we value not, nor can conceive how
any one would dream of delivering up so important a post
as this at present; from Cannon we have nothing to fear, if
there should be no sudden storm. If, Sir, you will send us
a reinforcement tonight of 100 or more men, it will certainly
be a great means of the salvation of this garrison. A floating battery of the enemy appeared this morning. We have
silenced her for the present. I am &c
"SIMEON THAYER Com⁴.

"P.S.—A Boat with a number of men deserted from our
fleet but this minute—they may give some unfavorable
account of our state, and insinuate some notion of our
evacuating the fort. All well—none hurt since my arrival
here—The garrison in good spirits."

CAPTAIN LEE TO WASHINGTON.

"Nᵒ 14ᵗʰ 77
"SIR:

"I have just returned from the lower counties on Delaware. In our excursion thro' that country, the several
landings on the river were visited, but to our satisfaction, we
learned that the intercourse between the inhabitants & fleet
was totally broke up. Lord Howe has positively forbid the
least connexion under severe penalties.

"I should have proceeded down as far as Dover, in order
to destroy some small craft, that were employed in furnishing
the enemy with fresh provision fuel &c, from Duck creek,
but this business being completed by Gen Patterson, I concluded the route unnecessary, & returned to my former
station. Thirty eight sail of Transports arrived in the
delaware while I was down & joined the fleet off Chester.
It was expected they had troops on board from N. York, but

none could be discovered as they passed up the river. I am &c.

"Hen^r Lee."

"At Mr Morris, Nov. 14th 8 oClock P.M. 1777

" Dr. Sir.

" We have just returned from reconnoitering the grounds about Darby, the Islands below and up to the middle ferry— we purpose to go out again in the morning—from the present view Darby appears the only eligible position for the army for the purpose of their crossing the river. It is the opinion of several of the gentlemen that the enemy may be kept dislodged from the Islands by detachment, others are of opinion that it would be dangerous unless the party was covered, by the Army, but all are of opinion, it is practicable either the one way or the other and considering the good consequences that will result from it, it ought to be attempted. Darby is not the most eligible post I ever saw, but it is not so dangerous as to discourage the attempt to relieve fort Mifflin.

" The flag was flying at Fort Mifflin at sunset this evening, there has been a very severe cannonade today.—inclosed is a letter from Col°. Greene respecting the condition of the fort. The enemy have got up two or three vessels into the Schuylkill, they were attempting to get up a two and thirty gun frigate, between hog Island and Province Island—by the best observation we could make her guns were taken out and follow'd her in a sloop.—She did not get up, but what was the reason, I know not.—The Commodore should be directed to sink a vessel or two in the new channel as soon as possible, and the fort encouraged to hold out to the last.—There is but one bridge over the Schuylkill and that is at the middle ferry. I examined the river myself from the falls to the mouth.

" The enemy have got a chain of redoubts with Abatis between them from one river to the other, part of this is from information and part from my own observation—The

Schuylkill is very deep and rapid, too deep for foot to ford it—the bridge at Matteson's ford is not in so great forwardness as I could wish, the commanding officer sais it will be done in three days—but a bridge of waggons can be thrown over for the foot to pass if that should not be done.

" The enemy are greatly discouraged by the forts holding out so long, and it is the general opinion of the best of the citizens that the enemy will evacuate the city if the fort holds out until the middle of next week.

" There is plenty of forage in this country, especially about Darby—we purpose to examine the ground a little more about Darby tomorrow, and if possible return tomorrow evening—From the best accounts we can get there is but five ships with troops on board in the river.   I am &c

" Nath. Greene."

COMMODORE HAZELWOOD TO WASHINGTON.

" Red Bank, Nov' 15th 1777

" Sir.

" Agreeable to your Excellencys request by letter to me of 13 Nov', I have inclosed you the opinion of myself & Officers in Council of War held of[f] Red Bank the 14th Ins', a copy of which you have inclosed, where your Excellency will see we are all unanimously of opinion in regard to our holding this Station with the Fleet.   While we were on this business their Fleet came up & attacked this Fort. I immediately carried all our force against them, & after a long & heavy Cannonading, with the assistance of a two Gun Battery, we drove or caused their Ships to drop down, but they getting their Ship Battery & a Sloop Battery up in the inner Channel close under our Fort Mifflin & under cover of all their Cannon & Bomb Batterys, & keeping up such a warm & hot fire, it was impossible for the Fort & that brave & good Officer to hold it longer, without that Ship could be destroyed.   I ordered one half of our Galleys with as brave an officer as I had, to destroy the Ship & Sloop, but he returned & said it was impossible while they was so well supported by all their Batterys, so at last that brave &

good Officer Major Thayer was obliged to set fire to their works & quit the Fort. Our Fleet has received much damage, & numbers kill'd & wounded, which cannot now be exactly ascertained, but as soon as I can get a return made out, shall send it. We shall hold our Post as long as possible, & shall anxiously wait to have your answer to this, Whether your Excellency approves of our determination. Our Men & Officers behaved with spirit & bravery. Having not to add for the present, am &c.

"JOHN HAZELWOOD."

"In Council of War held on board the Chatham Galley, Nov' 14th, 1777, summoned by Commodore Hazlewood to deliberate on a letter wrote him by his Excellency Gen¹ Washington dated Whitemarsh, 13th Nov' 1777.

"After maturely considering the contents of his Excellencys Letter, this Council are unanimously of opinion, That should Fort Mifflin be evacuated & so fall into the enemys hands, it will be altogether impracticable for our Fleet or any of them to keep their present station, or to prevent in such case the enemys raising works at the aforementioned Fort Mifflin, as in their present situation they are within reach of Shot & Shells from the enemys Batterys on Province Island. But should such evacuation on our side, & possession on that of the enemy take place, this Council are of opinion, that by the Batterys raised & to be raised on this the Jersey Shore on the upper side of Mantua Creek, & above that opposite the Chevaux de Friez, the passage of the enemys Shipping especially those of any considerable force, will be altogether obstructed, as without raising, or removing the Chevaux de Friez, it is impossible such Ships can have a passage.

"Much, indeed all depends on our keeping possession of the Jerseys, for should the enemy prevail there, it is our opinion, that our Fleet will be altogether annihilated, as in that case our retreat & resources will be entirely cut off.

"Should we be by the enemys getting possession of Fort Mifflin, be obliged to retire further up, we have a sure retreat into Timber Creek where all our Fleet may shelter in safety, from whence the Galleys might in a very short time salley out & we trust defeat any light Vessels of the enemy, for which the pass thro' in the intervals between the Chevaux de Frieze might be practicable, but those Vessels in such case must meet with many obstacles not only the risque of venturing thro' almost impracticable passes, but be also exposed to the fire of those large Batterys of ours on this the Jersey Shore.

" We of the Council are therefore unanimously of opinion, That on our Forces keeping possession of the Jerseys, depends altogether the preservation of our Fleet, & consequently every expectation to be formed from its Manœuvres in future.

" JOHN HAZELWOOD	ISAAC ROACH
" JOHN RICE	JOHN MITCHELL
" RICHARD EYRES	JAMES JOSIAH
" THOMAS MOORE	EDWARD YORK
" NATHAN BOYCE	JOHN HARRISON
" HUGH MONTGOMERY	ROBERT HARDIE
" BENJAMIN DUNN	WILLIAM WATKIN
" THOMAS HOUSTON	ISAIAH ROBERTSON
" WILLIAM BROWN	—— WARNER
" JEREMIAH SIMMONS	PETER BRUSTER."
" GEORGE GARLAND	

CAPTAIN CRAIG TO WASHINGTON.

"FRANKFORD, 15ᵗʰ Novʳ 1777

" SIR :

" I believe your Excellency may Depend upon the enemy's force being drawn to Attact the Fort to day, a very severe and heavy firing began this morning about 10 oClock and has continued ever since, the Enemy Dread the Northern Armys joining your Excellency and have been making every preparation to attact before the N—— army joyn'd, and have not been prepared before today.   I have the honor &c

"C. CRAIG."

BRIGADIER-GENERAL VARNUM TO WASHINGTON.

"FORT MERCER 15ᵗʰ Novʳ 1777 6 oClk P.M.

" SIR

" The Firing is universal from the Shipping Batteries &c. —We have lost a great many Men today—a great many of the officers are killed and wounded—My fine Company of Artillery is almost destroy'd—We shall be obliged to evacuate the Fort this Night. I am &c

" J. M. VARNUM.

" Major [Silas] Talbut is badly wounded, Major Fleury is wounded also. It is impossible for an Officer to possess more merit than Major Thayer, who commands the brave little Garrison." [1]

BENJAMIN RANDOLPH TO WASHINGTON.

"BURLINGTON, 15ᵗʰ Novʳ 1777

" SIR

" Being apointed by General Warnan to take charge of the Flag with Docter Glentuth, yesterday we atemted it. the Capton of the Friggat Rec'd it & detained us til he sent it to General How who Return'd for ansur we could not be Receved must return back to the warf at Coopers &c.

" at 9 oClock in the morning just as we got to the ferry I heard a univrsal Ratle of their drums in town and all moveing downwards below town. I likewise heard from a Quaker that Just Left it & the ferryman that brought them over, that on the 7ᵗʰ Inst. the Enemy Brought Stoors from their Shiping to last them for two weeks, that they sayd no more could come for two weeks after that on acc't the moon-light nits, they said they were hail'd by our men on the fort three times as they were Passing up. Likewise heard them cry out Allˢ well as they Passd, likewise told me the enemy ware moveing some Boats down towards the mouth Schul-kill. The officer of the Friggot told me they had just been sending two floting Batteries down the Schulkill with four 32 Pounders on board to assist against our fort that they

[1] " Major Ballard carries this."—*Endorsement by Brigadier-General Varnum.*

ware in want of Provisions but expected their Shiping up
in two or three days—he wanted to no wheather General
Putnam was Likely to Join your Excellency soon or not, I
could not tell anything about the matters of that sort, they
seamed much concerned it apeared to me.   I am &c
" Benj^a Randolph."

BRIGADIER-GENERAL VARNUM TO WASHINGTON.

"Woodberry, 15th Novr 1777 11 oCk A.M.
" Sir

"I was a great part of last night in Fort Mifflin; It is
greatly shattered, but very defensible, had we the Men mentioned in my letter of yesterday.—I shall send two Hundred
Militia in this night.   They will be able to work & fight
upon Occasion.—What put it into the Enemy's Head, I
cant say.   But they kept up a constant cannonade and
Bombardment all night, so as to prevent in a great Measure,
the necessary Repairs in the Breaches.—I am under the
Necessity of beseeching your Excellency to send a General
Officer, whose concurring Sentiments, or Orders, should he
be of superior standing, will be very advantageous.   The
Objects here are so various that I cannot fully do what I
know is essential to the Service.—The Militia are without a
Commander.—It is very difficult getting Matters done in a
speedy Manner.   I am obliged to attend every department
myself.—I do not make this Request because I am not fond
of commanding,—But from a Consciousness that the service
demands it.   We want another commanding Officer of
Artillery, & more Artillery Men.   Indeed, I think a Field
Officer of Artillery should be here.   Capt. [James] Lee will
do all that a brave, good Officer can, but a Shot may claim;
then we should be badly off indeed.   I am just informed
the Shipping are in Motion—Our Battery below has just
opened.   I am &c
" J. M. Varnum.

" N.B.—Should the Shipping play upon the Island, we
must evacuate it, But I am in hopes we shall keep them
down."

WASHINGTON TO BRIGADIER-GENERAL VARNUM.

"HEAD QUARTERS, 15 November, 1777

" SIR :

" I have received your Letter of yesterday inclosing the opinion of Maj. Thayer, the present Commandant at Fort Mifflin respecting the defence of that Post—and am happy to find that he and Maj^r Fleury coincide in their Sentiments as to the practicability of maintaining it in spite of the Enemy's Land and Floating Batteries. Their perseverance, however, may expose them to falling a sacrifice in case of an Attack by Storm, unless the necessary materials be furnish'd them from your side of the River, for repairing the daily destruction caused by the Enemy's Cannon. There should be a never failing supply of Fascines & Palisades— large Gabions will be useful—and a quantity of earth loaded in bulk on board of Flats, will be very serviceable in correcting the oozy nature of the soil on which they are obliged to work. They are likewise in want of Ammunition for their 32 pounder, for which they have been obliged to use the Cartridges of their eighteen Pounders.—A stock of Fire wood, an indispensible Article at this season of the year should be laid in at every convenient opportunity, so that they may not be deficient in it, in case of the Communication between them and the main being interrupted by high wind or bad weather. One or two of their gun carriages are dismounted, which will require the presence of such Artificers as you can spare. Mr Fleury seems desirous of retaining the Cannon on the Island. I cannot at this distance decide as to the propriety of suffering them to remain, which must depend upon the State of the Works, and the prospect of reestablishing some essential parts of them. Your visit to the Island will enable you to speak decisively upon this and other matters of importance.

" Genl Greene in a Letter received from him this morning informs me that the Enemy are attempting to get a Frigate thro the Channel between Hog Island and Province Island. This passage may be render'd impassable for Vessels of a respectable size by sinking a hulk there, or throwing some other obstruction in the ways. It will be proper therefore that you should have a conference with the Commodore upon this subject immediately, and consult with him upon the best means for frustrating the Enemy's Designs.

" With respect to the Enterprise upon Province Island which I recommended in my last—I must observe that tho my expressions gave it a great Latitude and that I proposed the ruin of the Enemy's works as part of the End in view —yet I should be content if nothing more could be effected to have the Cannon of those works, or any part of them, spik'd. A resolute body of Voluntiers and chosen men I still think might be employed with success in this Undertaking—and tho the time gain'd by us and the Embarrassment occasioned the Enemy would not be so considerable as in the other case, yet it appears to me worth the attempt, especially as by the means of surprise, the service might be done before the party could be opposed in force—and at all events the Retreat is easy.[1]

Gen¹ Greene in his Letter calls the Channel in question the *New* Channel. I am not certain which he means, but you will be able to determine. I am &c.[2]

"G° WASHINGTON."

COLONEL SMITH TO WASHINGTON.

"WOODBERRY, 15 Nov' 1777

" SIR:

" My Arm will this Night or tomorrow Night permit me to take the Command at fort Mifflin. I was there last Night,

---

[1] This attempt, suggested in Washington's letter to Varnum, dated November 13, 1777, *ante*, probably led to the proposed expedition outlined in Wayne's letter to Richard Peters, of November 18, printed in Stillé, " Major-General Wayne and the Pennsylvania Line," p. 105. I can find no evidence that the suggestion came from Wayne; and I think it more likely that when Varnum raised difficulties, Washington undertook the matter, and selected Wayne as a fit man to lead. He determined to await the re-enforcements from the north, and the opportunity was lost. This reconciles the statements of the two men as given by Dr. Stillé.

[2] In manuscript of Lieutenant-Colonel John Laurens.

it is now one Heap of Ruin & must be defended with mus-
quetry in Case of Storm. I presume the Enemy will continue to cannonade for four or five days & then they will be
obliged to storm. When they do, I am of Opinion they
will succeed. With 600 Men I think we could defend it as
an Island. Our great dependance must be their being to
much afraid to storm. I hope it will hinder them from
the Attempt untill your Excell^y can send such Number as
will give the Men a Relief every 3 Days—in that Case I
think we might defend it as an Island, & I Hope your Ex-
cell^y will soon be able to attempt Something that will hasten
their Departure to their Shipping—such parties of Men
would rebuild in the Night what they destroy in the Day.
I have the Honor &c

" SAM SMITH.

" Gen. Varnum has been oblig'd to send Capt Lee to take
the Command of the Artillery at fort Mifflin. Mr. Comstoc[1]
who took the Command after Capt Treat was very unfit, we
want a good Officer & more Artillery Men very much—We
are oblig'd to fire much Powder away & shall want Cartridges
for 12^s, 18^s & 32 pounders immediately."

BARON ARENDT ON FORT MIFFLIN.

" As long as we have a design to prevent a Junction between the Enemys Fleet and their Army, the maintaining
Fort Mifflin is indispensibly necessary—not that this place
in itself hinders the Junction, tho it certainly contributes to
that valuable purpose, but it gives Security to our Fleet,
which could not keep its present Station if the Enemy
should make themselves masters of the Fort & raise batteries against it—this is the opinion of the Commodore
whom I consulted upon this subject.

" Although therefore this post ought to be maintained to
the last extremity, yet I grant that there are many difficulties
in the way—the fatigue and inclement weather to which
the Garrison is exposed, are not the least considerable.

---

[1] Probably William Comstock, of Rhode Island.

" The Design of the Enemy seems to be to make themselves masters of the Island, by constant bombarding and
cannonading so as to ruin the works and either drive out
the Garrison, or exhaust them by keeping up a fire at night
—if however they find themselves disappointed it is probable
they will venture another attack with Troops.

" Whatever be their designs, we have only two points in
view—the Preservation of the Garrison—and repairing as
much as possible the ruined works. I propose this expedient which is not impracticable, because frequently used in
besieged Fortresses.

" 1. To preserve the Garrison let it be disposed in the most
secure places—this has been done hitherto by placing the
men behind the Stone Wall, but as it is considerably damaged and begins to fall, it can't afford shelter much longer.
My opinion is that the men ought to go out every morning
at day break, and lie down in order to be better conceal'd
upon Planks behind the Bank which is opposite to Province
Island—they should make no fire, but keep themselves warm
with their blankets, and have their victuals either cook'd
over night, or on the eastern side of the Island—to keep
them in spirits there should be an additional allowance of
Rum or strong-beer—especially as the Soil and Water are
exceedingly unwholesome—it is morally certain that the
Enemy will not fire upon the spot proposed, but direct their
shot against the Fort—where there should be only a few
Centries left, and a few necessary hands to serve the
Artillery.

" 2. The Garrison should be relieved as often as possible—
Gen¹ Varnum says he has not men enough to relieve every
night, but that it might be done every 48 hours—which is
sufficient—thus the Health of the Soldiers will be preserved,
they will not be worn out with Fatigue, and their Courage
will be renew'd—The Garrison ought always to be 400 strong
—the Commanding Officer and Engineer ought likewise to
be relieved.

" 3. For repairing the works, and in order to spare the
Garrison, it would be well to send every night for fatigue a

Detachment of 100 Militia with their Arms, they would be so many fighting men—they should carry with them Palisades, Fascines and Gabions—the work to be done, will depend upon the Damage sustain'd in the course of the day—I am of opinion that a Parapet of Fascines and Gabions should be substituted to the Palisades, it might be made under cover of them, and would be infinitely more serviceable—they might afterwards be taken away.

"It has been proposed to construct a battery upon the same bank, which I have pointed out above as Shelter for the Garrison,—and it is thought that this would change the direction of the Enemy's Fire so as to divert it from the Fort—but my plan would be inconsistent with this, and besides many of the Balls intended to take the battery proposed obliquely and in flank, would go beyond it and batter the Fort.

"4. I think that the heavy Cannon, which are not pointed against the Enemy's batteries, should be removed and placed in the battery lately open'd on the other side of the River—there they would be out of the reach of the Enemy's balls, and would be more dangerous to their Shipping—as they would give a plunging Fire—the Commodore is of the same Opinion.

"5. As to Ammunition and Provision I think a sufficient quantity for a few days only should be left at the Fort and the rest deposited in some vessel or vessels.

"6. For the Security of the Garrison in case of extremity, the Commodore should be required to send upon a conventional signal being given at the Fort, all the Vessels and boats to take them off.

"Lastly to hinder the Communication which still subsists between the Army and Navy of the Enemy, and is kept up by means of little boats upon which Fort Mifflin has fired without success—there is no other method that I know of than having armed boats and Gallies stationed in a proper place for driving away the Enemys boats.

"BAR. ARENDT.

" I have communicated most of these Ideas to Gen[1] Var-num and Col. Smith." [1]

SUBSTANCE OF BARON ARENDT'S LETTERS.

" General Varnum informed me this morning, that Col° Smith had sent him word by an officer, that he thought it impossible for the Fort to hold out longer than till tonight —and asked my opinion upon the subject.   It was that the Fort should be maintained to the last extremity, but that the Cannon of the Battery should be brought off with all the superfluous Provision and Military Stores—that the Cannon brought off might be placed with advantage else-where—and that provision and Ammunition for two days only should be left in the Fort.

" I went to Fort Mercer, with a design to cross to the Island and resume my Command, but my strength was not equal to my Good Will." [2]

COLONEL GREENE TO GENERAL POTTER.

" RED BANK, 15 Nov. 1777

" SIR

" Since my last the Cannonade has been very severe upon Fort Mifflin—this Day the Ships have come as near as the Chevaux de Frize would allow them.   A floating Battery with 18-24 p[n] came up between Fort Mifflin & Province Island, and the Fire from Them togather with that of their Batteries has dismounted all the Guns but two, Almost destroyed the works—and have killed and wounded a very considerable Number—Among the latter is Major Talbut and two Cap[s] of Co[1] Durkee's Regm't.   Our Shipping have kept up a warm Fire, and a two Gun Battery about $2\frac{1}{2}$ miles from this has annoyed the Enemy very much—We have sent Boats to the Brave Major Thayer, who has discretionary Orders to maintain the Post as long as he thinks practicable

---

[1] In manuscript of Lieutenant-Colonel John Laurens.   The endorse-ment shows it to have been written on November 15.

[2] An undated sheet in manuscript of Lieutenant-Colonel John Laurens.

—that the brave Garrison may have a secure retreat when the Post is no longer tenable —— —— 'tis too true that the boat deserted, another run away the next morning—We apprehend Nothing here.   I am &c.

" C. GREENE."

BRIGADIER-GENERAL POTTER TO WASHINGTON.

[" 16 November, 1777.]

" Dª SIR

"I am sorey to be the mesenger of Bad news last night at Ten oClock our Breve Garrison at fort Mifflin set fier to the Barrucks and set off to Ridbank   this Intiligance I have by my express that Brought me the in Closed—I see myself that our Barricks are Burnt and the enemys ships Viglint and a sloop are leying a long side of the Island   this moment I Receved your favour of this day and will observe the Contents.   I am &c

" Jaˢ POTTER" [1]

BRIGADIER-GENERAL VARNUM TO WASHINGTON.

" WOODBERRY ¼ after 11, A.M. 16 Novʳ 1777

" SIR

"Agreeable to what I wrote you last Evening, we were obliged to evacuate Fort Mifflin.   Major Thayer returned from thence a little after two this morning.   Every Thing was got off, that possibly could be.   The Cannon could not be removed without making too great a Sacrifice of men, as the Empress of Russia, alias *Vigilant*, lay within one Hundred Yards of the Southwest part of the Works, & with her incessant Fire, Hand Grenades & Musketry from the Round Top, killed every Man that appeared upon the Platforms.—The Commodore gave positive Orders to six Gallies to attack, and take that Ship.   They warp'd over to the Island, & there held a Council, lost a few of their men, & then returned without attempting any Thing, I left the Com-

---

[1] On November 28 Congress directed an inquiry to be made by General Washington into the loss of Fort Mifflin, on the river Delaware, in the State of Pennsylvania, and into the conduct of the principal officer commanding.

modore since one this Morning. He had positively ordered six Gallies, well manned, to attack the same Vessel—how they succeeded, I am not inform'd, but, according to Major Thayer's Sentiments, we could have held the Island, had the Ship been destroy'd.—I dont think the Shipping can pass the Chevaux de Frize while we keep this Shore.—The two Gun Battery, near Manto Creek, annoy'd them very much Yesterday. It is still firing slowly; but the Shipping having remov'd out of direct Distance, too much firing would be Profusion.—We are erecting a Battery, directly opposite the Frizes, w°h I believe will be finished to-day— I am not of Opinion that the Enemy can possess themselves of the Island without too great a Loss. Whether we shall keep a Guard upon it or not, I cannot determine 'till, from a critical Observation, I shall be furnished with new Circumstances. While we keep the Shipping down, our Navy will be safe; but should our Defences prove ineffectual, we shall take out a Part of their Guns, & let the others attempt passing the City.—Our Troops are so extremely fatigued that no time will be lost in knowing your Excellency's Orders, whether the Troops commanded by Col° Smith shall remain here, or return to Camp. The Officers seem anxious to join the Army, as their Men are much harrass'd—However, they have had two Nights Rest, & are necessary here, should we attack Billings Port—As a great part of my own Brigade have been lost at Fort Mifflin I shall not be able to make any hostile Attempt this Night; but am of Opinion that the Enemy should at all Hazards, be dispossess'd of this Shore.—We shall want the large Howitz, w°h I mentioned before.

" Your Excellency's Letter of yesterday came to me this Morning early—I am just told the Gallies last order'd to attack the Vigilant, did nothing: That misfortune will prevent us from keeping Men upon the Island. I am &c

" J. M. VARNUM.

" P.S.—Col° Greene offered to Officer and Man three Gallies, that would destroy the Empress of Russia, or perish to a Man. Capt Robinson, of the continental Fleet, offered to go himself & the Commodore proposes a fine Disposition, but cannot command his Fleet."

COLONEL SMITH TO WASHINGTON.

"Woodberry, 16th Novr 1777

" Sir

" Gen. Varnum will have inform'd your Excell^y of the Evacuation of fort Mifflin. I am extremely sorry for the Circumstance. Major Thayer defended it too bravely.

" My party taken (as your Excell^y knows) from the picquet, think they have done their Tour of Duty, & hope for your Excell^y permission to join their respective Regiments, who (they say) want their immediate Attention—the Officers have no Cloths with them. My Arm is yet very painful. Major Fleury is hurt but not very much, he is a Treasure that ought not to be lost. Capt [Edmund B.] Dickinson of the first Virg^a Reg^t deserves much Attention—he stayed with & assisted Fleury—he is a brave, industrious good Officer. Capt [George] Walls of the 4th Virg^a has distinguish'd himself on every Occasion, for a brave, industrious & prudent Officer. Capt [William Dent] Bell of the 6th Maryland has much Merit. I have the Honor &c.

" Sam Smith."

JOSEPH REED TO WASHINGTON.

" Capt. Lee's Quarters—near Springfield
" Meeting House, 6 Miles from Darby
" Nov. 16, 1777

" Dear Sir :

" General Green will give you so perfect an Idea of what he has seen here as to make any Remark unnecessary from any one else. I hope & believe it is not yet too late to give the Forts some effectual Relief, but every Moment is precious, in the present advance Season & after the Injury so heavy a Cannonade must have done them.

" As I know you are pleased with having the Sentiments of every Person who gives himself the Trouble of reflecting, I have no Difficulty in giving you mine as to the Mode of Annoyance. I am much inclined to think that unless the

Attack upon the Works in the Islands is either a total
or partial surprize it will fail—should they take Alarm at
any Movement of ours, & throw over a Body of Troops
on the Islands, the Approaches are so difficult that I think
the Attack will fail or at least will be attended with great
Loss.—The late heavy Rains have broke one of the Dams
& the Meadows are much softer than they were when this
Matter was under Consideration formerly.—But I should
hope these Difficulties may be obviated by Gen¹ Potter's
moving down to some convenient Distance—a Detachment
of at least 3000 Men moving over to him with Artillery, the
latter if concealed by a Night march I think the better.
The Time of Attack previously fixed & the main Body of
the Army to cross agreeably so as to destroy the Bridge, &
cut off all Communication of support at the same Time.
Should the Surprize fail I still think the whole Force of the
Army may be drawn to a Point so as to make the Islands
too warm but I think it will be effectual & more likely to
bring on a general Action which it seemed to be a general
Sentiment should be avoided, & which I also in our present
Circumstances am of Opinion we ought not to seek.

"I shall trouble your Excellʸ no farther at present. Capᵗ
Lee will give you an Account of the Observation of the
Day, which affords a happy Prospect. I am &c

"J. REED.

"P.S.—General Cadwallader desires me to mention that
a Party will go from Gen. Potter tomorrow to meet the 12
pounder & Howitz which are expected for the purposes Gen.
Cadwallader suggested." [1]

BRIGADIER-GENERAL VARNUM TO WASHINGTON.

"FORT MERCER, 17ᵗʰ Novʳ 1 oClk P.M., 1777
"SIR:

"In Consequence of the Enemy's armed Vessells, laying
at Fort Mifflin, their Provision Vessells pass unmolested up

[1] See a letter from Colonel Christopher Greene to Washington, dated
Red Bank, November 17, 1777, in Sparks's "Correspondence of the Revolution," Vol. II. p. 43.

to the Mouth of Schylkill, between Mud Island and Province Island. A considerable Number of Shipping have moved up this Day & anchored off Billingsport. It is probable they may intend landing the Troops from New York, w°h in Addition to those already there, (I mean Billingsport) their Force may be such as to put it out of my Power to prevent a Siege.—It is my Opinion, if your Excellency intends taking Possession of Province Island, this Post should be held. If you give up all Ideas of preventing the large Shipping's going up the River, this Post is of no essential Consequence ; Batteries along the Shore, between this & Manto Creek, might annoy greatly, or totally prevent the Shipping from raising the Cheveau de Frize, if the Troops besieging should be dislodged.—If your Excellency should think of establishing a strong post at Cooper's Ferry, I imagine all the large Cannon should be removed to Mount Holley. In that Case the Troops here would be of great Service.—It will require a large Force to keep the Shore so as to play directly upon the Shipping—Was our Fleet to continue under the Cover of this Place, the Enemy's Shipping would be in a worse Situation ; but, as they seem to be upon the Wing, the Enemy will soon be able to open Bomb Batteries from Fort Mifflin. This would not be terrible in itself, but connected with an Investiture, would deprive the Garrison of that Cover, w°h might otherwise be derived from the Bank of the River.—Col° Greene will write you the Sentiments of the principal Officers of the Garrison, upon their present Situation. Provided the Enemy should attempt crossing Timber and Manto Creeks at the same Time, Woodberry will be a more ineligible Situation than Haddonfield, as it will throw my Troops between the Enemy's Front and Fort Mercer; and prevent that Communication w°h would be necessary. However, in that Case, I shall act according to immediate Circumstances.—I hope your Excellency's Earliest Orders may be given upon these Matters.— It is a great Misfortune, that we have lost Fort Mifflin; Nothing but the undaunted Bravery, & persevering Prudence of Major Thayer, prevented a much greater Effusion of Blood, than has taken Place.—The Ground was held until the principal Cann[ona]de was over, when the greater part of the Garrison were put off. The Major with a rear Guard of about forty Men, remained, 'till with amazing Address, he had sent off the most part of the Stores, he then came away. Had the Garrison been bro't away in the Day time, the Loss must have been very great, as the shipping would have sunk many of the Boats. I mention these Circumstances, in repetition of what was said in my last, as it may be said by some, that the Major continued too long upon the Island.—If that was the Case, the Fault was mine, not his. I can say from my Conscience, I think never did Man behave better.

" I have called for an exact return of the killed & wounded, w°h will soon be transmitted; It is not so great as was imagined or expected.

" I am &c.

" J. M. VARNUM."

CAPTAIN CRAIG TO WASHINGTON.

" FRANKFORT, 18th November, 1777

" SIR :

" I have not been able to gain any intelligence of Consequence since I had the Honour of Addressing your Excellency.

" The enemy intend some Grand Menouver in Jersey very shortly which I hope to be informed of—the[y] have been making small enquiries respecting the Northern Army, and what number of Men your Excellency has in Jersey.

" Enclosed is a rough Draught of the enemy's lines. I have been so unfortunate as to meet with an Accident which prevents my being so active on the lines as I wou'd wish to be—shoud anything new Transpire I shall embrace the earliest Opportunity of communicating it. I have &c.

" CHARLES CRAIG.

" I have this Moment received information of Lord Cornwallace' crossing in Jersey last night with four thousand

Men. I shall write more particularly this evening. I
have &c.

"C. CRAIG.

"½ past 11 o'Clock.

"Since my last I have had I believe a True Acct. of Lord
Cornwals⁰ˢ rout. Last night about 12 o'Clock his Lordship
Marchd from the City with Two thousand Granadiers, &
light Infantry, he intends his march for Willmington where
he is to Cross the river and march up the other side and
make an Attackt on Red Bank Fort. I have the Honor &c.

"C. CRAIG.

"NEAR FRANKFORT, ½ past 3 oClock."

LIEUTENANT HEARD TO WASHINGTON.

"FRANKFORD, 18ᵗʰ Novembʳ Half past 2 P.M.

"SIR

"I am just now creditably inform'd by Mʳ Petre, direct
from the City, that last Night at 11 oclock, a large Body of
the Enemy under the command of Cornwallis, march'd to
the Neck.   their intentions are to cross over the River
below the Fort. Mr. Cooper further adds, that this detachment has so much weaken'd them, that they have not now,
in the City, Men sufficient to Man their Lines. I have
receiv'd various Accᵗˢ of this, which, tho' in themselves they
do not all agree, yet all in this, that a large Number has
actually gone off.

"Mʳ Cooper received this piece of Intelligence from a
Sergeant, who supposing him & two or three who were with
him to be well affected to the Royal Army, had communicated this to him. As Capᵗ Craig is now absent & I now
command, I have thought proper to send this. I have the
honor &c

"JOHN HEARD."

BRIGADIER-GENERAL POTTER TO WASHINGTON.

"SQUAIR, Novʳ 18ᵗʰ Eight oClock P.M., 1777

"SIR :

"You have been informed of the enemys move to Chester last night and of Generals Reed and Cadwalder & me

Reconnitring them—by Reeds letter of this day from Darbey I am now to inform you that the[y] are all Imbarked on Bord there ships and gon over to the Jarsey—Redbank must now fall. I am &c

"Jas. Potter.

"P.S.—I send you enclosed the Deposition of Mr. Sellers."[1]

JOSEPH REED TO WASHINGTON.

"Lewis Davis's 5 miles from Darby & near "Springfield Meeting House, Nov. 18, 1777 "½ past 9 oClock.

"Dear Sir :

"Since I wrote you this Afternoon we have got Intelligence, out of Chester, which may be depended on that the Troops at Chester began to embark at 11 oClock this Morning & past over to Billingsport with their Cannon, Waggons, &c.—they made no Secret of their Intentions to attack Red Bank—They gave out their Number was 5000 & the Inform[t] says there was certainly a great Number chiefly British.

"They said they would storm it to night if practicable but they were so late that the Informant thinks they could not effect it to night. He farther adds that Troops went from on Board the Ships on the same Errand. L[d] Cornwallis commands this Detachment. We have thought it best to despatch this Intelligence this Evening that you may be fully apprized of every Circumstance necessary for your Excell[y] to form a Judgment of what may be proper to be done in our present Circumstances.

"Gen[l] Cadwallader supposing from the Position of the British Troops that his Scheme was wholly frustrated, had directed Proctor to return & proposed crossing the River to Head Quarters tomorrow morning, but upon this Intelligence he has determined to stay. You may depend upon it that every Precaution will be taken for the Safety of the

---

[1] Nicholas Sellers, of the borough of Wilmington, a shallopman, and lately a prisoner with the English. The deposition refers to the cruel treatment meted out to prisoners, and the efforts of the British to starve them into enlisting on their side.

Pieces, & I make no Doubt they will be safely returned.   I am &c [1]

"Jos: Reed."

WASHINGTON TO BRIGADIER-GENERAL VARNUM.

"Head Quarters, 18 November, 1777
"10 o'Clock P.M.

"Dear Sir:

"A Body of the Enemy marched last Night from Philadelphia, across the Bridge at the Middle Ferry and proceeded to Chester.   Their number is variously reported, being from 1500 to 3000, but I imagine the former is most likely, although some people, from the city, think their numbers are much lessened upon their lines.   They this day embark'd their Horses from Chester on Board Ships and Brigs.   This would seem as if they were going away, but in my opinion it is only a feint, and that they intend to cross over to Jersey and pay you a visit.   Therefore keep a good look-out below; if you do this, they cannot surprise you because they must make a tedious debarkation of their Horses.   To all matters contained in yours of yesterday I refer you to the Generals St. Clair, Knox and Kalb, who went down to consult with you and the Commodore.   I expect a report from them to govern me in my operations, towards assisting you.   If you could get some countrymen to go into Billingsport with a small supply of provisions, he might learn something of their intentions and numbers.   I am &c [2]

"G° Washington."

---

[1] From Major Clark's letters I obtain the numbers of the regiments, exclusive of the Hessians and light infantry, which enable me to give the names of the colonels:

Fifth Regiment, Hugh, Earl Percy.
Fifteenth Regiment, Richard, Earl of Cavan.
Seventeenth Regiment, Hon. Robert Monkton.
Thirty-third Regiment, Charles, Earl Cornwallis.
Fifty-sixth Regiment, John Irwin.

[2] In manuscript of Lieutenant-Colonel Tench Tilghman.

WASHINGTON TO BRIGADIER-GENERAL GLOVER.

"HEAD QUARTERS, 19 November, 1777
"11 o'clock P.M.

" SIR :

" The Enemy having thrown a considerable part of their force over Delaware, with an Intention as I suppose of making an attack upon our Fort at Red Bank, occasions me to Reinforce the Garrison & troops already their with a large Detachment from this Army—in addition to which it is my desire & you are hereby order'd to March by the most convenient Route after receipt of this to Join the Continental Army which may be in the Neighbourhood of Red Bank under command of Major Gen¹ Greene, or any other Officer there commanding, & take his directions with respect to your conduct at that Post. You will take the Necessary precaution for the Subsistance of your Troops on their march to this place by Detaching Commissaries &cᵃ, to provide for them. Your first Route should be Directed to Haddonfield & from thence as Circumstances will require. I am &c

" Gᵒ WASHINGTON."

WASHINGTON TO THE COMMANDING OFFICER OF EITHER POOR'S
OR PATERSON'S BRIGADE.

"HEAD QUARTERS, 19ᵗʰ November, 1777

" SIR :

" Instead of proceeding to Coryels Ferry which I imagine is your intended Rout, I desire you will march down as far as Trenton, and there wait my orders before you cross the River. The moment you receive this, dispatch an Officer to me, to inform me where you are, when you will be at Trenton, & by what Road you will march, that I may send orders to meet you. I am &c.

" Gᵒ WASHINGTON.

" If this should reach you between Flemington and Coryels Ferry, you are not to march towards Trenton, but cross at Coryels, as first intended.¹

¹ In manuscript of Lieutenant-Colonel John Laurens.

WASHINGTON TO BRIGADIER-GENERAL VARNUM.

" HEAD QUARTERS, 19 November, 1777

" DEAR SIR :

" In Consequence of advices rec^d since I wrote you last
Night, I have ordered Genl Huntington to march to your
Assistance. You will please to direct the detachment that
went first down to Fort Mifflin under the command of Col°
Smith to return to camp, they are in so much want of
Necessaries that it is impossible for them to remain longer.
Let the Militia that are with you be put in the best order,
that they can be. I wish they had a good officer at their
Head to arrange them properly. I am &c

" G° WASHINGTON.

" P.S.—It would not be amiss to collect all the Militia
you can in the Country adjacent." [1]

WASHINGTON TO COMMODORE HAZELWOOD.

" HEAD QUARTERS, 19 November, 1777.

" SIR

" I am favor'd with yours of 15th Instant covering the
Resolution of a Council of War held the preceding day
upon the Subject of my Letter of the 13th.

" The General officers who have been sent from here
to Examine into & determine upon the Measures to be
adopted in that quarter have, I expect, by this time put
things in such a Train as will be most conducive to the
public Interest, & agreeable to the Officers concerned.
Should any matter be left undetermined by them, I shall
be able from their Report to form my Opinion thereon &
shall immediately communicate it to you. In the mean
time I have no doubt but you will afford every Assistance
in your Power to repell any attempt which may be made to
clear the channell or reduce the Fort.

" Inclosed you have a Letter from Presid^t Wharton
which he requested might be forwarded to you. I am &c

" G° WASHINGTON."

---

[1] In manuscript of Lieutenant-Colonel Tench Tilghman.

WASHINGTON TO BRIGADIER-GENERAL VARNUM.

"19 November, 1777

" SIR :

" The Generals St. Clair, Knox and Kalb returned to Camp this Evening—they are all clear in their opinions that keeping possession of the Jersey shore at or near Red Bank is of the last importance.[1] I have therefore determined to make such an addition to the Reinforcement that marched this morning under Genl. Huntington that I am in hopes you will be able to give an effectual Check to the force which the Enemy at present have in Jersey. Gen¹ Greene will take the command of the Reinforcement—Very much will depend upon keeping possession of Fort Mercer, as to reduce it the Enemy will be obliged to put themselves in a very disagreeable situation to them and advantageous to us, upon a narrow neck of land between two Creeks, with our whole force pressing upon their Rear—Therefore desire Colonel Green to hold it if possible till the relief arrives. All superfluous Stores may be removed if it can be done after this reaches you; that in Case of Accident as little may fall into the hands of the Enemy as possible. While we hold the fort it will be necessary for some of the Gallies to lay close under the Bank to keep the Enemy from making any lodgment under it, and it will also secure your Communication with the Water, which perhaps may be essential, for I do not remember whether there is a Well in the Works. There can be no danger to the Galleys while we keep the Bank above them, and if we evacuate, if they cannot get off, they may destroy them and put the Men on Shore. I have recommended this upon a supposition that they will be very serviceable to you; if you do not think they will, you need not keep them.

" Altho I am anxious to have the fort kept, I do not mean that it should be done at all events so as to endanger the

---

[1] Joseph Reed gave to President Wharton another account of the conclusion of these generals, saying they " were of opinion that the fort would not be tenable against regular approaches, and that the galleys would be of no use."

safety of the Men without any probability of success. I am &c[1]

"G⁰ WASHINGTON."

CAPTAIN CRAIG TO WASHINGTON.

" SIR :

"I received various Accounts yesterday respecting the Enemy's Measures for making an Attack on Red Bank   in my last Letter to your Excellency I mentioned the Enemy's intending to march by Willmington, having receiv'd that information from the City, But I think it very improbable— That Cornwallace is march'd with a party of Troops is a Certainty, said to be two Thousand Granadiers and Light Infantry.   But where he intends Crossing I am not able to learn.   The Enemy were last Night alarmed, and Drew in their Piquets.   Nothing New has Transpired since my last. In that Sketch of the Enemy's lines I sent yesterday is mentioned a Compʸ from each Regᵗ being Draughted— Those men were Draughted before the reduction of Fort Mifflin.   I have the Honor &c.

" C. CRAIG.

"FRANKFORT, 19ᵗʰ Novʳ 1777

"Since my last Letter I have received a Certain Account of a Number of Highlanders crossing to Jersey last Night about nine oClock.   The[y] cross'd at Coopers ferry—their Piquets were Drawn in last night, their lines very weak by every information.   I am &c.

" Wednesday one o'Clock"

BRIGADIER-GENERAL WAYNE TO WASHINGTON.

"TWO MILE STONE, 2 oClock P.M. 19ᵗʰ Nov. 77

" DEAR GENᴸ

"The light Infantry who were Encamped on the Right between third & fourth Street have struck their tents this morning—their Picquets are drawn in—we took possession of the advanced Redoubt made of Rails, where they vacated this day.   I am just proceeding along the line to the left.

[1] In manuscript of Lieutenant-Colonel Tench Tilghman.

They have turned out the Guards from a house near the City with a few of their Horse, but don't seem Inclined to Advance—there is no *Abettu* to the Right. I am &c

"ANT.ʸ WAYNE."

BRIGADIER-GENERAL VARNUM TO WASHINGTON.

"HADDONFIELD, Nov. 19ᵗʰ 5 P.M., 1777

" This Morning my flying Camp was removed from Wood-berry to this Place, as a more fit Situation for benefiting Red Bank. One principal Inducement was a Concurrence of Reports that the Enemy from Philadelphia were to form a Junction with those from Billingsport. In wᶜʰ Case we have a proper Position for attacking the Party first men-tioned, & thereby facilitate the Retreat of the Garrison over Timber Creek, wᶜʰ otherwise would be impracticable.—My Videts have just informed me from Manto Creek Bridge, Sunton, that the Enemy moved, three Hours since with about one Thousand towards that Bridge, but as it was taken up, which they could not fail knowing, I imagine their Principal Manœuvre was filing off from their Rear to their Right, in Order to cross five Miles above, where the Creek is easily fordible. Should this be the Case, I fear the Garrison must retreat in the Morning. However, I am this Moment going to Red Bank, & its Vicinity to satisfy myself more fully, & consult with Colᵒ Greene. I am so fully of Opinion that they will bend their whole Force to get full Possession of the Jersey shore, rather than [1] I shall recommend holding the Post longer than otherwise, think-ing that you will contend with them here, in great force, rather than suffer their Points to be carried. Nevertheless, not knowing what your Result may be, I shall not suffer the Garrison to be sacrificed upon Conjecture; but continue them as long as I can cover them—That most of the Troops have left Philadelphia, appears in Corroboration of your Excellency's 'Intelligence,' by daily Deserters who come to me. I have no Doubt of it, and am fully of your Opinion respecting their Intentions.—I have Accounts

[1] In turning the leaf the general seems to have omitted some words.

from Billingsport, by Deserters, two of whom came to me last Night, of the sixty-third Regiment, that their Force consists of three British Regiments from New York, fifty five Rank & File in a Company. I am induced to believe the Calculation true in part, as all the recruits from England have joined in New York—Some Companies of Guards, three and an half Hessian Battalions, two Green Coats & Preston's Regiment of Horse. These in Addition to those before there. I have nothing more to add, but that I am &c.

                              " J. M. VARNUM.

" By Major Ward, I now have your favor of this Day; am much obliged for the Reinforcement proposed; but can not think much of the Militia of this part of Jersey. A Reg^t from the Eastern part has left us to Day, but another, larger, came to us."

BRIGADIER-GENERAL POTTER TO WASHINGTON.

                              "Novr 20th 1777

"I am under the disagreeble necessity of Informing your Excilancey that on the eighteenth Instant one of my picquats that Consisted of 1 Capt 2 sub^s 50 privits had 28 privits, Lieut. & 2 Sarg^t taken prisners, and 3 wounded. as to the perticulars I Refare you to General Cadwalder. I am &c.

                              " JA^s POTTER."

WASHINGTON TO BRIGADIER-GENERAL POOR.

                    "HEAD QUARTERS, 20 November, 1777
" SIR

"Upon receipt of this you are to direct your march towards this Army, and to be as expeditious as possible in forming a Junction. I am &c

                              " G^o WASHINGTON.

" If in consequence of yesterday's orders you should have filed off towards Trenton, continue that Rout and give me notice of it by a Messenger. He will probably find me at the Crooked Billet." [1]

WASHINGTON TO BRIGADIER-GENERAL PATERSON.

"HEAD QUARTERS, 20ᵗʰ November, 1777

" SIR

" I yesterday wrote you a Letter with conditional directions relative to your march; upon receipt of this, you will proceed by the way of Coryel's Ferry and join this army as expeditiously as possible. I am &c

" Gᵒ WASHINGTON."

CAPTAIN McLANE TO WASHINGTON.

"DICKESON HOUSE, Novʳ 20ᵗʰ 1777

" SIR

" Intelligences this day agree that the Enemy have but few Troops in the City   its currently reported that our people have avaccuated Red Bank last night   this Evening I fell in with one Thornton as he was going to his family near the lines   he is a [   ] to the Gallys & left them this morning in Bristol   he left the River opposite Red Bank this morning at 3 oClock   he thinks that the fort was then in our Posission and that our people had received Intilligence that their was a reinforcement Comeing to their assistance he saw last Tuesday a Great Body of the Enemy Cross over province Island to Billingport   this day the Enemy's advance Sentrys consist of horse and they are on a line from delaway to Schuylkill distance about one & half miles from the City— no Picquits of foot his discovered this day outside their lines this Evening I heard a smart fire of small Arms for about one Minute   it appeared to be across the Delaway towards Cooper's ferry. Inclosd you have a few lines from the same person that sent the last—this morning one Thomas Smith of my party deserted to the Enemy   he was one of the Sixth Maryland regiment   has many of my party are Bare of Cloaths & desire to be Actife [?] if his Excellency

---

[1] In manuscript of Lieutenant-Colonel John Laurens. The letter to General Paterson contained the same P.S. as that to General Poor.

thinks propper I will be prepared to receive the relief in German Town tomorrow Evening. I remain &c.

"ALLAN M^CLANE.

[*Enclosure.*]

"The Meadows Before the Redouts under water fortification acrost the roads of 2^d & 3^d Streets Intrenching along the Brow of the hills all the rest of works as before mentiond The longer you Delay the more Difficult it will be."

BRIGADIER-GENERAL VARNUM TO WASHINGTON.

"HADDONFIELD, 20th Novr 11 A.M., 1777

" SIR

"Upon my Arrival at Red Bank last Evening, I found that Col° Greene had rec^d the same Acc^{ts} wch I mentioned to your Excellency in my Letter of yesterday; he was farther informed that the Enemy were actually crossing the Ford, In Consequence, he had given Orders for an Evacuation. The Powder by Capt Duplissis, was strewed over the Fort. However, upon an Apprehension that your Excellency might make a great Effort to save it, the Garrison agreed to remain; Hoping to take up the scattered Powder by Day Light. Immediately they were alarmed by the rowing of many Boats near the Shore. This changed the Scene and induced us to bring off the Men, leaving a strong rear Guard to fire upon the Boats. Upon the Approach of this Party the Boats retired. This caused a diversity of Opinion at first; But, it was finally the prevailing Sentiment, that the Boats retiring was a feint to draw the attention of the Garrison, & lull them into Security, 'till a Party from the Ford should throw themselves between Tim[b]er Creek and the Fort. From these Considerations, added to a dismal Circumstance that the firing a single Musket in the Garrison would blow it up, or the bursting of a single shell,—it was concluded to take away the Men, leaving a small Number to set Fire in Case of Necessity, & trust to their Fate.—We have bro't off many Stores; a large Number of Waggons have gone this Morning for the same Purpose. I believe the Possission will be ours 'till we can get away every thing valuable, except the heavy Cannon, or till a strong Force might again be sent in. I am now ascertained the Enemy's Reason for not attacking us here before. By a young Gentleman, who left Philadelphia last Evening, It appears that General Howe imagined there was a very large Force in New Jersey, commanded by Gen¹ Greene. He has therefore ordered all the Grenadiers down, with some other Troops to join Gen¹ Willson: Lord Cornwallis commands the whole. It is given out that they will take Red Bank or sacrifice their whole Army—This Young Gentleman farther adds, that he verily believes there are not to exceed one Thousand Men in Philadelphia. ½ past 12. Your Excellency's Favor of yesterday is delivered to me.—We shall send some Men into the Fort. The Gallies have gone past Philadelphia.— I cannot think the Enemy will attempt the Force, [fort?] after being once convinced that we are equal, or superior to them in the Field. Should General Greene arrive before they attack, & have sufficient Force to move over Manto Creek, they must fight us, before they make any other Attempt. If we beat them, Billingsport as well as red Bank will be ours. Should they possess themselves of Red Bank previous to General Greene's Arrival, that will not prevent an Action, as the Fort will contain but few Men, and, in the Result, will be his who conquers in the Field. I am &c

" J. M. VARNUM."

BRIGADIER-GENERAL VARNUM TO WASHINGTON.

"MOUNT HOLLEY, 21ˢᵗ Novʳ 1777

" SIR

" Last Evening Fort Mercer was evacuated. Some of the Shipping burnt this Morning. Most of the Stores bro't safely off. The Enemy, part at Billingsport, part between Manto & Timber Creeks, and some at Fort Mercer. We have moved to this Place as the first safe Position on Account of the Creeks. From hence we can move by the Head of the Creeks, go down upon the Enemy, secure both

our Flanks by the Creeks, and by the same means, secure a
Retreat in Case of Disaster. It is a fit Situation for making
a Junction of the respective Cors. Gen¹ Huntington has
already joined me. Gen¹ Greene is at Burlington. The
Militia amount to Twelve Hundred. Three Hundred here,
seven Hundred at Haddonfield. I have ordered them here,
but am just told 'they dont like the Manœuvre.' Two
Hundred at Coopers Ferry & Gloucester: They are to join.
With the Great Force you have ordered, we shall be
superior, I believe, to the Enemy in the Field. We have
the Advantage by being at the Head of the Creeks; & it is
my firm Sentiment we ought & shall attack them to Advantage. The Success of that Manœuvre, as I mentioned before,
will determine the Possession of the Forts. I am &c.[1]

"J. M. VARNUM."

MAJOR-GENERAL GREENE TO WASHINGTON.

"BURLINGTON, 5 oClock P.M. Nov. 21. 1777

" Dᴿ Sɪʀ.

" General Varnum this moment acquaints me that fort
Mercer was evacuated last evening—Commodore Hassel-
wood informs me also that the greater part, if not all the
fleet except the thirteen Gallies were burnt this morning;
one or two of the smallest vessels attempted to pass the
city and could not effect it, one was set on fire and one
other fell into the enemies hands owing to the matches
going out—the People made their escape. My division
arrivd on the other side of the river about ten this morning, but the want of scows to get over the waggons will
prevent our marching until this morning the greater part
of the night if not the whole will be employd in geting
over the baggage & Artillery.

" General Varnum has retreated to mount Holly. I purpose to see him and General Huntington early in the
morning if it is practicable to make an attack upon the

[1] See a letter of this date from Joseph Reed to President Wharton, in
Reed's "Life of Reed," Vol. I. p. 338, where it is wrongly dated the
25th.

enemy it shall be done; but I am afraid the enemy will put it out of my power as they can so easily make us take such a circuitous march by taking up the bridges over timber creek—I cannot promise any thing until I learn more of the designs of the enemy, their strength and the position they are in. If it is possible to make an attack upon em with a prospect of success it shall be done.

" Col. Shrieve [Israel Shreve] was with me this afternoon about turning out the Militia. I wish he may succeed, but from the temper of the People, there appears no great prospect—I have heard nothing from General Glover's brigade. I hope Col. Morgan's Corps of light troops will be on in the morning and Capᵗ Lee's troop of light Horse.

" The fleet are greatly disgusted at the reflections thrown out against the officers; the Commodore thinks the Officers are greatly injured, he asserts they did their duty faithfully. I am &c.

" N. GREENE.

" N.B.—The Commodore this momᵗ informs me there is three Sloops & a Brigg past safe by the City." [1]

INTELLIGENCE.[2]

" The lines at the North End of the City are nearly compleat, they are ditch'd & facin'd from Delaware to Schuylkill, between each Redoubt—They have dam'd the Run at the upper end of second street, in order to keep the back water in, the more to obstruct your coming up to their works— On Monday night Lord Cornwallis & Sir Wᵐ Erskine, with a large detachmᵗ some say four, some 5 thousᵈ men marchd thro' Derby downwards, cross'd the Delaware & took Red bank which was evacuated before they came to it, in Con-

---

[1] " *Resolved*, That an enquiry be made into the causes of the evacuation of Fort Mercer, on the river Delaware, and into the conduct of the principal officers commanding that garrison; and that a committee be appointed to report the mode of conducting the enquiry."—*Journals of Congress*, November 28, 1777. The members of the committee were William Duer, Francis Dana, and Francis Lightfoot Lee.

[2] From a new correspondent.

sequence of which, our brave little fleet were put to the rout. I believe all the Gondelows & two topsails made a safe retreat up the River, the others are all burnt—this morning 21ˢᵗ Novʳ 1777.

"One o'clock P.M. Just now a boat came from Wᵐ Cooper's ferry with a flag of truce, Bringing a Hessian Doctor & four Ladies over, soon after she left the wharff, the Delaware Frigate fired a Shot at her, she proceeded, till the frigates Boat met her took them all out & made the officer & his Crew prisoners, the passengers were sett at liberty & the others took to jail. The reason of this Violation I cannot guess, perhaps the flag was not properly authenticated by a General Officer, or they were Exasperated at the Burning our Fleet.

"They continue getting up Provisions by way of Schuylkill, they sell Rum at a Guiney pʳ Gall: pork they [have in] plenty, Beef & Butter they have none, their flower all very Musty—they begin at the Chevaux de frees tomorrow—they say Cornwallis is to scower the Jerseys, whilst How is to maintain this City with about 3000 men, they appear to be in the greatest security, notwithstanding I have the greatest reason to believe from every Accᵗ that they do not exceed that Number.

"Their different preparations plainly denote their determination of wintering here.

"They have pulled down peal hall & all the rest of the houses facing their Redoubts. They have ordered all the wood within their lines to be cutt for the use of the Army, they are takeing up houses & when the empty ones are full they quarter the rest on the Inhabitants—Beef in Market is sold for 5/ pʳ lb. paper, & 3/9 hard money—thank God, the Quakers Idol is fallen ¼ already, & I hope soon will to nothing; 'tis reported & I believe it to be fact the Quakers have lent them 90,000 pounds the better to carry on the war & some of them at this time refuse to take it for goods.

"The army are very healthy & very saucy, say they have men enough to defend their Lines whilst Cornwallis clears the Country.

"I hope His Excellency General Washington will soon convince them to the contrary."

MAJOR-GENERAL GREENE TO WASHINGTON.

"MOUNT HOLLY, Nov' 22, 1777

"D^R SIR

"I came to this Place yesterday morning—the Difficulty of crossing the Baggage over the River prevented its coming up last night. The Boats & Scows at Burlington are under very bad Regulations.—Gen. Varnum had retreated as I wrote your Excellency before to this place. He left a Party of Militia at Haddonfield: I am afraid there has a very considerable Quantity of Stores fallen into the Enemies Hands, but principally belonging to the Fleet. The Enemy and the Militia had a small Skirmish at little Timbercreek Bridge, the Enemy crossed there in the afternoon & encamped. They say they are going to take Post at Haddonfield to cover the lower Counties & open a Market from thence; Those Counties are some of the most fertile in the State, from whence great Quantities of Provisions can be drawn—A large Number of Boats went up to Philadelphia from the Shiping yesterday morning—there were some Soldiers on board of them.

"Col° Morgan's Corps of Light Infantry advanced this morning for Haddonfield. If the Troops can be got in Readiness I intend to put the whole in motion this afternoon. We are greatly distrest for want of a Party of Light Horse. I must beg your Excellency to forward some as soon as possible.

"I have heard nothing from Glover's Brigade. I sent an Express to the commanding Officer yesterday, but from the present Situation of things, I believe it will be best not to wait their coming up.

"Every Piece of Intelligence necessary for my Information with Regard to the Movements of the Enemy in the City, I must intreat your Excellency to forward to me by Express.

" Col° Shreeve will attempt to turn out the Militia, but the Commissary's Department is in such a bad Situation & the People so unwilling to furnish Supplies, that it will be difficult to subsist a large Body.

" A considerable Body of light Horse would be very useful here.

" Your Excellency's Letter of the 22ᵈ Insᵗ is just come to Hand. You have in this, all the Intelligence which I have received. I am &c.

" NATH. GREENE."

WASHINGTON TO MAJOR-GENERAL GREENE.

" HEAD QUARTERS, WHITEMARSH, 22 November, 1777

" DEAR SIR :

" I am favᵈ with yours of yesterday afternoon from Burlington. As you have crossed the River, an attack upon the Enemy's detachment, if it can be made with success, would be a most desirable object. But I must leave the propriety of it entirely to your own judgment. I have heard nothing more of Glover's Brigade than that they are advancing down the Road from Morris Town. I sent an Express to meet them, and to turn them down towards you, but I think you had better despatch one of your family or an Officer to guide them to you. There are not more than one hundred and seventy of Morgan's Corps fit to march as they in general want Shoes—they went yesterday and will join you I suppose this day. Capt. Lee's Troop are not yet come from the other Side of Schuylkill, but they are expected every instant, and will be sent immediately over to you. If you can procure any account that you think can be depended upon of the Number that the Enemy detached from Philadᵃ, I beg you will send it to me. Or if they send any part of their force back, let me know it instantly. I shall be anxious to hear of every movement of you or the Enemy, and I therefore wish to have the most constant advices. I am &c.

" G. W.

" P.S.—I shall order an express to be stationed at Bristol to bring on your despatches." [1]

WASHINGTON TO CAPTAIN ALLAN McLANE.

" HEAD QUARTERS, 22 November, 1777

" SIR :

" I have this moment received your Letter containing the Proposals of some of the Inhabitants near the Enemy's Lines. I will undoubtedly accept their offers of service on condition that they give in a list of their names, and engage to be under the absolute command for the time specified of such Officer as I shall appoint. This precaution is necessary, for otherwise they may only receive the Public Money without performing the Duty expected of them. I am &c.[2]

" G° WASHINGTON."

WASHINGTON TO BRIGADIER-GENERAL VARNUM.

" 22 November, 1777.

" SIR

" I have rec^d your favors of 20 & 21st Inst. by this Express I shall write to Maj. Genl Green from whom you will receive your Instructions respecting your Operations on that Shore.

" I am at a loss to determine upon what Principle the Powder was strewed over the fort at Red bank as I expected that if an Evacuation was found necessary it might be brought off, & if that was impracticable I considered the best mode of destroying it was to throw it into the River unless it was determined to blow up the Works with it, which could never be effected by the mode which was adopted.

" As the Destruction of the Fort would naturally accompany the Idea of being obliged to Abandon it, I shall be much disappointed if I hear it has not been executed. I am &c

" G° WASHINGTON."

[1] In manuscript of Lieutenant-Colonel Tench Tilghman.
[2] In manuscript of Lieutenant-Colonel John Laurens.

WASHINGTON TO MAJOR-GENERAL GREENE.

"HEAD QUARTERS, 22 November, 1777

"DEAR SIR.

"I have received your Letter of this Day's date—it does not appear from any account worthy of credit, that any part of the Detachment which cross'd the Delaware under Lord Cornwallis has return'd to Philadelphia. I am inclined therefore to wish that you would advance to meet it as much in force as possible—and that for this purpose you would use every means to hasten the junction of Glover's Brigade. I am at a loss to account by what mistake Capt. Lee's Troop is not with you; that was originally intended for the Service you mention, as it was esteemed the best calculated for it. As a party of horse appears so essential, that or some other will be ordered to join you immediately. I am &c

"G° WASHINGTON.

"By an officer from Glover's Brigade I was informed that it reached Morris Town the evening of the 20th. I sent a message to him to urge them forward and have reason to think they are by this time in your Neighborhood."[1]

THE NAVY BOARD TO WASHINGTON.

"CONTINENTAL NAVY BOARD
"BORDEN TOWN, 23d Nov' 1777

"SIR :

"It is with the greatest Concern we inform you of the total Destruction of the Continental Fleet at Red Bank; having been burned by our own Officers in Consequence of a Determination of a Council of War. We have not yet had an Opportunity of making a regular Enquiry into the Reasons of so desperate a Measure. As far as we can collect from the Officers and Crews here, it was occasioned by the Assurances of the Commander of the Land Forces, that they must expect no further Protection from his Army; not even to secure a Retreat in Case of Emergency. But

[1] In manuscript of Lieutenant-Colonel John Laurens.

this must be the Subject of future Enquiry. Be the Cause what it may, the Loss seems at present, to be irreparable.

"We request the favour of your Excellency to let the enclosed Packet go with your next Despatches to Congress, & are &c.

> "FRAˢ HOPKINSON.
> "JOHN WHARTON."

COLONEL JOSEPH ELLIS TO MAJOR-GENERAL GREENE.

"[HADDONFIELD], Novʳ 23ᵈ 1777

"By a Woman who came thro' the Enemy encampments this day, says, that their main Body lay at Woodbury & Lord Cornwallis quarter'd at Mʳ Coopers—That they have a large encampment at Great Timber Creek Bridge and their advanced picquet consisting of about thirty are posted at Little Timber Creek Bridge.—They give out that they have 10,000 Men, but she thought they had not half the number; most of the Troops she saw were cloathed in Greene—she thought they had between 80 & 100 Light Horse."

[Unsigned.]

MAJOR-GENERAL GREENE TO WASHINGTON.

"MOUNT HOLLY, Novʳ 24, 1777

"Dᴿ SIR

"I have nothing new to communicate to your Excellency with Respect to the Motions of the Enemy—they remain or did remain last night at Woodbury, with a Guard at Timber Creek, consisting of about six hundred men. The Boats that went up, mentioned in my former Letter, I conjecture had on Board the Baggage of the Army; the Soldiers seen on board, were the regimental Guards to the Baggage.

"The Militia of this State is dwindling to nothing. Gen. Varnum says, there was upwards of 1400 a few days since —they are reduced now to between seven & eight. Colᵒ Shreeve is gone out to see what Impression he can make upon the People, and to endeavour to draw together as large a

Number as possible; but I cannot flatter myself with any considerable reinforcement.—I will endeavour to inclose your Excellency a Return of our Strength in Continental & Militia this Afternoon if possible.

"We are all ready to advance; but the General Officers think it advisable to wait the Return of the first Express sent to Glover's Brigade; to learn the strength & time the Junction may be formed with that Brigade.—I have heard nothing where it is, notwithstanding I have sent three Expresses.—Capt. Lee is not arrived, neither have I heard any thing of him—I could wish if possible, some Horse might be sent, as every Army is an unwieldy Body without them; & in this Country, they are more immediately necessary, to prevent the Enemy from sending out theirs to collect Stock.

"Col° Cox who is with me at this Place, says, if the Enemy can open a Communication with the three lower Counties, they will be able, independant of all the surrounding Country, to draw Supplies of every kind, necessary for the Subsistance of the Army & Inhabitants of the City of Philadelphia.

"Your Excellency observes in your last, you must leave the Propriety of attacking the Enemy to me. Would you advise me to fight them with very unequal numbers. Most People, indeed all, agree they are near or quite 5000 strong —Our Force is upwards of three, exclusive of the Militia, which may be from seven to eight hundred at most. The Situation the Enemy are in, the Ease with which they can receive Reinforcements, & the Difficulty of our knowing it, will render it absolutely necessary, whenever we advance from this Place, to make the Attack as soon as possible.— I had much rather engage with three thousand against five, than attack the Enemy's Lines, & there is a much greater prospect of succeeding, but still I cannot promise myself victory, nor even a Prospect of it, with Inferior Numbers. I have seen of late, the difficulty your Excellency seemed to labour under, to justify the Expectations of an ignorant Populace, with great Concern. It is our misfortune to have an Extent of Country to cover, that demands four times our Numbers—the Enemy so situated as to be very difficult to approach, and from pretty good Authority superior to us in numbers. Under these Disadvantages, your Excellency has the choice of but two things, to fight the Enemy without the least Prospect of Success, upon the common Principles of War, or remain inactive, & be subject to the Censure of an ignorant & impatient populace. In doing one you may make a bad matter worse, and take a measure, that, if it proves unfortunate, you may stand condemned for by all military Gentlemen of Experience; pursuing the other you have the Approbation of your own mind, you give your Country an opportunity to exert itself to supply the present Deficiency, & also act upon such military Principles as will justify you to the best Judges in the present day, & to all future Generations. For my own Part, I feel Censure with as great a Degree of Sensibility, as is possible, and I feel ambitious of doing every thing that common Sense can justify; but I am fully persuaded, in attempting more you may make a temporary a lasting Evil.—The Cause is too important to be trifled with to shew our Courage, & your Character too deeply interested to sport away upon un-military Principles.—

"For your Sake, for my own Sake, & for my Country's Sake I wish to attempt every thing which will meet with your Excellency's Approbation—I will run any Risque or engage under any Disadvantages if I can only have your Countenance if unfortunate. With the Publick I know Success sanctifies every thing and that only. I cannot help thinking from the most Dispassionate Survey of the Operations of the Campaign that you stand approved by Reason & justified by every military Principle.—With Respect to my own Conduct, I have ever given my Opinion with Candour & to my utmost executed with Fidelity whatever was committed to my Charge.

"In some Instances we have been unfortunate.—In one I thought I felt the Lour of your Excellency's Countenance, when I am sure I had no Reason to expect it—It is out of my Power to command success, but I trust I have ever endeavoured to deserve it.

" It is mortifying enough to be a common Sharer in Misfortunes, but to be punished as the Author, without deserving it, is truly afflicting.

" Your Excellency's Letter of the 22ᵈ, but I suppose it was of yesterday, this moment came to hand. As I have wrote so fully upon the Subject I have nothing to add, only, that to advance from this place before Glover's Brigade joins us, unless we attack the Enemy without them, will rather injure than facilitate our Designs. But if your Excellency wishes the Attack to be made immediately— give me only your Countenance & notwithstanding it is contrary to the Opinion of the General Officers here, I will take the Consequences upon myself.

" Inclosed is a copy of a letter from Colo. [Joseph] Ellis at Haddonfield.

" The Hospitals in the Jerseys are greatly complained of —they prove a grave for many of the poor Soldiery—principally oweing to the Negligence of the Surgeons who have the Care of the Hospitals. How far these Complaints are well grounded I cannot pretend to say—but I would beg leave to recommend the sending of good trusty Officers to inspect the Management of the Hospitals & to remain there until regularly relieved. I am &c.

" NATH GREENE.

" Major Burnet has just returned from Glover's Brigade —they will be at the black Horse to Night—Eight miles from this place.

" half past three oClock."

COLONEL ELLIS TO MAJOR-GENERAL GREENE.

" HADDONFIELD, Novʳ 24ᵗʰ 1777

" DEAR SIR

" In complyance with your Letter of yesterday, I send you a state of the Militia under my Command, which is

about 400 Effective at this place, and about 100 in the
neighbourhood below Manto Creek; the time of service for
which they came out will for the greater part expire in a few
days; Orders are out for Assembling the other Classes, so
that I hope to keep up the number.—As to the Enemy, from
the best discoveries we have been able to make, their main
strength is at Woodbury, and their lines extend from Manto
Creek, to Little Timber Creek, an extent of six or seven
miles: their whole force about 5000, consisting of Brittish,
Hessians, and Marines; The Marines are employ'd in destroying the Works at Red Bank, when that is effected they
give out, they intend moveing their Army upwards, to Burlington and Mount Holly; Their Post at Woodbury is advantageous & difficult to attack.—Thus you have an Account
of matters in this quarter. If any thing interesting comes
to my knowledge, I shall transmit it with all possible speed.
I am &c.

" Jos: Ellis.

" N.B.—The Enemy have 8 or 9 Field pieces on the different Roads near Woodbury.

" Just now receiv'd Intelligence by a Person who came
thro' part of the Enemy's lines on the upper-side of Great
Timber Creek, who says there is about 300 at and between
the two Timber Creeks."

BRIGADIER-GENERAL WEEDON TO MAJOR-GENERAL GREENE.

" Haddonfield, Novr 24, 7 oClock
" Dr General.

" We only arrived here a few minutes ago. Some of our
parties have taken 9 prisoners, which will get to you early
to morrow. From them we have had I believe pretty exact
accounts of their numbers, which the Marquis will enclose
you a particular account of. They amount to 4250, 60
pieces of Artillery and 100 Light Horse. The Infantry
and artillery may be nearly right, but I doubt the information respecting the horse. They have this day advanced on

this side Great Timber Creek with their Main Body, and
have pitched on this side of Little Timber Creek also—
Some of the prisoners were taken within two miles of the
town—They have no troops at Red Bank, and but few at
Billingsport. The prisoners say they intend crossing the
Delaware at Cooper's ferry. We shall look about us in the
morning, and shall communicate any thing of importance.
From yours very sincerely

                                          " G. Weedon."

[*On back.*]—" I have this moment rec⁴ your Orders to
return;—myself & Horse is so much fatigued, that can't
get further than Moors Town tonight. Shall join you early
in yᵉ Morning."

BRIGADIER-GENERAL POTTER TO WASHINGTON.

                          "Camp at the Squair, Novʳ 24ᵗʰ 1777

" Sir :

" I was at Chester yesterday the most of the shiping is
gon up the River as far as the Bend below Billingsport—the
enclosed lines I Received from a good honest whig that
would not assart a falce hood knowing it to be such he lives
in the City."

                                          [Unsigned.]

[*Enclosure.*]

" Sir

" I Received yᵉ Beef & Return thanks till better paid.

" The troops in thee Jerseys under Comand of Lo⁴
Cornwalis are not come back Neither is any others arrived here, but Shipping with Stores for army. No accᵗ
at all from yᵉ Jerseys their Numbers here I cant find out
but I Beleave it takes one third part Daily for Guards in
& about town.

" The meaning of that fire you see was the Americans

set fire to their fire ships & the reports of their guns when the fire had got to them & the great Explosons of Magazines on board the Galleys all got up safe to Burlington." [1]

WASHINGTON TO MAJOR-GENERAL GREENE.

"HEAD Q^{ᴿˢ} 24 November, 1777

" D^ᴿ SIR :

"If you have not moved from Mount Holley when this comes to hand, I wish you to wait there till you see Col° Meade, who will set off immediately charged with some important matters which I thought it improper to commit to paper. This, however, you are to understand under this restriction—That I do not mean to prevent you a moment from prosecuting any Objects you have immediately in view that promises success. I am &c [2]

" G° WASHINGTON."

[1] This was from the same correspondent as gave the lines printed on page 156.

[2] In manuscript of Robert Hanson Harrison. A council of war sat on November 24 to consider the possibility of attacking successfully the enemy in Philadelphia. No decision appears to have been reached, and Washington requested each officer to submit his opinion in writing.

[NOTE.—To properly understand the importance of the following documents, it is necessary to recall the political position occupied by Washington. The success of Gates at the northward had directed public attention to his supposed capacity as a commander. The plot which has passed into history as the Conway Cabal originated some time before Conway had anything to do with it, and was in its nature political rather than military. The idea entertained by some members of Congress, notably those from the Eastern States, of the necessity of having two commanders instead of one, offered a basis for scheming in the military line. Did anything happen to Washington, it was felt there was no man to take his place; and Gates, at the head of the northern army, reaping the benefits of the preparation and leadership of others against Burgoyne, gave promise of a brilliant military future, and thus presented himself as a legitimate successor to Washington. This was early the feeling among certain members of Congress, and their prepossessions were used in an illegitimate way to further the ambitions of men wishing to advance themselves by means of Gates. There is not enough evidence to prove that Gates was a party to any scheme having a definite purpose to supplant Washington; but there is abundant evidence of a wish on the part of certain officers in close connection with Gates to push him for the chief command of the American army. In seeking this they sought even more their own advancement and advantage, and it is to Conway and Mifflin, out of Congress, and to Samuel Adams, James Lovell, and, as is generally supposed, Richard Henry Lee, in Congress, that the alleged Cabal owed a support and encouragement that eventually led to an actual plot to advance Gates even at the expense of removing Washington.

The surrender of Burgoyne directed attention to Gates. To accomplish that object Washington had so far depleted his own army as to be in no position to offer effective resistance to the advance of Howe upon Philadelphia. The battle of Brandywine and the reduction of Fort Mifflin practically determined which army should hold the city, and the general public, seeing only defeat in one quarter and a brilliant success in another, jumped to the conclusion that the one was due to inefficiency, while the other was caused by splendid military ability. It was, therefore, easy to foment an opinion that Washington had been derelict in his share of the campaign; and as day after day passed with the two armies almost within gunshot of one another, yet no engagement taking place, the populace clamored for action. They could not understand why, with forces supposed to be nearly equal in strength, an assault upon the British in Philadelphia should not be attempted. They could not know how much Washington had sacrificed of his strength to assist Gates, and they did not know that the force returning from the northern army after its success did not rejoin Washington until after Fort Mifflin had fallen. It was only when Glover's brigade and Morgan's corps had joined the main army that Washington felt himself strong enough to entertain an assault upon the city. Not only did he wish to make this assault, but he was urged to it by the popular clamor, as it was thought that good political results would follow a striking military success. He knew that he had enemies in the army, and felt that he had them in Congress. The sentence from Conway's letter gave him knowledge of the one, while his friends in Congress kept him advised of the other. It was to determine whether his idea of an attack on the British was practicable that he called a council of war and requested the opinion in writing of each general officer. These opinions are now published for the first time, and must be considered in the light of something besides military policy, although they are naturally concerned more with the military than the political features.

One bit of evidence which I believe has not been heretofore known is to be found in a report submitted to Congress by the Board of War on November 21, or three days before this council was held. The military questions in Congress had been under the control of a " Board of War and Ordnance" until October, 1777, when a " Board of War" was established, to consist of three persons not members of Congress. As a beginning of a separation of executive from legislative functions, this was a decided step in advance. It was on October 17 that the report constituting the Board of War was adopted, or about two weeks after the knowledge of Gates's victory had been obtained. On November 7 the members of the Board were elected: Major-General Thomas Mifflin, Colonel Timothy Pickering, and Colonel Robert Hanson Harrison. Mifflin and Pickering accepted their appointments. On November 17 Congress determined to add two members to the old Board of War, and selected Mr. Dana and Mr. J. D. Smith. This old Board, composed of members of Congress, met on the morning of the 21st of November; and, by a strange oversight, the report they laid before Congress contained the name of Major-General Mifflin as present and apparently taking a full part in the proceedings as one of the members. This error was afterwards corrected and his name stricken out. In this report is to be found the first suggestion formally made that Gates should be the President of the new Board. It also contained other matter of such interest as to warrant its publication in full. It will be seen that the paragraph applying to Gates was postponed, as well as that which provided for the retention of Richard Peters as Secretary to the Board. Six days later Congress proceeded to the election of three Commissioners for the Board, and elected Major-General Gates, Joseph Trumbull, and Richard Peters as the Commissioners, and specially appointed Gates as the President of the Board. It is thus established that it was due to Mifflin that Gates received this high appointment to a place in which he could more easily work upon the sympathies and influence of the members of Congress, led rather by the ambitions of others than by his own wishes. The general impression to be gained of Gates, from his correspondence, is that of a rather dull, well-meaning, and easily influenced man, such a man as would readily become the tool of others possessed of greater capacity and more unscrupulous.

Nothing could be more cutting to Washington than the terms of this report urging the claims of Major-General Gates to the position of President of the Board. The principal matter urged by Washington upon Congress as essential to future operations—a measure on which the future of America would depend—was the formation of a new army of competent number and engaged for the war, or for a longer service than twelve months. As the end of the year was approaching, he found himself once more face to face with the formation of a new establishment. He had been providing for this contingency for months, and after an experience of short enlistments through two campaigns, had become so convinced of the attending evils as to see no safety in any other course than in a reasonably permanent force of sufficiently long service to become disciplined and accustomed to their officers,—a prime necessity in an efficient army. Nothing could have hurt him more than to have one intoxicated by an unusual success cut in under him with the remark that his policy was a "theory" and that there were other things more important. The committee urged Gates's military skill as competent to suggest "reformations" in the different departments of the army, while his "character and popularity in the army" would facilitate the execution of such reformations,—" a Task in the opinion of this Committee more arduous and important than the formation of any new Establishment, however wise it may be in Theory."

Fortunately, no such language was used in a formal resolution ; for it is hardly possible to believe that Washington would have remained at the head of the army under such a studied rebuke of his policy. Congress rejected the words of the report, and on the 27th passed the following :

Resolved, That Mr. President inform Major-General Gates of his being appointed president of the new constituted Board of War, expressing the high sense Congress entertain of the general's abilities and peculiar fitness to discharge the duties of that important office, upon the right execution of which the success of the American cause does eminently depend ; that he inform general Gates, that it is the intention of Congress to continue his rank as major-general in the army, and that he officiate at the Board, or in the field, as occasion may require ; and that the general be requested to repair to Congress with all convenient despatch, to enter on the duties of his new appointment.

WORTHINGTON C. FORD.]

REPORT OF THE BOARD OF WAR.

" At a Board of War, y° 21ˢᵗ Novʳ A.M. 1777.

" Present, *Major General Mifflin*, Mʳ Lee, Mʳ Duer, Mʳ Jones, Mʳ Harvey, Mʳ Williams & Mʳ Dana.

" The Board beg leave to report to Congress

Agᵈ

" That they have had a Conference with General Mifflin on the late Establishment made by Congress for conducting the War Department, and are unanimously of opinion, that a sufficient number of Commissioners have not been appointed for giving due weight to the execution of the Regulations which may be recommended by the Board, and adopted by Congress, and particularly for enabling one of the Board of Commissioners to visit from Time to time the different Armies, Posts, or Garrisons in order to see that the Regulations adopted by Congress are carried into Execution, and to examine what are the wants of the Army, and what Defects or Abuses prevail from time to time in the different departments.[1]

Prio Qʸ

" That it wou'd further greatly tend to facilitate the Business of the Department, especially at the Commencement of the new Establishment, to secure the Continuation of the Services of the Secretary of the late Board of War, who in their Opinion has discharged the Duties of an arduous and complicated Department in its Infant stage, with Honour to himself, and much Disinterestedness, and with Fidelity and advantage to the Public.

[1] Printed in the *Journals of Congress*, November 24, 1777.

Postp^d

" "The Board further beg leave to represent that General Mifflin has express'd a warm Sollicitude that Major General Gates shou'd be appointed President of this Board, from a Conviction that his Military Skill would suggest Reformations in the different Departments of the Army essential to good Discipline, Order & Œconomy, and that his Character and Popularity in the Army would facilitate the execution of such Reformations when adopted by Congress; a Task in the opinion of this Committee more arduous and important than the formation of any new Establishment, however wise it may be in Theory.

Ag^d

" On these Principles your Committee are of opinion

" That two additional Commissioners should be appointed to execute the Department of the War Office in P^rSuance of the Resolution of Congress of the [17th of October[1]], and that any three of the said Commissioners should be a Quorum to transact Business; anything in the former Resolutions respecting the Board to the contrary notwithstanding.[2]

" Extract from the Minutes.

" Jos. Nourse

" *D. S. B^d War.*"

Endorsed by Thomson as " passed." In the handwriting of Richard Peters is added:

" The Board are further of Opinion that the Resolution pass'd on the   Inst. relative to the Execution of the War Department should be annull'd; and that the *Members* former *Committee of Congress* Board of War should be authoris'd to proceed on the Business of that Department,

---

[1] In manuscript of Charles Thomson.
[2] Printed in the *Journals of Congress*, November 24, 1777.

till such Time as a Quorum of the Commissioners of the War Office shall attend."

OPINION OF MAJOR-GENERAL GREENE.

"MOUNT HOLLY, 9 o'clock Nov. 24, 1777

"D" SIR

"I received your favor by Col. Mead who has communicated to me the design of an attack upon Philadelphia, the consequences if successful are so desireable that I wish it appeard to me more practicable.—In war there must be always something left to chance and I would always recommend to trust some consequences to the spirit and bravery of the troops. An excess of caution which councils of war are generally productive of, often deprives a country of the advantages of a due exertion of the spirit & bravery of the troops—but I have viewed this subject in and out of council, I have weighed the good and bad consequences—I have surveyd it in a Historical point of light, I have examind it from my own observations in the course of the war, and I cannot think there is that degree of probability of the attempts succeeding that will warrant the undertaking. I have not time without detaining Col. Mead too long to give my reasons against the attack in full detail, but I think it a hazardous attempt and will terminate to the injury of the Continent and disgrace of the army.—I am sensible that many things pronounced impracticable before they were attempted have been crowned with success in the undertaking—But prudence forbids that being made a principle which necessity alone can justify—I wish that it was in our power to give that Army some capital wound—the reputation of the Army and the happiness of the country loudly call for it—but in consulting our wishes rather than our reason, we may be hurried by an impatience to attempt something splendid into inextricable difficulties.

" The depreciation of money, the corruption of the people and the dislike to service that prevails throughout the army will justify measures at this day that might wear the complexion of rashness under different circumstances. How far these considerations may authorise the attempt I cannot pretend to say. One thing I would beg leave to recommend, that is if your Excellency thinks of attacking the City this winter improve the present moment for sure I am whatever reinforcements of militia may be drawn in to aid the army they cannot render it so formidable and equal to the attempt as it is at this hour. I am very willing to lay aside my own private Judgment and second the attempt—you may depend upon it Sir that I will as freely embark in the attempt if your Excellency thinks it warrantable as if I was of the same sentiment, and whatever may be the event my opinion never shall be known.

"The troops here are under marching orders—Glover's Brigade will join us in the morning—I intended to advance in the morning at nine, but Col. Mead's coming and recommending the postponing the march until I hear further from your Excellency, and as the troops coming in will want one day's rest I thought it best to countermand the orders for marching until I hear from your Excell^y and I am further induced to the measure because I dont apprehend the difficulties of attacking Lord Cornwallis will be increasd from one or two days delay. The Enemy give out they are 10,000 strong and that they intend to march to Burlington.

"I wish your Excellency to weigh the subject coolly and take your measures accordingly—I shall be perfectly satisfied be the result what it may.

"I am &c.

"N. GREENE."

OPINION OF LORD STIRLING.

"CAMP, Novr 25th 1777

"SIR:

"In Compliance with your Excellency's request that each of the General Officers met in Council yesterday Evening, should give you their Sentiments in writing on what Measures had best be pursued in the present Exigency of our affairs; I must now beg leave to give it as my opinion that as all the reinforcements we had any reason to expect, have now Joined the main Army, and as a Considerable body of the Enemy's army is detached into New Jersey under the Command of Lord Cornwallis, a favorable opertunity is presented for an immediate Attack of the Enemy. That other Circumstances render this measure absolutely necessary. That from all I have heard said, or that has occurred to me on the Subject, I think the following plan of Attack most feaseable, 1ˢᵗ That the Enemy's Lines on this side Philadelphia be attacked at Daylight by three Columns properly flanked and supported. 2ᵈ That two thousand men be drawn from General Green and embarked in Boats at Dunker's ferry, to proceed to philadelphia, land at or near Spruce Street, push thro' to the Common, endeavour with part to secure the Bridge over Schuylkill, and with the remainder to Attack the Enemy in the Rear of their Lines. 3ᵈ That five hundred Continental Troops with the Millitia under General Potter possess such of the hills on the other side of Schuylkill as command an Infilade of the Enemy's Lines, and while part of them carry on a Brisk Canonade in that place, the rest of them proceed to the Bridge over Schuylkill and wait an oppertunity of attacking the Works there in front, when the party from Spruce Street make an Attack in the Rear. The Landing of the party at Spruce Street should he effected if possible just before day light, as it would greatly facilitate their passage thro' the Town and bring the Alarm to the Rear of the Enemy's lines in time to Cooperate with the main Attack in front. These are outlines of the plan I would propose, and submit it to your Excellency & am with great Regard and Respect

" Your Excellency's most Humble Servant

" STIRLING."

OPINION OF MAJOR-GENERAL SULLIVAN.

" CAMP, WHITEMARSH, Novemʳ 25ᵗʰ 1777.

" DEAR GENERAL:

" Agreeable to yʳ Ordⁿˢ of Last Evenᵍ I have consᵈ the practicability of making an Attack upon the Enemy in Ph—— & weighed its probable Consequences in every view That occurred to me.

"In order to Determine whether such an Attempt is Likely to succeed it is necessary to consider the Enemys situation— The Manner of our making the Attack on the Lines—the Mode of Attack we must adopt for carrying the city after we have made ourselves masters of their Lines & the probable method the Enemy may adopt to Render our Designs abortive. The Right of the Enemy is secured by the Delaware, their Left by Schuylkill & their Rear by the Junction of those Rivers. Their front is partly secured by an Inaccessable Pond & the Residue by a Chain of Redoubts strengthened by Abbatties in part & partly by circular Works—These Redoubts being 14 in number. The Attack upon them must be total or partial if the whole are to be attacked, as works cannot be carried but by Columns. The attacking part of your force in Front must be Disposed in fourteen Columns to carry 14 Redoubts manned with 100 men each. After carrying those they are to assume a Different Form to attack the city which will then be on their Left Defended by 4600 men, even if we suppose the Enemys whole Force in Philadelphia to amount to no more than 6000. If a partial attack is made upon these Redoubts, it must be on these Left, for if these Right be attacked & carried those Redoubts which remain on their Left will with their field pieces play obliquely on the Rear of y^r Troops while Forming & making the attack on the city. Should then their Left be attacked & carried & your Troops pass them & form agreeable to your most Sanguine Expectations & advance towards the city they will have the chains of Redoubts on their Left, the Schuylkill in their Rear, the city & the Delaware in front & the Delaware & Schuylkill on their Right. When your Troops advance to the city in Line they will find the wall of Brick Houses opposed to ye right of their Line, The upper stories of those Houses well filled by musqueteers & the main streets by which alone they can penetrate filled with men, Drawn across of sufficient Depth to oppose any part of your Line that may come against them, & the whole Defended by a Train of artillery surely (?) superior to any you can possibly bring against them, & this artillery being placed in front of the Houses makes no Interval in their Line & is compleatly covered by The Musqueteers occupying the upper Lofts of The Houses. This Disposition will oblidge you once more to form Columns to penetrate the Streets, in Doing which your Troops must the moment they enter the city expect a Fire in front from the Troops opposed to them & on both Flanks from the Houses : These circumstances must occur to the party attacking in Front. How far they may be assisted by a party thrown into the city by water I will not Determine. If the party in front is successful they may be saved—if not they are inevitably lost—before we promise ourselves Success from this Stratagem it will be proper to consider how far this plan will be Likely to be Discovered by the Enemy in Season to prevent its Effects. Every person who has attended to the Noise made by a Fleet of Boats Rowing in the Night must be sensible that they will be heard at Lest two miles & the Noise will Direct the Enemy where to make their opposition—It cannot be supposed that the Enemy will be stupid enough to Let their whole army run to oppose them—they have alarm posts which they will repair to & send a sufficient Number of the Reserve with field pieces to oppose or entrap them. It will be far from having the Effect Designed by a Feint which answers no other purpose but to Induce the Enemy to suppose your whole force being thrown to a point with an Intention to make your most vigorous effort there & by this means Draw them from the posts you wish to carry. They will easily know that you have not boats to Transport any considerable part of your army to the City by water, nor would it be prudent in you so to do. They will therefore consider this as a Feint & Treat it accordingly while they prepare to Receive your Real Attack in Front which this Feint will sufficiently announce to them— with Respect to the probability of carrying the Lines & afterward the City Defended by an army almost equal in Number to that part of yours which you can expect anything from is what both reason & experience speaks Loudly against. I have sometimes Read of Lines & partial Retrenchments being carried but in the course of my Reading (which has not been Inconsiderable) I have never Read of a Chain of Redoubts Covering the whole Front of an Army being carried (even where they had not as in the present Case rivers covering every other side of them). I cannot help observing that some Gentlemen who think we can easily carry those Redoubts say that if we are Defeated we have a Strong and secure Camp to Retreat to. how it can be supposed that a Camp without Lines or Redoubts can be better Defended by a Defeated army against a victorious one than Lines & Redoubts can with Troops, against others upon equal footing only is beyond my Conception. I know it is Said that these Redoubts are weak, but it would be absurd to suppose that the Redoubts they have been Labouring at six weeks are not as perfect as those Thrown up by Peter the Great in one night which Defeated the best army in the world or equal to that single Redoubt which Ruined the British Army at Bunkers Hill. Mr. Howe has never attempted a Redoubt since but at Red Bank & was Defeated —he was several Days with Double your numbers within musket shot of y^r Lines on Long Island & White Plains & feared to attack you—he has no Conception that Lines are so easily carried but if in this he is mistaken all military writers agree that the attack of a village is the most Hazardous Enterprise in war, & has seldom been attended with Success. Experience has so far convinced the King of Prussia that he is determined never to attack another. if it be said we must Reduce it by Cannonnade my answer is that must be a work of time, especially as they have more cannon & heavier mettle than we.

" I know the world expect something from this Army & our affairs call for it, but no Caprice of the Greedy Multitude should induce us to Sacrifice the Army—a Defeat will be so far from helping that in my opinion it will ruin our affairs. The common people will Discover Howes superiority to both our armies without Considering the advantage he had against them—those who have sense enough to Discover the advantages he had against them will condemn the attempt as unwarranted by Reason or Experience—so that from Different views the Country will become universally Discouraged, which I fear will end in the Ruin of our Cause— Upon the whole I think the most certain method to retrieve our affairs, to strengthen our friends & Discourage our Enemies as well as to establish the Currency of our money will be to put the army in such a Situation as will render it necessary for Mr. Howe to fight us or Loose his honor & the confidence the people have in his arms. Once it is known that by avoiding you he acknowledges your Superiority in the field his very friends will Despise him for his weakness & Deceit. Yours will be encouraged & value your money at a high rate when supported by those Arms which (this hitherto) arrogant Invader dare not Attack.—There is still another mode of attack upon the Enemys Lines which is to pass your Columns between the Redoubts. if this should be attempted & the Enemy should retire & Draw up in Rear of their Works Leaving in them a sufficient Number to man them your Troops must advance under a Front & Two Flank Fires till they have passed the Redoubts when they will have an additional one in their Rear from the Redoubts they have passed & after Enduring all this they will have to attack the City under all the Disadvantages before mentioned, in which if they are successfull they will do what no other Troops have ever accomplished.

" I know it is said by some that your Excellency's character & that of the whole Army will suffer if something is not attempted as the Northern Army is called to our Assistance, &c. I am far from thinking so. But Let us consider what foundation there can be for censure. It is beyond a Question that General Howe has been much Superior to you in Numbers thr° the whole Campaign. Yet you have fought him & th° the field remained his the victory was yours—he to add to his Force & to get a Decisive Superiority over you in the field called for a Reinforcement & you to counteract him did the same. You by this means became 13000 strong & he remains at Least twelve. if your additional militia will make up for the want of Discipline in your young

Troops I think it is all we can expect.   Where then is this Superiority in numbers on your side which will warrant your making an attack so Likely to Compleat the Ruin of your Currency : an attack condemned by every military writer & unwarranted by Reason or Experience ?   Actions always take their Character from the Success that attend them, & those Gentlemen who urge this matter to save the Credit of the Army Deceive themselves & you; for if you are unsuccessful the Credit of the Army will be Destroyed & the Confidence of the people Lost beyond recovery & your own Character must suffer.   It has been urged that these works may be carried by Surprize : I have ever understood that works were constructed to prevent a Surprize & never once conceived it possible to surprize & carry 14 redoubts especially when the Enemy's first line is encamped in Front of them—it would be needless to give your Excellency instances of such attempts upon Redoubts alone and unfortified Villages being rendered abortive.   Military Books are full of them   those writers tell us that a single Stone House, mill or Church if well defended cannot be reduced by [but?] by cannon.   if this be true with respect to one a Regular Line of them opposed to your whole Front must be much more Difficult.   What success a Cannonnade from Troops in the open field is Likely to have upon others covered by a village & redoubts & possessed of a Superior Train of artillery requires no great share of military knowledge to Determine.   I have mentioned some unfortunate attacks upon Redoubts that have fallen within our own knowledge.   I will at present mention but two that have proved so upon villages not Defended by Lines or Redoubts.   One was in Corsica the first campaign made by the French ag^t it, where the whole French army were cut to pieces in storming a small village defended by Paschal Paoli's Brother with a Handful of Corsicans & at German Town one Stone House snatched from us a victory which was about compleated.   I am therefore clearly of opinion that the attempt would be Hazardous & must End in Ruin to the Army & to the American Cause.   but should y^r Exce^y think the attempt practicable I shall cheerfully give up my opinion & use every effort in my power to carry it into Execution with Success. I have the honor to be your Excey⁸ most obed⁺ Serv⁺

"JN° SULLIVAN."

OPINION OF MAJOR-GENERAL ARMSTRONG.

"CAMP AT WHITEMARSH, 25ᵗʰ Novʳ, 1777

" SIR :

" Without such an acquaintance of the Enemies lines as wou'd discover to you where they are more or less accessible, I cannot well approve of an attack upon them, nor can I conceive the opposite numbers at Philadᵃ under six thousand or upward.—And question whether an attack can be successful if the lines are not penetrated in so short a space of time (perhaps some seven or at most ten minutes) as will render it impossible for the party thrown into the City shou'd the first attempt on the lines fail, to contribute any effectual influence. The principle upon which that part of the disposition is formed is perfectly just, but the numbers too few, and the contingencies various.

" In the present view of things I rather approve carrying the Army over Scuilkill & making tryal of any advantages that yet may be derived from a possession of the Islands &c. &c., by which means either the Enemy may be drawn out or the Scuilkill pass'd to advantage on the Ice. At the same time I am totally submissive to yʳ Excellency's commands, beging leave only to add that whether the attack is made or not, but especially if it is, the far greater part of yʳ force in the Jersey may suddenly be recalled and join the Army. And that I am with the greatest respect &c

"JOHN ARMSTRONG."

OPINION OF THE CHEVALIER DU PORTAIL.

"25 9ᵇᵉʳ 1777.

"To attack the Enemy in their Lines appears to me a difficult and dangerous Project. It has especially this very considerable Inconvenience—the exposing our Army in case it does not succeed to a total Defeat. This is easily demonstrated. One of the principal means proposed is to throw two thousand men in the rear of the Enemy—if we do not succeed these are so many men absolutely lost. As to the main body of the Army which is to attack in front, it must pass through the Intervals left between the Abattis and Redoubts, which they say form very narrow Passages—if after penetrating we should be repulsed can Troops in disorder return easily by the Passages through which they were introduced—will it not be very easy for the English to cut off their Retreat. Our whole Army then may be destroy'd or made prisoners. Now does it become this Army which is the principal one, to run such Risques—*does it become it to stake the Fate of America on a single Action?* I think not. For my part I never would place this Army in a Situation where its Rear was not perfectly free, much less where it will be inclosed on all sides without means of Retreat. To justify such an Enterprise the success must be almost certain. To judge of this we have only to take a view of the Dispositions which must be made for this attack. This View will render the Difficulties evident. First—two thousand men are to be introduced by a River of which the Enemy are wholly Masters. If we embark them near the Enemy the noise may alarm them—if at a distance, the cold which they will undergo, will render the use of their Arms exceedingly difficult in the morning—besides can we flatter ourselves that the River side is unguarded. Let us reflect that a single man is sufficient to make this project miscarry and cause us the loss of two thousand men.

"As to the Attack in front—these are nearly the Dispositions which would be followed—We should march upon as many Columns as there are Roads leading to the Enemy —upon our arrival in their presence, each Commanding Officer of a Column, according to the size of the works before him, and the number of men which he judges are contained in them, divides his Troops into two parts, one of which surrounds the works and attacks them vigorously, while the other marches boldly through the Intervals and falls upon the troops in the Rear. But every one sees how much harmony is required in all these dispositions. How much presence of mind in the Superior Officers—how much firmness in the troops who have to execute all their manœuvres under the fire of an Enemy who are in a great measure cover'd.

" If the Enemy's works are not inclosed, the Enterprise would be much less dangerous—if they are, the Enterprise is too hardy.

" His Excellency I think desired us to say a word respecting the operations in Jersey. In general it seems to me that we can do nothing better than to endeavour to attack the Enemy's Force there with superior numbers—but there is a very important Observation to be made, which is that we should not weaken ourselves too much here; for we are to consider that the Enemy may recross their Troops in one night and attack us by day break with their whole force.

" If however an attack be determined upon, the Enemy's Works should be more particularly reconnoitred.

" The Chevalier Du Portail." [1]

OPINION OF BARON DE KALB.

" According to His Excellency General Washington's orders, and desire of having every Gentleman's opinion on the Subjects laid before the Council last evening.

" Mine is to attempt an attack on the lines & City, as soon as the Plans thereof can be properly laid, all necessary dispositions and calculations made, as to the mode & time. In respect to the Plan much must depend on intelligences of the Enemy's Position & collected or separated forces, and the whole Enterprise on secrecy and Expedition.

" Two essential points would be necessary to be known.

" 1° Whether a passage for a Column will be practicable on the Bridge or middle ferry on Schuylkill river, to make there a strong attack, or whether the Ennemies take down the Bridge in night time. In this case a small body of

---

[1] This opinion was given in French. I have used a translation made by Lieutenant-Colonel John Laurens.

troops and some artillery would be sufficient on the right bank of that river to disquiet & annoy them in their Lines, and the whole army to be Employed to attack in front with different Columns.

" 2° Whether the Key & City Shore of Delawar be not strongly defended, either by Pickets, intrenchments, row Gallies, floating and other Batteries, and whether the Noise of the Boats to be employed there, will not prevent or defeat the Execution of a landing, for if th' attempt should fail by such obstructions, the boats could hardly be brought off and these troops would be in great danger of being either sunk or taken. If on the contrary no such obstacles were to be feared, a surprise on that side and a well timed attack in the rear of the lines woud undoubtedly insure a compleat Victory.

" Many more things could be said on this subject.

" As for myself and Division we will do our best in what ever part of the Enterprise and attack, His Excellency will find proper to Employ me.

" Baron de Kalb.

" At Camp, 25 9ᵇᵉʳ 1777"

OPINION OF BRIGADIER-GENERAL IRVINE.

" Whitemarsh, Novʳ 25ᵗʰ 1777

" Sir :

" I have seriously revolved in my mind the subject that was debated in Council last night, and notwithstanding the present disagreeable situation of our affairs, cannot think that we are yet reduced to the necessity of hazarding the total destruction of the army by a general attack, on the very ground that general Howe would wish to fight us on ; to attack redoubts &cᵃ with any prospect of success, we should be much superior in numbers to the enemy and at least equal to them in discipline, were we possessed of these advantages, & had boats sufficient to throw about 3000 men into their rear I should chearfully vote for the proposed attack, as in my opinion the defeat of genˡ Howe would then be as certain, as, I am afraid ours would be were we to attack him with our present strength.

" I could therefore wish that the army was placed in such a position (either on this or the other side of Schuylkill) as to invite or oblidge general Howe to leave his strongholds & seek us in the field, as the probability of success in a general action then, would be more in our favour with equal numbers, than in an attempt upon his lines with our present triffling superiority.

" I have had but little experience in war, & therefore give my opinion on this important question with diffidence, should your excellency or the major part of the council determine on the attack, I shall chearfully sustain the part assigned to me, & exert my utmost abilities to procure success.   I have &c.

" JAMES IRVINE."

OPINION OF BRIGADIER-GENERAL MAXWELL.

" SIR :

" Agreeable to your Excellency's request of last night that I should give my opinion this morning in writing concern-ing the making an attact on Philadelphia immediately—I am not for attacting it at present, and will proceed to give some reasons why I would not, viz : It is but a few days ago ; before General Green & Huntington crossed the Dellaware that we determined in a full council that an Attact on the Enemy in their Fortifycations &c. was by no means eligible, and I think we was as strong then as we are now on this side.   It is urged that if we do not make an attact on the Town we must be put to the greatest difficultys to raise another Armey, keep up our credit, &cᵃ.   I am of opinion if we throw the Armey away we have, without some good appearance of success we are much more likely not to get another one nor support the Credit of our money.   I am for attacting and Harrassing them by every means in our power; by any other method than that of attacting them in their works.   I am &c.

" Wᴹ MAXWELL.

" WHITE MARSH, 25ᵗʰ Novbr. 1777.

"N.B.—I have heard that the Enemy has got up 2 or 3 small armed Vessels to Philadelphia by people that came out yesterday."

OPINION OF BRIGADIER-GENERAL PATERSON.

"Nov. 25, 1777

"SIR :

"The proposed attack on Philidelphia in my Opinion will be so hazardous that we cannot be justified in prosecuting of it, as a Failure will most certainly be attended with the loss of great Numbers of our Troops, which I am fearfull would be attended with Fatal Consequences My perfect Ignorance of the Country renders me intirely incapable of recommending any other Plan, but shall with Chearfulness do my utmost to put in Execution this or any other your Excellency shall think adviseable. I am &c.

"JN° PATERSON."

OPINION OF BRIGADIER-GENERAL POOR.

"November 25th 1777

"SIR :

"I am sencable that the Situation of our Country loudly Calls for the Exertions of this Army.

"But fear an atact upon the Lines Round the City of Philidelphia will be unsuceful therefore dont advize to it.

"as I have jest arived to Camp & not acquainted in the Countrey beg to be Excused from proposing a new Disposistion of the Army. I am &c

"ENOCH POOR.
"*B. G¹.*"

OPINION OF BRIGADIER-GENERAL SCOTT.

"WHITE MARSH, 25th Novʳ 1777

"SIR :

"I am for making an attack, so soon as things Can be put in readiness. As to the plan I can Think of none better than that propos'd by Gen¹ Cadwalader, with this Alteration, that the partie proposed to land in the City be detached from Gen¹ Green and not taken from this army. I Have two reasons for this, the one is that those men with him are the Flower of the army, and that it will requier the best men we can pick to effect the landing if opposd. My other Is that we cant well spare them from this army. I have &c

"CH⁸ SCOTT."

OPINION OF BRIGADIER-GENERAL SMALLWOOD.

"CAMP, Novemb^r 25th 1777

"SIR:

"I have revolved in my Mind the Subject of your Requisition last Night, and placed it in every Point of View, and must confess I am much embarrassed. I see the Propriety and Necessity of an Attact, I view with Pain the pressing Expectations of the Public, the Reputation of the Army at Stake, the depression of our Money, the difficulty & hazard of the proposed Attact, and the Misfortunes, and I may add the almost inevitable destruction which must ensue upon a Defeat,—and upon due Reflection let it suffice to say I am against an Attact on the Enemy's Lines, from an Impression that our Troops are not equal to it, unless there was a moral certainty of throwing in the Parties proposed, down the Delaware & across the Schuylkill, to alarm & make a Diversion on the Flanks & in their Rear, but I think this Event wou'd be doubtful & uncertain, as well as extremely hazardous for the Delaware Party & might in general subject the Army to too great a Sacrifice upon such a Contingency.

"I shou'd therefore think it more eligible to manœuvre, and endeavor to draw Genl Howe out of his Lines to an Engagement, wch I shou'd judge is both Practicable, and probable. I have the Honor &c.

"W. SMALLWOOD."

OPINION OF BRIGADIER-GENERAL WAYNE.

"CAMP AT WHITE MARSH, 25th Novem. 1777

"SIR:

"After the most Dispationate & Deliberate Consideration of the Question your Excellency was pleased to propose to the Council of General Officers last Evening; I am Solemnly and Clearly of Opinion—that the Credit of the Army under your Command, the Safety of the Country—the Honor of the American Arms—the Approach of Winter which in a few days will force you from the field, and above all the Depreciation of the Currency of these States,—Points out the Immediate Necessity of giving the Enemy Battle. Could they possibly be drawn from their Lines, it's a Measure Devoutly to be wished.

"But if that cannot be Effected, It is my Opinion that your Excellency should March tomorrow morning and take post with this Army at the Upper or North End of Germantown—and from thence Immediately Detach a Working party to throw up, or effect to throw up some Redoubts under the direction of your Engineers.—this Intelligence will reach the Enemy—they will Conclude that you Intend to make good your Quarters there, and however desirous they may be to dislodge you—yet it will take up some time to withdraw their force from the Jersey.

" by this Manœuvre you will be within Striking Distance, the Enemy will be deceived by your Works, your Troops will be fresh and ready to move the same Night so as to arrive at the Enemies Lines before day light on thirsday Morning Agreeable to the proposed plan of Attack—with great part of which I am in fellowship—the outlines are good —they may be Improved to Advantage and Crowned with Success.

" It has been Observed by some Gentlemen that the Attack is Hazardous—that if we prevail it will be attended with great loss.

" I agree with the Gentlemen in their Position—but however hazardous the Attempt—and altho some Loss is certain, yet it is my Opinion—that you will not be in a worse Situation—nor your Arms in less Credit, if you should even meet with a Misfortune—than if you were to Remain Inactive.

" The eyes of all America are fixed on you, the Junction of the Northern Army—which Obliged Gen¹ Burgoyne to lay down his Arms, gives the Country & Congress some expectation, that a vigorous Effort will be made to Dislodge the Enemy.

" Its not in our Power to Command success—but it is in our Power to produce a Conviction to the World that we Deserve it. Interim I am &c.

" ANT^r WAYNE, *B. G.*"

OPINION OF BRIGADIER-GENERAL WOODFORD.

" DEAR GEN^L

" I cannot help viewing the purposed attack upon the Enemy's Lines as attended with many Hazards & Dificulties. But these are over Ballanced by the following considerations vizt first the necessity that something should be attempted by this Army before it retires into Winter Quarters, both for its own C^r & the support of our paper currency.

" Secondly that from my knowledge of the State of the soldiery we are not likely to be in a better condition, if so good a one, at any Future time.

" Thirdly, that all the Force we expected is arrived—and lastly, that the present Detach'd situation of the two Armys promises a fairer prospect of success than is likely to present itself whilst we are able to continue in the Field.

" I am therefore for making the Attack so soon as your Excellency & some of the Genl Officers have had sufficient time to Digest a proper plan. I have &c.

" W^x WOODFORD.

" Novr 25th, 1777"

OPINION OF BRIGADIER-GENERAL KNOX.

"PARK OF ARTILLERY, CAMP, WHITEMARSH 26th Novr 1777

" SIR :

" I exceedingly lament my want of experience and ability to fill properly the important station in which I am, and I am more particularly distress'd when such important Questions are referr'd to my decision as those which your Excellency gave us in Charge the last evening. The happiness or misery of the people of America may be the consequence of a right or erroneous judgment.

" Much lately has be[en] urg'd concerning the reputation of our arms, as if we had long been a warlike nation whose existence like the antient Romans depended on their military Fame. I confess I view the matter differently and cannot bring myself to believe (how much soever I may wish it) that we are upon a par in military knowledge and skill with our enemies. Indeed it is not possible and the sensible part of mankind well know it.

" We set out in the contest with notions and sentiments very different from these. We then considerd we were contesting for our *all,* for everything dear to humanity : But it now seems otherwise with many persons, whose anxiety for military Fame seems to absorb every other consideration.

" I have also heard it urg'd that your Excellency's reputation would suffer. I freely confess an Idea of this kind pains me exceedingly and were I fully to believe it, I should be impelled to give my opinion for measures as desperate as I conceive the attempt to storm the enemies works and Philadelphia. I am not of opinion that your Excellency's character suffers in the least with the well affected part of the people of America. I know to the contrary, the people of America look up to you as their Father, and into your hands they intrust their *all* fully, confident of every exertion on your part for their security and happiness—and I do not believe there is any man on Earth for whose welfare there are more sollicitations at the Court of heaven than for yours.

" I believe perfectly that there are some people who speak disrespectfully of your Excellency, but I as perfectly believe that these are people who have never given any unequivocal evidence of their attachment to our rights; or whose boundless ambition has been check'd by your well try'd patriotism.

" The state of the depreciation of our Currency has also been urg'd as a principal inducement to some desperate attack—That its value diminishes every day. It is but too true that the large emissions and some other causes have effected a diminution of the value of our paper currency. Had the same enormous emissions taken place in a time of profound peace and flourishing Commerce as have taken place during the war, without sinking any part of them by taxes, I do assert that the Currency would be equally depreciated as at present.

"The circumstances of the respective states would not permit them 'till lately to endeavor to sink their proportions of the paper currency—butt now almost every state on the Continent are making large strides towards it. The Currency in the eastern States from their large taxes will increase in its value every day. I cannot therefore perceive the force of the argument urg'd, deriv'd from the consideration of the failure of the currency.

"The Gentlemen who urge the desperate measure of attacking the enemies Line, Redoubts and city of Philadelphia seem to forget the many principles laid down by people experienc'd in the art of war against our engaging in General actions upon equal terms—against our risquing our all on the event of single Battles—In the beginning of the Contest our friends in England urg'd the impropriety of such conduct, giving instances of numbers of States who lost their liberties by means of them. It is an invariable principle in War, That it cannot be the interest at the same time of both parties to engage. It is also another fix'd principle that the invaders of a Country ought to bring the defenders of it to action as soon as possible. But I believe there is not a single maxim in War that will justify a number of undisciplin'd troops attacking an equal number of disciplind troops strongly posted in redoubts and having a strong city in their rear such as Philadelphia.

"It is proposed to attack the enemies redoubts without being perfectly acquainted with their number, strength, or situation, with troops of whom we have had the experience in two capital actions, that it was impossible to rally after they were broken. By the mode of attack propos'd we are to stake the Liberties of America on a single attempt in which the probability of success is against us, and if defeated of sacrificing the happiness of posterity to what is call'd the reputation of our arms.

"It has been agreed that the enemies Force consists of

10,000 rank and file fit for duty—it is said Lord Cornwallis has taken with him from 1,500 to 3000.   Suppose the number 2500, which is 500 more than I believe he has—there remains 7,500 rank and file fit for duty.   Our returns are 8000.   (I say 8000 because I hold the militia in case of an attack of this kind useless entirely, for we know they will not stand within the range of a Cannon ball.)   We are to attack 7500 strongly posted in redoubts, having batteries and a strong City in their rear.   In this instance the Idea that is necessary among disciplined troops of having three to one to storm works is laid aside, not because our troops are *better* disciplined than the enemies, but because from a concurrence of circumstances our affairs are in a *desperate* situation, and we must retrieve them or perish.

"Marshall Saxe says redoubts are the strongest and most excellent kind of field Fortification, and infinitely preferable to extended lines—because each redoubt requires a separate attack, one of which succeeding does not facilitate the reduction of the others.   Charles the 12th with the best troops in the World was totally ruin'd in the attack of some redoubts at Pultowa, altho he succeeded in taking three of them.

"The Character of the British troops in Europe is far above mediocrity—and the experience we have had of their discipline and valor by no means proves them contemptible. In the commencement of the War they storm'd an unfinish'd work on Bunker Hill, but the experience gain'd there has entirely prevented them from making any similar attempts. Indeed the Germans lately made an attempt on red Bank, the event of which will hardly give them a favorable opinion of the attack of redoubts by storm.

"The situation of the American army on long Island after the Battle of the 27th Augt was exceedingly ineligible, and the enemy must have known it; but they did not attempt to carry our redoubts by storm, altho' had they succeeded in one instance and made a sufficient opening for the introduction of a large Column of troops, the greater part of our army then on the Island must have fallen a sacrifice or have been taken prisoners.

" From the experience deriv'd from reading and some little service and the knowledge of the strength of the enemies works, my opinion is clearly, pointedly, and positively against an attack on the enemies redoubts, because I am fully convinc'd a defeat certain and inevitable.

" My opinion is to draw our whole strength together, take post at and Fortify Germantown, considering it as our Winter Quarters.—When the Works there are in a tolerable state of defence, I should propose taking our whole force (except one brigade to guard the redoubts) and proceed near the enemies Lines, offering them Battle, which if they declin'd would in the opinion of every rational man fully evince our superiority in point of strength—if they should come out, fight and defeat us, we have a secure retreat and Winter Quarters.

" I have thus offer'd my sentiments to your Excellency with freedom, but if a contrary disposition should take place and an attack be resolv'd upon, I shall endeavor to execute the part that may be assign'd me to the utmost of my ability. I am &c.   H. KNOX,
                                        "B. Gen¹ Artillery."

WASHINGTON TO MAJOR-GENERAL GREENE.

" HEAD QUARTERS, 25 November, 1777
8 o'clock P.M.

" Dᴿ SIR :

" Colᵒ Mead delivered me yours this morning, as I was upon my way to reconnoitre the Enemy's Lines from the West side of the Schuylkill. I had a full view of their left and found their works much stronger than I had reason to expect from the Accounts I had received. The Enemy have evacuated Carpenters Island and seem to be about doing the same by Province Island. Accounts from the city say Lord Cornwallis was expected back today or tomorrow, which corresponds with the information sent you by Gen. Weedon. All their movements make me suspicious that they mean to collect their whole force while our's is divided, and make an Attack on the Army on this side. I therefore desire (except

you have a plan or prospect of doing something to advantage)
that you will rejoin me with your whole force as quick as
possible. I have ordered all the Boats down to Burlington
to give you despatch and when you have crossed, all those
not necessary for the common use at the Ferries, should be
immediately sent up to Coriels again. Yours of yesterday
that appears to have been written before that sent by Col°
Meade has reached me since I got Home. The Hospital at
Burlington deserves your consideration. If you leave it
uncovered and Lord Cornwallis should detach a party, the
patients will certainly be made prisoners. I therefore beg
you will endeavour to have them removed, or think of some
way of giving them protection by posting some Militia or
leaving some Other Troops while the Enemy remain in that
Quarter. The Hospital at Princeton also will be left naked
if the Enemy should move farther up, You will therefore
leave them some cover, if you think there will be occasion.
I am &c.[1]   G° Washington.

"P.S.—As leaving a Guard at Princeton will still divide
our force, if the patients could be removed further from
thence, I think it would be for the better. I told Dr Ship-
pen when he fixed it there, it would be dangerous."[2]

MAJOR-GENERAL GREENE TO WASHINGTON.

"Mount Holly, Novr 25th 4 oClock

"Dr Sir

"This moment received intelligence the enemy are embarking from Glocester and crossing over to Philadelphia.
Col. Comstock sends this intelligence and says it may be
depended upon.—I have order'd General Varnum's & General Huntington's brigade to advance immediately to fall
upon the enemies rear and prevent their geting off their
stock. I wait your Excellencies orders to march where you
may think advisable. Colo. Sheppard[3] got into camp about
noon—the whole body of the troops will be ready to move

[1] In manuscript of Robert Hanson Harrison.
[2] In manuscript of Lieutenant-Colonel Tench Tilghman.
[3] Colonel William Shepard, in command of Glover's brigade

at a moments warning—The Riffle Corps & about 600 militia are upon the enemies flanks.

" A detachment from Capt Lee's Horse took nine prisoners yesterday, the first account I ever had of their being in this quarter. I am &c. N. GREENE."

MAJOR-GENERAL GREENE TO WASHINGTON.

"MOUNT HOLLY Nov. 25th 12 o'Clock

" D^R SIR :

" I wrote your Excellency this afternoon that the enemy were crossing from the Jerseys to Philadelphia and that the intelligence came from Col. Comstock—he is stationd at Haddonfield to collect intelligence.—I have received two letters from the Col. today the first dated at 12 o'Clock the last at three both of which I have enclosd.—It appears to me the enemy are crossing their Cattle, but I much doubt whether any part of the troops have crost the river—perhaps they may begin in the morning—I am divided in my mind how to act—If your Excellency intends an attack on Philadelphia our moving down to Haddonfield will prevent our co-opperating with you—but if the enemy are crossing, the attack upon the city would not be warrantable now if before, without our whole collective force at least, and as part is below and part here, I wish to move forward for the support of the troops below and attack the enemy if practicable.

" I expected before this to have received your Excellencies further Orders but as I have not and from the intelligence there appears a prospect of attempting something here I have ventured to put the troops in motion—if I should receive orders to the contrary I can speedily return.

" If the enemy cross to the city they may be attackt at any time hereafter as well as now—if they have not crost and are in a situation to be attackt we shall have an opportunity to attempt something. I am anxious to do every thing in my power and more especially as the People seems to be dissatisfied at the evacuation of red bank fort. I am &c. N. GREENE."

COLONEL COMSTOCK TO MAJOR-GENERAL GREENE.

" Sir :   " HADDONFIELD, 25 Nov. ½ past 12, 1777

" This moment I arrived from a reconnoitering tour near
Little Timber Creek Bridge, sent a smart young woman
who had a sister in Gloster as a spy to Gloster; she has
returned and I believe has rec[d] no other damage than
receiving a kiss from the Hessian General (this is as she
says).   She reports that a very large number of British &
Hessian troops are in Gloster, that they are embarking in
boats & going to Philadelphia, and that her sister there in·
formed her they had been embarking ever since early in the
morning.   That Lord Cornwallis quartered at Col. Ellis'
house & the Hessian General in a house opposite—who
asked the young woman where the Rebels were?   She
answered, she could not tell—she had seen none of them!
She said she passed many sentrys before she came to little
Timber Creek Bridge where she passed the last.

" I doubt not this information.   I fear they will be too
quick for us.   Col. Hart's Reg[t] is here.   With great esteem,
                                           " ADAM COMSTOCK."

COLONEL COMSTOCK TO MAJOR-GENERAL GREENE.

                               " HADENFIELD, 25th November, 1777
" Sir   3 oClock P.M.

" Seven prisoners just arrived here from the Enemy taken
by the Militia, about 3 mile from this place on the Road to
Glos'ter.—the prisoners I have examined.   Two of them
are Gunners and 2 Matros, belonging to the first Reg[t] of
Artilary, the other 3 belong to the 33[d] Reg[t]—they were
about ½ a mile from their Picket plundering, those belonging to the Artilary had 3 of the Artilary Horses with them
marked G. R. which are also taken.   This Express rides
one of em.   The Prisoners on Examination say the Main
Body Lye about 4 Mile from this on the Gloster Road
encamp'd that their Line form a Tryangle, that they are to
wait there till they have embark'd all the Stock for Philadelphia, which will take em all Day, & that the Army expects to embark tomorrow and go into winter Quarters, that

they have 2 6 pounders in front, 2 ditto in the Rear & some smaller in the Center, that they were not in the least apprehensive of any of the American Army being within 10 miles of them, otherwise they should not have been taken in the manner they were. This moment 7 Hessian Prisoners arrived here taken in the same manner. I have not examined them. I could wish your Army was here now, for I think they may be supprised very easy. They give various Acc^{ts} of their Numbers, from 5 to 8 thousand. They mostly agree that Billings Fort & Fort Mercer are leveled.—O how I want to give em a Floging before they Leave the Gersey. With every sentiment of Esteem & Respect &c

" ADAM COMSTOCK."

MAJOR-GENERAL GREENE TO WASHINGTON.

" HADDONFIELD, Novr 26th 4 o'clock P.M. 1777

" D^R SIR

" Your Excellency's letter of the 25th reached me at this place—I halted the troops on the receipt of it, those that had not got into the town—Genl Varnum's & Huntington's Brigades got to this place before the letter came to hand. I am sorry our march will prove a fruitless one—the enemy have drawn themselves down upon the Peninsula of Gloucester—the Ships are drawn up to cover the troops—there is but one road that leads down to the point, on each side the ground is swampy, & full of thick underbrush, that it makes the approaches impracticable almost—these difficulties might have been surmounted, but we could reap no advantage from it—the Shipping being so posted as to cover the troops, and this country is so intersected with creeks, that approaches are rendered extremely difficult, and retreats very dangerous.—I should not have halted the troops, but all the Genl Officers were against making an attack, the enemy being so securely situated—and so effectually covered by their Shipping.

" We have a fine body of troops & in fine spirits, & every one appears to wish to come to action :—I proposed to the Gentlemen drawing up in front of the enemy, & to attack their Picquet and endeavour to draw them out, but they were all against it, from the improbability of the enemies coming out. The Marquis with about 400 Militia & the rifle Corps, attack'd the enemies Picquet last evening, kill'd about 20 & wounded many more, & took about 20 prisoners—the Marquis is charmed with the spirited behaviour of the Militia & Rifle corps—they drove the enemy above half a mile & kept the ground until dark—the enemy's picquet consisted of about 300 & were reinforced during the skirmish—The Marquis is determined to be in the way of danger.

"From the best observations I am able to make & from the best intelligence I can obtain it is uncertain whether any of the enemy have crossed the river, the boats are constantly going but I believe they are transporting stock—there is as many men in the returning boats, as there goes over—by tomorrow it will be reduced to a certainty.—I believe the enemy have removed the great Chiveaux de frize—there went up 60 sail of Vessels this morning. If the obstructions are removed in the river it accounts for the enemies evacuating Carpenters & Province Islands as they are no longer necessary—the prisoners say the enemy are going into Winter quarters as soon as they get up the river.

"Inclosed was our order for battle, with a plate agreeing to the order.

"I purpose to leave General Varnum's brigade & the rifle corps at this place for a few days, especially the rifle men who cover the country very much.—Gen¹ Varnum's brigade will return to Mount Holly tomorrow or the next day.—I will make further enquiry respecting the hospitals, & give such directions as appear necessary.

"My division, Huntington's & Glover's Brigades will proceed with all despatch to join your Excellency—I could wish the enemy might leave the Jersies before us.[1]

"I am &c.

"NATH. GREENE."

[1] The body of the letter is in the manuscript of J. Burnet, V. aide-de-camp. Greene's other aides at this time were William Blodget and James Lloyd.

MAJOR-GENERAL GREENE TO WASHINGTON.

"MOUNT HOLLY, Nov. 27, 1777

" D^R SIR

" Your favor of yesterday [1] I received last night about 12 oClock. The greater part of the troops returned to this place last night and marched early this morning to cross the Delaware—I staid at Haddenfield myself with General McDougal's division to give the necessary Orders to the Militia—I have left the rifle Corps at Haddenfield and Capt Lee's troop of light Horse to encourage the Militia and awe the enemy; to prevent their coming out in small parties— Col. Olney had orders to make an attack upon their Piquet this morning but they drew them in so close to their main body, and there being but one road he could not effect it— their Piquet consisted of about 300 men—I am much afraid the withdrawing the troops will greatly alarm the Country— Any position below this with any considerable force would be very dangerous—the country is so exceedingly inter- sected with creeks; and lies so contiguous to Philadelphia— I think any body of troops may be surprised from the city at Haddenfield in five hours, and at almost any place in its neighbourhood.

" The Hospitals will be in some danger at Burlington, Burdenton & Princetown if all the troops are withdrawn from this state, but if the sick were ordered to be imme- diately removed, it would still increase the alarm in the country, for which reason I would risque what are there at present and order the Director General not to send any more there.

" I shall set out immediately for Burlington—I have given Lt. Col. Abale orders to procure waggons and send off all the spare ammunition to Huntingdon, the heavy cannon to Bordenton—At my arrival at Burlington I will enquire of the Commodore respecting the matters by you directed.

" General McDougal's division will quarter here to night and march at five in the morning for Burlington—I think

[1] Printed in my " Writings of Washington," Vol. VI. p. 220.

there are as many troops gone forward as will be able to get over to day.

" I shall push on troops as fast as possible without injuring their health. I sent forward one of my aids to Burlington early this morning to superintend the embarkation of the troops & baggage—I am with sincere regard & due respect &c.   N. GREENE."

CAPTAIN CRAIG TO WASHINGTON.

" SIR

"I have this moment been Honoured with your Excellency's Letter—and embrace this opportunity of returning an Answer. By every Account, Lord Cornwallis is returned, it is a Certainty that a number of Troops are Arived at the City—both Horse and foot. I wrote y^r Excellency this Morning the Enemy ware under march^g orders, it is expected the[y] will March tonight. Your Excellency may Depend on the earliest information of their Movements— by some Accounts the enemy intend to send their Boats one way, and the greater part of their Army another, it is thought the boats are intended for Delaware. I have the Honour &c.   C. CRAIG.

" FRANKFORT, 28th Novr 1777. "

MAJOR-GENERAL GREENE TO WASHINGTON.

" BURLINGTON, Nov. 28th 9 oClock, 1777.

" D^B SIR

" Three Brigades are now on their march for Head Quarters, my division & Glover's Brigade—General McDougall's division is not yet come to town—they had orders to march at four this morning and I was in hopes they would have been in town, by the time Glovers brigade got over the River—I am afraid the want of provision has detained them this morning. It is with the utmost difficulty we can get bread to eat—the Commissary of purchases of flour is very ill managed—there is no magazines of consequence, and the army servd from hand to mouth—The Baggage cannot be got over by tomorrow night.

" Mr. Tench Francis an uncle of Col. Tilghman was brought to me a prisoner this morning—he was taken at

Glocester—he sais Lord Cornwallis' detachment consisted of about 6,000, that none embarked until yesterday—he also adds that the reinforcement consisted of about 2500 from New York. General Howe designs to make an immediate attack upon the Army unless the weather is bad—this is the general conversation of the Officers of all ranks—Mr. Francis sais he thinks the enemy design to burn and destroy wherever they go—Germantown is devoted to destruction—The enemy plundered every body within their reach, and almost of every thing they had. It is the common conversation among the officers of all ranks that they design to divide our lands as soon as the Country is conquered—The obstinate resistance they say made at Mud Island has broke the campaign. I am &c.   N. GREENE."[1]

THE NAVY BOARD TO WASHINGTON.

"CONTINENTAL NAVY BOARD
"BORDEN TOWN, 28 Nov 1777

"SIR

" We are under a Necessity of drawing your Excellency's Attention once more to the Frigates at this Place.—Notwithstanding our Endeavours, we have not been able to raise the Effingham—she still lyes on her Beam Ends in a very disagreeable situation. After the Destruction of our Fleet at Red Bank, the Officers & Crews of the several Vessels came up to this Place, to the Amount of between three & four Hundred. We are much at a Loss for Accommodations for these Men; but if we had our Frigates afloat, this Difficulty would be obviated. As we have now so many Hands at Command, we are of Opinion, we can with Certainty get these Ships ready for their Reception; & at the same Time have the Plugs so fixed that they might be drawn at a minutes Warning & the vessels sunk, should the Enemy make an attempt upon them. Nevertheless, however safe or convenient this Plan may appear to us, we do not think proper to put it in Execution without your Approbation.

[1] For a letter from Washington to Greene, written at seven o'clock on the evening of this day, see my " Writings of Washington," Vol. VI. p. 228.

As the winter is now approaching fast & must soon put an End to all our Water Schemes, we request your Excellency's Answer by the Return of the Bearer (Capt Pomeroy). Whatever your Advice may be in this Matter, you may depend on our strict Compliance with it.

" Several Captains of the Vessels lately destroyed have saved some of their Sails, Stores &c. We wish to know whether you are of Opinion they may be kept here with Safety or not.

" A Report is circulated & again contradicted respecting a French War. We should thank your Excellency for Information, whether it is so or not. We have &c.

" Fra^s Hopkinson
" John Wharton

" P.S.—We are sorry to trouble you with Letters to Congress; but hope it will be attended with no great Inconvenience; apprehending that you have frequent Occasions to send to York Town & that our Packets may go with your Despatches."

WASHINGTON TO FRANCIS HOPKINSON AND JOHN WHARTON.

" Head Quarters, 29 November, 1777

" Gent^n

" I am fav^d with yours of the 20th. I see no Reason for changing my former opinion in respect to sinking the Frigates to ensure their safety. If they are weighed again, and converted into Barracks for the Seamen, they must be brought near the shore and when the Frosts sets in, they cannot be sunk should the Enemy approach at such time. I however, leave the Matter to your judgment.

" The Hulks of the Vessels will be all that are necessary for Barracks, if you should determine to put them to that use. The sails, Rigging and all other Stores of them and the Vessels that have been burned should be removed to some distance from the Water Side. I am &c.[1]

" G° Washington."

[1] In manuscript of Lieutenant-Colonel Tench Tilghman.

COUNCIL OF WAR.[1]

[The following papers were overlooked and therefore are not in the place they would have occupied had a strictly chronological order been followed.]

" At a Council of War held at Head Quarters at Whitpain 29th October 1777.

" Present

" His Excellency The Commander in Chief

" Major Generals—Sullivan   Brigadier Generals—Maxwel

" Greene	Smallwood
" Stephen	Knox
" Marquis Fayette	Varnum
" McDougall	Wayne
	" Mughlenberg
	" Weedon
	" Huntington
	" Conway
	" Pulaski

" His Excellency informed the Board, That the enemys whole force according to the best estimate he could form, founded on general returns of their Army which had accidently fallen into his hands bearing every mark of authenticity, and from probable calculations of such changes as may have happened since the date of them, amounted to abt. 10,000 rank and file, present fit for duty. That their main body by the last accounts were in and near Philadelphia. That they had established several batteries on Province Island, opposite to Fort Mifflin, from which, they continually annoyèd the garrison there; but hitherto without any material effect,—That they had on the 22d instant attempted to carry Red Bank by storm, but were repulsed with considerable loss. That the day following several of

---

[1] The call for this council is printed in my " Writings of Washington," Vol. VI. p. 143, and did not contain the question of an exchange of prisoners, suggested by the letter of Lieutenant-Colonel Persifor Frazer. An opinion by Brigadier-General Wayne is in Stillé's " Wayne," p. 109.

their ships of war drew up against Fort Mifflin; which, in conjunction with their batteries before mentioned began a severe attack upon the fort; but were compelled to quit the enterprise and retire with loss—That however, notwithstanding the obstacles they encounter in the River obstructions, they have found means to open a communication with their ships by way of Tinicum Island.

" He further informed them, That our whole force at this time amounted by the last returns to 8313 Continental troops and 2717 Militia rank and file present fit for duty. That besides these, were the garrisons at Fort Island and Red bank, the former consisting of about 300 Continental troops, the latter 350; in addition to which a detachment of three hundred Militia marched the 26th to reinforce the two posts—also the troops on the other side the Schulkill in number about 500—Militia, under Brigadier General Potter.

" That this force was likely soon to suffer a diminution of 1986 Militia, by the expiration of the term of service for which those from Virginia and Maryland engaged.

" That on the other hand, He had called upon the State of Pennsylvania in the strongest terms, to afford all the assistance and reinforcement in its power to this army; and that he had also written to Generals Dickinson, Foreman, and Newcomb, pressing them in the most earnest manner, to endeavour to collect all the militia of the State of New Jersey, that can possibly be spared from other objects, in the neighbourhood of Red bank, as an additional aid and security to that post; but was uncertain what degree of success these different applications might have.

" He finally informed them that by advices from the Northward, it appeared that General Burgoyne and his whole Army had capitulated to General Gates, on condition of being permitted to return to Great Britain, and not bearing arms again in North America during the present contest.

" That by a letter of the 25th instant from General Dickinson, there was reason to believe Sir Harry Clinton and the forces with him had returned down the North River; and that the troops heretofore stationed at Rhode Island were arrived at New York—That he was not able to afford any precise information of the dispositions made by General Gates and Putnam, in consequence of the forementioned events; but had heard that General Gates had detached two brigades to join Governor Clinton at Esopus.

"Observing, that under these circumstances, he had called a Council to consult and resolve upon the measures, best to be persued; He accordingly requested the sentiment of the Gentlemen present on the following subjects—

Questions.	*Answers.*
"1ˢᵗ Whether it will be prudent in our present circumstances and with our present strength to attempt by a general attack to dislodge the enemy from Philadelphia?	It will not.
"2ᵈ If prudent — and in case we are unsuccessful— Where shall we retreat to?	Precluded by the above answer.
"3ᵈ If not thought eligible —What general disposition of the army had best take place, till the season forces us from the field?	The army should take post on the ground a little to our left, which has been reconnoitred and reported by the Engineers; and sufficient reinforcements should be sent to the garrisons of Redbank and Fort Mifflin, to complete the number of men requisite for their defence.
"4. Supposing the enemy to keep possession of the City—Where, and in what manner, shall the Continental troops be cantonned, when they can no longer keep the field?	Deferred.

" 5. What measures can be adopted to cover the Country near the enemy and prevent their drawing supplies from it during the Winter?

Deferred.

" 6. Can any—and what succours may with propriety be drawn from the Northern armies at this time?

Succours should be drawn from the Northern armies to Consist of twenty Regiments—fifteen of Massachusetts—three of New Hampshire and Lee's and Jackson's regiments.

" The deliberations on the foregoing subjects finished,— The Commander in Chief proceeded to the following questions—

" As the whole time of the Adjutant General seems to be engrossed with other duties—Will the office of Inspector General to our army for the purpose principally of establishing and seeing practiced one uniform system of manuel and manœuvres, be adviseable?

Such an office is adviseable. The Manuel Manœuvres or any regulations to be established, previously to be settled or agreed to by the Commander in chief, or a board of officers, appointed by him for that purpose.

" Should Regimental promotions extend only to the rank of a Captaincy or to that of a Majority?

Promotions should be regimental as high as Captains inclusively. All from that rank in the line of the State.

" Will it be consistent with propriety or policy to allow soldiers the reward offered to others for apprehending deserters?

The reward should be allowed to soldiers.

"The Commissaries complain of the number and disproportion of the rations issued to the troops, and at the same time of the exorbitant price of all kinds of spirits, owing to the impositions of the suttlers on the soldiery—What regulations or remedies can be applied to rectify these abuses?	Deferred.
"Col. Frazer, in a letter of the 9th instant having represented that he had 'liberty to mention it as General Howes earnest desire, that a general exchange of prisoners should take place on equitable terms, or that the officers, prisoners of War on both sides should be released and have liberty to go to any place in possession of their friends on their paroles' — What measures might it be proper for us to take in consequence of that information?	Deferred.

"Jno. Sullivan
"Nathl Greene
"Adam Stephen
"Le M$\underline{q}$uis de Lafayette
"Alex^{r} McDougall
"W. Smallwood
"H. Knox
"J. Varnum."

An^{ty} Wayne
P. Muhlenberg
G. Weedon, B. G.
Jed Huntington, B. Genl
T. Conway, B. G.

[NOTE.—With the failure of any plan for attacking the British in Philadelphia the question of future operations became of importance. The popular view was still in favor of some active measure which should give the enemy an idea of the fighting ability of the Continental army, and this view found support in Congress, where it was urged as much on political as on military grounds. No one denied the expediency, even the necessity, of a partial victory to inspire the States with a little energy, infuse a little vitality into the sinking currency, and wipe out the depressing atmosphere of a retreating and somewhat disorganized army. But this was only one side of the question. It appeared to Washington that a present and temporary advantage might be obtained at too great a cost. A defeat or failure might complete the ruin of the army, give strength to the jealousies and rising plots among the officers, and, by dispersing the army, scatter throughout the continent the seeds of complaint, of fancied wrongs, and suffering under inaction and defective commissary and hospital service, which would obstruct the enrolling of a new army. However brilliant a successful dash might be, it was too late in the season to retrieve the fortunes of war, and the husbanding of the existing force, seasoned and disciplined as it was, seemed of greater moment than devising an attack on the issue of which all might depend. To consider the question of winter-quarters a council of war was called, and the following are the opinions.

WORTHINGTON C. FORD.]

OPINION OF MAJOR-GENERAL SULLIVAN.

"CAMP AT WHITEMARSH, Decem^r 1, 1777

" DEAR GENERAL

" Agreeable to your Excellenceys Commands I have Considered upon the most suitable place to Canton the Army During the winter. The several places proposed in Councill have their Advantages and Disadvantages but that which has the Least objections ought to be fixed upon. The Intentions of the Board is to take that Station which will answer best to cover the Country, Refresh the Troops & Discipline the Army & by adding to the Numbers by Recruits & otherways prepare it to take the field with vigour Early in the Spring—in order to Determine what place will be most Likely to answer this purpose it will be proper to consider the several places proposed with the objections that may justly be made to each: The first is The Great Valley on the other side of Schulkill. There it is proposed to Hutt the Army for the winter. The second is to canton the Troops in Wilmington & its Neighbourhood. The Third is to canton them from Lancaster to Reading.—

" The first place proposed will cover the Country west of Schulkill, provided Large Detachments are kept near the Schulkill & on the Delaware to prevent the Enemy from making Inroads and Collecting Forage &c. in the Neighbourhood of Darby, Chester & Wilmington but in case the Enemy should take post with a large party at Wilmington, you must send a Force superior to theirs to attack them, or move a large part if not the whole of your Army near that place to prevent them from Foraging & Drawing provisions, in which Case your Huts must be forsaken & of Course become useless. One great objection to Hutts is that they are exceeding unhealthy and are at Best but a miserable Shelter from the Inclemency of the weather.— The mortality among the Hessians at Brunswick Last Spring as well as common observation will justify this assertion. Should you be able to cover the west side of the Schulkill by adopting this plan it must be by making a Winters Campaign ; but it is to be Rememberd at the same time that you Leave Exposed the State of New Jersey and all that part of Pensylvania which Lies on the East of Schulkill, and put it in the power of the Enemy to render your Communications with the Eastern States across the Delaware very Difficult, if not impracticable. The second post proposed namely Wilmington & its Environs will not only Leave New Jersey & the Eastern part of Pensylvania, with most of your Hospitals & Stores Exposed but even the Western part of Pensylvania will be in great Measure Exposed unless you keep a Force near the Schulkill to prevent the Incursions of the Enemy. This will also occasion a Winter's Campaign, without answering any other purpose but that of covering part of Maryland & the Delaware States & your Situation will put it in the power of the Enemy compleatly to cut off your Communications with all the States east of Schulkill. In addition to those Difficulties There is another of great weight in my mind, which is that Though it is not Easy to Surprize the post, it is by no means Impracticable. This will necessarily Increase our out Guards & Pickets, & make the Duty of the Soldiers something severe—& to add to it Mr How by a move of his army up the Schulkill towards y^r Stores may compel you to move your Army as often as he chuses to repeat the manoeuvre. If, therefore either of the before mentioned posts are taken a Winter's Campaign must be the Consequence. This in my opinion ought if possible to be avoided. The most warlike nations in the World both in Ancient and Modern times have endeavoured to avoid them, even when they had a sufficiency of Cloathing for their Troops, & were in Climates much more temperate than ours, Experience convinced them that the gain was by no means equal to the Loss and though in most Instances whole Provinces have been given up, this Consideration has not been thought of sufficient weight to keep Armies in the Field through the winter Season.

" The Situation of your Army will be scarcely Tolerable if placed in the warmest Houses During the winter the whole of them without Watch Coats one half without Blankets & more than a Third without Shoes Stockings or Breeches & many of Them without Jackets. Indeed there are some without Coats & not a few without Shirts Even the Officers in sundry Instances are Destitute of proper Cloathing, some of them being almost naked. These Considerations should Induce us to avoid a winter's Campaign if it may be Done without the Greatest Inconveniencys.—The Third place will leave exposed the East & West Side of Schulkill near the Enemy & at the same time expose New Jersey. It will, however cover the Back parts of the Country give opportunity of Recruiting & Disciplining your Army & at the same Time furnish Houses that will supply the want of Comfortable Cloathing to your Troops, & give you & your officers a proper opportunity of turning your Thought to proper Measures for Regulating your Army & enabling it to take the field with vigor in the Spring. To secure the Country as much as possible one Brigade should be placed in New Jersey for the militia to collect to in Case of Invasion & scouting parties of the militia should be constantly near the enemy to intercept the small parties from making inroads into that State—at Potsgrove or Reading in Pennsylvania should also be another Brigade or Division for the same purpose & the militia of this State should be constantly scouting near the Enemies' Lines to keep them from foraging with impunity. This Disposition will cover your Hospitals & Stores & keep open your Communications with all the States—Though you may in taking the above Situation be under a necessity of Removing some Inhabitants who have fled from Philadelphia farther Back into the Country, yet this is a much Less Evil than Exposing the Army to be Ruined by the Inclemency of the Seasons & the want of Cloathing, but this may in some Measure be Remedied, as the Distance between you & the Enemy will permit you to canton your Troops in Towns considerably back of the Line which marks your Front. I know that there are also Objections against this Disposition which have great weight, among which is that of Leaving so much Country open to the enemy, but in every view of the Subject I think this the Least Liable to objection. I cannot help giving it as my opinion if we are to make a winter's Campaign, & our Force is Deemed sufficient to dispute the field with the enemy after the seven Virginia Regiments Leave us : that Germantown will be the most proper place for the purpose—as that & Beggars Town will afford cover for most of the Troops. The several Roads leading to it may soon be fortified against a surprize & Corps selected to defend the Houses which will supply in great measure our want of numbers. The proximity of our Situation to the Enemy will keep them within Bounds & by keeping a strong party of Pensylvania Militia on the west of Schulkill and 1 of the Jersey Militia on the East of Delaware, their Incurtions into the Country will be totally prevented. if a winters Campaign is to be carried on this will be the most advantageous and comfortable Quarters for the purpose—but if a winters Campaign is to be avoided, the other is to be preferred for the Reasons afore assigned. I know that both officers & soldiers Dread a winter's Campaign, the prospect of which Induces our officers to Resign in such Numbers & prevents privates from Engaging in the Service. With Respect to the post our Army takes previous to Retiring to Winter Quarters, I think it immaterial at present, for if Mr Howe Declines a general Action no situation we can take either on this or the other side the Schulkill will compell him to fight us as he has the Delaware open to furnish him with supplies, and if he is Determined to bring on an Engagement he will seek out the Army let their Station be where it will. Dr General, the above is submitted with all Due Defference & Respect by your Excellencey's most obed^t serv^t

"J^no SULLIVAN."

OPINION OF THE MARQUIS DE LAFAYETTE.

" Your excellency ordered me to give my· opinion about the three plans for winter quarters: 1° the chain from about the Sculckill till bethehem— 2° this from reading to lancaster—3° building hutts about and quartering in willmington.

" I must confess my being prevented of fixing my sentiments in a decisive manner by my want of knowledge about very interesting points among them are 1° how far we should distort and perhaps disaffect those persons who schould be turned out from the diferant places they are in.

" 2° how far we may expect to collect and keep with the army all the officers who perhaps will think themselves intitled to go home, to occupate themselves with theyr businesses or pleasures if we are not in a kind of warlike quarters, and then we will took the [   ] advantage of theyr being instructed and disciplined we schould endeavour to gaite [get?] in going into peaceful places.

" 3° What effect can it make upon the people our leaving the country entirely oppened to the execution, cruelties, and also to the seduction of the enemy, when we shall give them all the opportunities they can wish to draw all the provisions from everywhere and in the same time to inlist provincial soldiers.

" 4° if our giving a greater idea of the army in covering the country and laying near the ennemy will more facilitate our making recruits than if we were in good comfortable towns and not in a place and in a manner which shall seem to the eyes of the people a kind of winter campaigne.

" 5° till what point those different measures will please or distress the officers and (what is generally to the militur world the less attended to, and deserves the greater attention) our private soldiers.

" 6° till what point we may depend upon our intelligences and light troops to avoid equally and being surprised and tiring the troops by false alarms.

" 7° if we can hope that the soldiers will now receive cloathes &c. in order to be fit for some winter marches and operations, if in case where they schould be defeated we may hope to meet them again.

" Such are the points of knowledge which I am deprived of by my being stranger in this country, and my being stranger in the army, if I can speak to, for I have no officers no soldiers under my particular direction whom I could consult and know theyr temper theyr inclinations, and all what it is possible to expect from them.

" however I'l tell your excellency my very imperfect sentiments about the matter.

" 1ˢᵗ the first proposition seems to me the less eligible, and my reason for it is the scarcity of villages and principally the report of the commissaires and other gentlemen who know the country.

" 2° the second seems to me the most prudent : there we schall be quiete, there we can discipline and instruct our troops, we can be able to begin a early campaign, and we schall not fear to be carried into a winter campaign if it pleases General howe. therefore in consulting only prudence, and as far as my little knowledge can go, I am at lest certain that I'l have nothing to reproach to me in giving my choice to this second proposition.

" however (and in making excuses to your excellency for such an indecision and referring myself to your knowledge about the suppositions I will make) if it was not diswilling neither for officers neither for soldiers, if going to lancaster will disafect and make a bad impression as far as to prevent our recruiting, if we can keep better our officers when we schall be in a kind of encampment near the ennemy, if principally you think that we schould be fit for some winter march's we should be able to support some disadvantages then I am fully and with a great chearfulness of opinion that we must go to willmington my reasons would be these.

" 1° this position enable us to do in the course of the winter what we schall think proper to annoy, to deprive of ressources of every kind to attack if possible the ennemy.

" 2° this position has something shining and military like which will make the best effect and upon the continent and even in Europe.

" 3° the doctors, and americain ones who know the manners and phisik constitution of our soldiers say that nothing is so comfortable as well made hutts.

" prudence orders me to choose lancaster, but if the inconveniences I fear (without being able to know them) if those inconveniences I explain to your excellency are not as strong as they can be, if principally our civil situation ask from us something shining and perhaps bold then I give all my wishes and all my choice to willmington.

" THE MQUIS DE LAFAYETTE
" M. G."

OPINION OF BARON DE KALB.

" Rest, Recruiting & Cloathing being most necessary to the army I am of opinion that taking winter quarters at Wilmington almost behind the Ennemy, will not answer the purpose, because every movements the Ennemies will make up Schuylkill river we must follow their motions or be cut off from our Stores, or forced to fight whether it will suit us or not. I am apprehensive this position will of necessyty bring on a Winter Campaign.

" It appears to me, unless His Excellency has very strong reasons, to maintain Delawar State & part of Chester

County, that more tranquility & safety could be expected between Lancaster & Reading by building partly hutts for that purpose, if it is equally (as was observed by several Gentlemen) unavoidable to have hutts near & about Wilmington.

"BARON DE KALB.

"AT CAMP 1ˢᵗ Xᵇᵉʳ 1777."

OPINION OF MAJOR-GENERAL GREENE.

" Agreeable to your Excellency's command I shall in a few words give my Sentiments with respect to the necessity of puting the troops into winter quarters and the properest place to canton them in.—Every one that views the Condition of the army and is acquainted with the severe duty they have gone through will readily agree that good warm comfortable quarters are necessary to supply the defect of cloathing, and that some relaxation is essential to give a proper tone to both men and Officers to prepare them for the ensuing campaign—In doing this we must have regard not only to the army, but the country.

" An army without a country is like an infant incapable of feeding or cloathing itself—Every part of the country whether Whigs or Tory that we suffer to be ravaged is a diminution of our strength, and an increase of theirs.—Men are essential in war, but provisions, cloathing and accoutrements are equally so.—The first and great object in cantoning the troops is to take a position secure from surprize; the next is covering; the third is a situation convenient for drawing forage and provisions for the subsistence of the army and the cattle belonging to it.—These are the great principles to be attended to in quartering the troops and cannot be dispensed with without certain and inevitable ruin to the whole military machine.—There are other secondary considerations such as covering the country and distressing the enemy in drawing their supplies; where a position can be found to answer all these valuable purposes is the object of enquiry.

" It is said by many that a total relaxation is necessary for the good of the army—for enabling the officers to recruit their Reg[ts] and to give the men time to recover their spirits. —I must confess if I was to speak from my own feelings and declare my wishes instead of my sentiments, I should be of that opinion—Pleasure is ever agreeable to human nature, but never more so than after long and severe duty an opportunity to unbend the mind must be the wish of every one, and it is not very difficult to accommodate our reason[s] to our wishes; but whether a total or a partial relaxation will be for the general interest of the army is worth enquiring into.

" If we retire so far back as to be totally out of danger, pleasure and dissipation will be the consequence. Officers of all ranks will be desirous of visiting their friends—the men will be left without order, without government—and ten to one but the men will be more unhealthy in the spring than they now are, and much worse disciplined.—The health and discipline of troops can only be preserved by constant attention and exercise—we must not flatter ourselves that going into quarters will recover the health or discipline of the troops without regard is paid to one and attention to the other.

" It is said we must carry on war upon the great Scale, and that particular interest must not be brought in competition with the general interest and that by attending to the minutiæ, we shall sacrifice the principle object. I readily agree that it is perfectly consistent with the maxims of sound policy for the lesser to give place to the greater—but is it necessary for us to throw open a great extent of country to give a necessary relaxation to the Army ? It is the country that feeds, cloaths, and furnishes us with troops. If the subsistance of the Inhabitants is destroyed they will be incapable of giving us the necessary aid—if the army in the winter season leaves the country unprotected—will it not be a discouraging circumstance to sending recruits to join us— which will be a diminution of their local security, if they can expect no protection from the collective force.—I am no advocate for taking measures from popular opinions, but it is necessary to preserve the confidence of the country;

for by the union and spirit of the people alone can the opposition be continued.—

"The Legislator is in some measure under the necessity of accommodating his measures to the prejudices of the people—mankind will only be subservient to your purposes in proportion as they conceive their interest and happiness connected with your measures—I have heard it remarked that the sufferings of the army spread in all directions throughout the continent, alarms the people and prevents them from entering into the service.

"The same may be said with regard to the poor plundered inhabitants.—It is true the eyes of all the continent are upon us for protection—but it is natural for man to reason, what is my neighbours condition may bye and bye be mine.—

"If the army seems disposed to exert its force to shelter the country from ravage; it is natural to expect the people will be anxious to strengthen its hands; but if the enemy are left at liberty to ravage at large, and the inhabitants of our State make the condition of another their own, it will be an alarming consideration. Therefore I think some regard should be had in taking our measures to afford as much cover to the country as possible without militating with the principal design—not for the sake of the particular spot that is covered, but to prevent the disagreeable influence it will have upon the surrounding Inhabitants.

"I cannot conceive a total relaxation to be necessary to recruit the army, or recover its spirits. I am fully persuaded that recruiting by voluntary inlistments is in a great measure at an end. The enormous bounties that are given so far exceed the american funds, and the continental bounty now allowed falls so far short of private bounties, that few if any recruits are to be expected through that channel—If this be granted then the recruiting service will wholly depend upon the exertion of the civil authority of the respective States, and this exertion doubtless will be in proportion to the reputation and confidence the legislative bodies place in the army—For it cannot be expected from the local prejudices of mankind that the several legislative bodies will be willing to strip themselves of their inhabitants, & lessen their own internal safety unless they are well persuaded the measure is essential to their own happiness and security.

" It is absolutely necessary the army should have an opportunity to relax and recover its spirits—but there is a great difference between constant duty and total relaxation —A proper medium between these two extremes will be found better adapted to restore the spirits of the army and preserve its discipline—We must be in a situation to take off that constant watching and yet not so remote from danger but that some attention to duty is necessary.

" Men are naturally apt to sink into negligence without there is something constantly to rouse their attention—The objects of pleasure are so much more inviting than those of Duty that without a restraint is laid on one and a necessity imprest to attend to the other it is ten to one that the objects of Pleasure steal the mind wholly from the discharge of its duty.—I do not mean to urge these reasons for taking a position near the enemy to oblige us to be constantly on the watch but to shew that a total relaxation may be dangerous—Remember Hannibal's army at Capua.—

" The general discontent among the officers of almost all ranks renders winter quarters essential to redress the prevailing grievances and new organize the army for the spring —but the fatigues and hardships of the campaign and the want of rest and relaxation are not the great sources of the discontent that prevails. It springs from a different fountain. It is the pay and subsistance which are found to be incompetent to the necessary demands of the officers to preserve their dignity and support their families.— This is the great evil and this must be remedied or else this army must and will dissolve.—There are some other things complained of—Such as, Rank, that military Jewel, being confered on almost all orders of men to the disgrace of rank, and great mortification of officers who find themselves often reduced to a level with persons they despise, from the prostitution of military dignity.—

" The manner of cloathing the troops is a subject of complaint.—There is no provision made proportionable to the demand of the army; and the difficulty of obtaining that which is provided has given great disgust to some and discontent to others.—These are some of the principal subjects of complaint—and a partial relaxation from military duty is necessary to put every thing in a proper train for opening the next campaign.

" It is necessary that an appearance should be kept up as much as possible of besieging the enemy, not only to cover the country, but to preserve the credit of our currency which will always rise and fall as our army appears superiour or inferior to the enemy. The enemy will also draw out of the country many recruits without they are kept within bounds. —All these are objects worthy our attention.

" There have been two plans proposed for cantoning the troops. One from Bethlehem to Lancaster, the other at Wilmington and it's environs.—There can be great objections raised to both.—It is said (with how much truth I know not) that all the back towns are crouded with inhabitants, refugees from Philadelphia; if that be true, to turn them out to make room for the Soldiery will bring great distress upon the inhabitants & be productive of no small discontent.—I have no doubt in my own mind but that there can be quarters procured in the proposed Line of cantonment from Bethlehem to Lancaster, but there appears to me to be many evils attending it.—It is a great distance back in the country and leaves the Enemy a great range in front and upon each flank. It must distress the back inhabitants. We shall be consuming the substance in the bowels of the country which should be always held as a reserve against a misfortune.—In withdrawing ourselves to so great a distance it will be improved abroad into a kind of dispersion into the mountains and among ourselves it will wear the complexion of a retreat, and many will be suing for Protection.

" I must confess however that, if safety and relaxation are the only objects under consideration, the geography of the country from Bethlehem to Lancaster is more favorable for a Cantonment than Wilmington—but I cannot help thinking that quarters can be got at Wilmington with much less distress to the Inhabitants of the State—that the position will be secure enough with the force cantoned in and about it—That provision & forage can be got easier and cheaper in that position than in the other—in this Position we can draw it from the enemy while the other will leave it for them—that this gives us a better opportunity to protect the lower Jersey and not less the upper—that this will distress the enemy in drawing supplies—and upon the whole cover a greater extent of country than any other.—For these Reasons I am for the Position of Wilmington, and if any part of our stores are insecure I would immediately have them removed.—I would have about a brigade of continental Troops in the Jerseys and about one thousand militia between the Delaware & Schuylkill, and about a thousand more at or near the Gulph—and an advance post at Chester —of continental troops.

" NATH. GREENE

" *M. G.*"

OPINION OF LORD STIRLING.

" CAMP WHITE MARCH, Decem 1, 1777.

" SIR :

"In agitating the General Question which your Excellency put to the Council of General Officers yesterday, there arose three propositions as to the Stationing of this Army for the winter, all attended with very great Inconveniences. That of placing it at Wilmington does not answer the purpose of Quartering the Army, as the buildings in and about that place are not Capable of receiving above one third part of the Army ; besides I think it is one of the most dangerous Scituations that I know of, for if the Enemy were to make a sudden movement and take post near Kennet Square or New Garden, our Army would have no Retreat, we should be reduced to the Necessity of fighting them, with the Delaware and two other Impassable Waters on our flanks and Rear. It is true it would cover the three lower Country's and part of Maryland from the Incursions of the Enemy by land, yet they would have what Communication they pleased with it by water, this advantage would therefore be trifling, & for it we should give up all pensilvania & New Jersey, for the Enemy to Ravage at large; and put it in their power Effectually to Cut of our Communication with all the Country to the Eastward of Delaware River: these are reasons I think sufficient to Induce us to drop all thoughts of Quartering the Army at Wilmington. As to the plan of putting the Army into Huts in the Township of Tryduffrin in the great Valley, I must acknowledge it is a Scituation well Calculated for Covering Chester & Lancaster Counties, and for Checking any Attempts the Enemy may design against Maryland & the Lower Counties on the one side and a Great part of the Country between the Schuylkill and Delaware on the other, the Communication with Jersey and the Northern States will be preserved, the Encampment will be easily guarded as there is but one Way to approach it from Philadelphia; But it is still only an Encampment. It is not going into Winter Quarters, It is not procuring for the Officers and Men that Comfort and Opportunity of recruiting which they richly deserve after a long and fatigueing Campaign; these perhaps are not in our power to give them anywhere, and should that be the Case, this may be as good a Scituation to hut in as any; provision can be handily brought in from all Quarters, but how it is for forage I know not. The third proposal was to Cantoon the Army in the Towns of Reading and Lancaster and the Villages between them or in their Vicinity. If this is practicable I should like it best of any, as the Men would have a Chance of getting better refreshed than by either of the other two proposals; but it has been objected that it is impracticable, as those towns and Villages are already filled with persons who have fled to them for Refuge, and if it is so we must be Content. If the Safety and Comfort of the Army is principally to be Considered, they can Easily be Cantooned in the Towns in New Jersey which are in a great Measure deserted by the Inhabitants. But I think it is also of high Importance to Cover as much of the Country as we can; and that the possition in the Valley will Cover as much or more of the Country than any other that can be pointed out; the Enemy will never Venture out as far as Chester on that side, as we Can Cut them off by taking post at Darby, to which there is a direct Road; nor would they be fond of penetrating far to the Northward of Philadelphia, least we might pass a body of troops over between them and the Town. Upon the Whole I should be for hutting the Army somewhere in or near Tryduffrin, especially if it is so fine and Rich a Country as has been represented. I am &c.

"STIRLING."

OPINION OF MAJOR-GENERAL ARMSTRONG.

"CAMP AT W. MARCH 1ᵃᵗ Decʳ: 1777.

"MAY IT PLEASE Yᴿ EXCELʸ:

"I beg leave to recommend that as early as it may be safe, to make such movement, the Army may pass over the Scuilkill & take for some time a position on that side.

"With respect to Winter Quarters for the Army—the longer I consider the measure pointed out in the back Villages of this State, the more inadmissable that step appears to be, as by the large lattitude thereby given the enemy thro' the winter & early part of the spring, every doleful & pernitious consequence must be expected—The hearts of good-men thro' all the States depressed, and this State in particular, little less than sacrificed to the whole without real necessity! Amongst the innumerable evils resulting from that situation, the imposition of the Oaths of Allegiance & an end to Government & the future aids of the Militia thro' great part of the State, must inevitably follow.

"I'm therefore of Opinion that in proper time, part of your Army take possession of Wilmington, and the Residue form a Chain from thence to Dowingstown & perhaps to White Horse on the Lancaster road, at these two some Cover may be had, & Hutts with some use of Houses in the intermediate space—these are the best outlines that appears to me, which may be corrected and better determined when the Army is on that Side. And am with perfect respect y^r Excellency's Most Obed^t humb^l Servt

" JOHN ARMSTRONG.

" P.S.—I hear that some part of the Bridge is already broken or carried off. G^l Potter is not yet come over, I suppose owing to the bad weather. I expect him today.

" J : A."

OPINION OF BRIGADIER-GENERAL MAXWELL.

" SIR :

" Agreeable to your Excellencys request of last evening, that we should give our opinion concerning the most eligible place for Quartering or incamping the Troops during the winter. As much has been said on the Subject of Quartering in different places some with a view of covering the Country, & others for recovering, recruiting, and gathering the Troops together, for another Campaign, and to ly at such a distance from the Enemy that they were not liable to be harrassed by them during the winter. If covering the Country is your Excellency's chiefest object I would recommend that our armey should be moved to the west side of Schoolkil, at the distance of about 30 miles from Phil^a with our left tolerable near that River, leaving a party of observation on the East side; and there Hutt in the most convenient place. But if the other part viz the refreshing and recruiting our Armey be your Excellency's chief object in that case I would recommend that our Armey should retire back in the Country on a line from Reading to Lancaster and in the Neighbourhood of that line, and try to collect all our scattered Troops of every sort near the main body, and take every Method in our power to get the Reg^{ts} filled up during the winter, and those well cloathed we have. If the last proposition takes place I would recommend that a party of observation be stationed one on the West S., the other on the East side of Schoolkill to prevent the Enemys partys from penetrating far into the Country.

" Likewise a party should be sent into New Jersey to

relieve the Militia there who has been a long time on duty & to give them an opertunity to fill up their Quotas in the Continental line. Those Troops might return in the Spring as soon as the roads was fit for traveling on, should it be thought necessary. This last Scheme I prefer to the first—and am your Excellencys Most Obedient Humble Servant

"Wᴹ Maxwell.

"White Marsh the 1ˢᵗ Decemʳ 1777."

OPINION OF BRIGADIER-GENERAL SMALLWOOD.

"Camp, Decemʳ 1ˢᵗ 1777

" Sir

"The Distresses of the Army, the Inclemency of the weather, & the approaching Season, combine to point out the Expediency of fixing on Winter Quarters; and in doing this all local Attachment ought to be sacrificed to the Public Good, to reduce the Enemy, & free ourselves, I wou'd chearfully resign myself to a Den the ensuing & many other Seasons if found necessary.—Three Positions have been pointed out—from Bethlehem to Lancaster—the Valley *in Hutts*—& Wilmington—three Capital Objects are in view— The Health & Security, the Discipline of the Army—& the support and covering the Country—the first Position would be incompetent to any other than the first of these Objects. The second wou'd not amply admit of, or be adequate to any other than the second Object, for it woud impair the men's Health, & leave not only the Jerseys, but also the Delaware Government & Eastern Shore of Maryland open, which the Enemy woud avail themselves of, & get fully suppli'd this Season.—The Third tho it does not fully coincide with our Views, yet in a more inlarged & general Degree, it answers the Object of our wishes, more than the preceeding or any other Position I know of under our present circumstances—I woud recommend sending the sick to the first mentioned Position, but I am strongly impressed that the hail & active part of the army ought to take post at Wilmington, to awe, & perhaps annoy the enemy, or at least

prevent and deter them from taking possession of, or drawing their supplies from such an extensive Tract of Country
as either of the other Positions than Wilmington wou'd
lay open to them—Wilmington & its vicinage will cover
more Troops, & is more compact, may annoy the Enemy,
will obstruct them, & cover more of the Country than any
other Position I am acquainted with under our present
Situation, & will admit of Exercise & manœuvring (from
the compact station) upon as large a Scale & as often as
may be necessary, & with respect to insecurity against surprize think no Post within a Night's March of the Delaware below Philad[a] cou'd be rendered more secure—a Post
that's perfectly secure is eligible, but I am induced to think
it wou'd have a bad Tendency on our Army. Officers of
all Ranks & Denominations wou'd be going Home, their Im-
portunities wou'd be irresistible, the Soldiers wou'd follow
their Example, & if Furloughs were not granted, Desertion
wou'd ensue, & in most Instances a Neglect of, & inattention
to Discipline.

"Being Officer of the Day Time admits not of my enlarging more on this Subject; or adding further than that I
have the Honor to be with great Respect, your Excellencys
most Obed[t] H[ble] Serv[t]

"W. SMALLWOOD."

OPINION OF BRIGADIER-GENERAL KNOX.

"PARK OF ARTILLERY, Dec[r] 1, 1777
" SIR,

" Your Excellency last evening referr'd to your General
Officers the consideration of the position proper for Winter
Quarters, and order'd us to give our opinions respectively
on that subject.

" I shall be concise in my opinion, establishing the proposition that Winter Quarters are indispensably necessary
for the Army in order to give it that rest and refreshment
of which it stands much in need—to repair the Carriages
of various kinds which are damag'd; to recruit the exhausted horses; to recruit and fill up the reg[ts]; to reform
the army in some essential particulars, in a word to put the

army in all its branches on such a footing as to be able to take the field next Campaign with the greatest probability of Success.

" The King of Prussia says ' the first object in Winter Quarters is Tranquility'—it is very evident if we take our Winter Quarters so near the enemy, as to be subject to frequent alarms and constant hard duty, we shall have but a small part of the present army to oppose to our enemies. Could a place be found about 30 miles distant from & North or N. W. of Philadelphia in which it was possible to quarter the troops, I should prefer it to a greater distance or different direction as by it we should be able to cover a greater extent of Country than by taking post at Wilmington or retiring so far back as Lancaster & Reading.

" Two Ideas present themselves in considering a place proper for Winter-quarters. The ease and safety of the troops and the covering the Country, thereby preventing the enemies deriving supplies from it. I consider the first the greater objects and all inferior ones should give place to them, and therefore give my opinion that the troops should at the time appointed retire into Winter Quarters, the right of the Cantonment to be at Lancaster & the left at Reading, provided a sufficiency of houses and good cover can be procur'd there—an officer of reputation on whose veracity your Excellency could rely can easily ascertain this matter.— parties of 500 or 600 to be kept out on command advanc'd 30 or 40 miles, under the command of active partizan Officers who should be directed to be constantly moving about to prevent the enemy making any disposition to surprize them.

" Advantages may by these means be taken of any smaller detachments sent out by the enemy—indeed the militia of the State may be kept considerably advanc'd, they being light troops, will cover the Country & be but in little danger of being surpriz'd.

" If the Cover in the range from Lancaster to Reading should be found to be insufficient, I should be for hutting the whole army about 30 miles distant from Philadelphia,

in some position which should have the Schuylkill about 10
or 12 miles on the right or left—the goodness of the position
to determine this. General Muhlenberg mention'd a position which comes within this description which perhaps
on examination might be found to be proper.

" I have the honor to be with the greatest respect
" Your Excellencys most obedient Humble Ser[t]
" HENRY KNOX,
" *B. G. Artillery.*"

OPINION OF BRIGADIER-GENERAL POOR.

" SIR,
" Monday, 1st December, 1777

" in answer to the questions propos'd yesterday, Rispect-
ing the Quartering Army this winter I am clear of apoinyen
that the grait Object is to secure our men from the Inclemency of the wather Incres our numbers Dissapline our men
and make our Army as Formadable as possable that we
may be able to take the field early in the Spring.

" I am not acquainted with this Country so as to point
out the most sutiable place—by Information do think that
the line from Lankester to Reading is the most Elagable of
the three places mention'd. I am Sir your most obedient
Humble Serv[t]

"ENOCH POOR, B. Gen[l]."

OPINION OF BRIGADIER-GENERAL WAYNE.

" SIR :
" CAMP AT WHITE MARSH, 1st Dec[r] 1777

" The procuring good and easy Winter Quarters for the
Troops under your Excellencies Command—and Covering
the Country from the Depredations of the Enemy as far as
Possible without too much fatigue to the Army—are Objects
of the first Consequence, & to which too much Attention
cannot be paid.

" A Chain of Cantonments has been proposed (and supported with very plausible Arguments) from Lancaster to
Reading and the Intermediate villages between them,—to
which Cantonments I can't agree for the following Reasons.

" Because by taking Quarters at the Distance of sixty miles west of Philadelphia, you at once give up to the enemy all the Delaware State, the Eastern shore of Maryland, the Counties of Phil[a], Bucks and Chester.

" Because by this access of fine Country the Enemy will be enabled to draw supplies, not only for the Winter—but to lay up Stores for the next Campaign—to vittual their Transports—carry Gen[l] Burgoyne's army to Great Brittain —and perhaps bring out an Equal Number to Re-enforce Gen[l] Howe early in the Spring.

" Because the sick and feeble of the Army in the Respective Hospitals will in a great Measure be left between the Enemy and us—Otherwise Intermixed with the healthy Troops—and subject them to the same Disorders that the Sick may be Infected with.

" Because you cannot in these Villages procure cover for more than one-third of your Effective's without casting to the Mercy of Weather and Howling Wilderness—those families who flew before the Enemy to these very places for Shelter—giving up ease & Affluence, for Liberty and Protection.

" Because other States are Subject to Invasion—who will naturally conclude if these are given up to Distruction— that it may be their case next, and will thereby be deterred from giving that aid, which they otherwise would afford— least they should first Irritate, & afterwards be left to the Mercy of a more than savage foe.

" Because the Eyes of the World are upon us—and we have given the Country some Ground to expect, some Protection—since the Junction of so great a part of the Northern Army.

" For these Reasons I am positively against taking Quarters at the places before Mentioned—but would propose making good our Quarters in a Posilion that will at once afford cover to the Country and enable you to draw supplies for your Army—from the Vicinity of the Enemy —in doing of which you will not only Distress them—but save for the use of the next Campaign those Stores which you would be necessitated to expend if Quartered at the Distance of Sixty Miles from the Delaware River.

" You will also leave such Houses as can be procured in that Country to be Converted into Hospitals for the use of the Sick and Convalescents—to which the feeble of the Army may be collected & Commissioned Officers sent (in Proportion to the Number of the Sick) to superintend them—who will not only preserve Order but Introduce Discipline amongst the Convalescents, by obliging them to appear clean on the parade and Manœuvre them whenever the weather will permit, which will be more conducive to their health and be a means of saving men's lives than the whole powers of the *Materia Medica*—they will also afford protection to our Stores by Detering any small party from attempting their Destruction.

" For these Reasons, and to sweeten the tempers of those Officers that at present may be a little sowered as well as for the ease & Conveniency of others, I am Induced to meet those Gentlemen in Sentiment, who are for Quartering the Army at Willmington & in its Vicinity—which with the aid of some Hutts will afford Cover sufficient.

" The Position is such as to give the Enemy the Greatest Annoyance—with the least fatigue to your own Troops.

" Your Excellencies own good Judgment will point out the proper Measures necessary to guard against that Surprize which some Gentlemen *Effect* so much to dread—I can only assure your Excellency that whatever Position you may think most proper, I shall always be ready to acquiesce with, & to serve you with the best Service of your most Ob^t and very Hum^l Ser^t

" ANT^Y WAYNE."

OPINION OF BRIGADIER-GENERAL VARNUM.

" WHITEMARSH, 1st Decr 1777

" MAY IT PLEASE YOUR EXCELLENCY !

" From a cursory view of the present state of your Army compared to the Position of the Enemy I am fully convinced that your Troops should immediately go into quiet, peaceable Winter Quarters. By the various Fatigues of the Campaign, your Men are dispersed thro' many parts of the Country, incapable of taking the Field at this advanced Season. The Hospitals are crouded with Sick and Invalids, occasioned, in a great Measure, by the want of clothing & Rest—Your Officers are very discontented, as their Families are suffering at Home, not being able to purchase the Necessaries of Life. The Credit of the Mony is so amazingly decreased, by the prevailing Avarice of the Times, that the recruiting Service rests upon a very precarious Basis. Your great Dependence must therefore be upon the present Army. To make it respectible, it is necessary to collect the feeble together; to nurse and cloath them, and give to the whole such a Spirit of Discipline and Order, as will make them truly formidable. The Enemy is in good Quarters, not to be attack'd, without the greatest Hazard. He will not attack you, unless he imagines he has a manifest Advantage. In this Situation, you have much to loose, nothing certain to gain.—As therefore another Campaign is morally inevitable, your Troops should be put in the best Situation, to open it early, with vigor & Activity. To fix upon the Line of Cantonment, is a matter of Perplexity. If you attempt covering the Country from the Excursions of the Enemy, you make a Winter's Campaign necessary. But that Position w°h will give them the greatest Check, consistant with the Ease of the Troops, is the most eligible. That part of Pennsylvania w°h lays between the Delaware and the Schylkill seems best calculated for this Purpose. While it preserves a Communication with the Southern and Northern States, it gives some kind of Security to New Jersey. A removal to Wilmington and Places adjacent, would give the Enemy the full command of the Delaware, and perhaps, Effect a Separation of the States. It cannot be supposed that the large Villages in the back parts of Pennsylvania are so crouded with Inhabitants as to give no Shelter to the Army. Should the Buildings be too scanty to receive all the Troops, the Deficiency might be made up

by substituting Hutts, wch would prove a sufficient cover
for the more healthy and robust.

" I am, with great Submission, your
"Excellency's most obed^t Servt
"J. M. VARNUM."

OPINION OF BRIGADIER-GENERAL WOODFORD.

"CAMP, 1st Decem^r 1777

"DEAR GEN^L

"Upon considering the several places purposed for the
winter cantoonments of the army, I think the Villages
from Reading to Lancaster, with the addition of some
Hutts, the most Eligable position for the Troops in their
present situation.

"Were the men warmly clad, I should give it as my
Opinion that Willmington, or some post nigher the Enemy
should be taken in preference to the above, where we might
annoy them in their Forrageing &c. in the course of the
Winter.

"But upon considering our present circumstances &
looking forward to the opperations in the spring, I think
the advantages we should give them of possessing a part
of this state & the Lower Countys, would be overballanced
by our having a vigorous army ready to take the Field
early in the next campaign, with sufficient Magazines of
provision & Forrage laid up in the course of this Winter.

"If the Range of Cantoonments I purpose should meet
the approbation of your Excellency, after hearing the sentiments of the Genl Officers, I would purpose that as much
Forrage & provisions as possible, of every kind, be immediately drawn from the Country between our Quarters &
the Enemy & that such as we had it not in our power to
remove be destroy'd, saveing a bare sufficiency for the
subsistance of the Inhabitants, & that the Country in our
Rear be kept as a Reserve.

"Previous to the removal of the Army, I would recom-
mend that one or more, Genl Officer go with the D. Q^r Master

Gen¹ to view the cover that can be procured for the Troops, & make their Report to your Excellency as speedily as possible.

" If these Villages are found too much crouded with the Refugees from Philadelphia & its neighbourhood, I should think it no great hardship for them to be obliged to remove to the Farm Houses contiguous, & that the D. Q' Master Gen¹ (after having ascertain'd their numbers), be order'd to assign them Quarters at a distance that it would be unsafe to squander the Troops in, & that the publick waggons remove their affects. I am with great respect your Excellencys most Obed' humble Serv'

" Wᴹ Woodford."

OPINION OF BRIGADIER-GENERAL WEEDON.

" Dear Sir :

" I have agreeable to your Excellency's direction, considered in every point of view I am able ' a proper position for this Army during the winter'—Three plans for facilitating this desirable purpose have been proposed, viz' Hutting, Drawing them down to Wilmington & its vicinity, or cantoning them in the back country from Reading to Lancaster.—In my opinion there will be great inconveniences attending any measure we may take—The first plan is certainly the most desirable, but I fear the least eligible; & both for reasons so obvious that they hardly need mentioning. Does not the present situation of affairs promise another Campaign? Tis true that by wintering your Troops within ten or fifteen miles of the enemy you might in some measure cover the country contiguous thereto, but would not this subject your Army to a winter campaign? Add to this the unhealthy quarters they would be confined to, rendered still the more so by the very nature of the materials which compose them. Our service has already driven us to this necessity on a former occasion, which proved more fatal to the troops than all the actions they fought during the campaign!—Let us benefit by experience.— Your army, Sir, is now much reduced by hard service & other sufferings during this Summer & Fall; I fear & believe, I may say with truth, (& consequently on this occasion with propriety) that a third of them tho' now in the field, are more fitting for the Hospital than the Camp: without Blanketts, without Shoes, & in short almost destitute of every comfort required by the strong & robust, much more the weak & feeble. What then must be the effects of keeping them out all winter in this dispiriting situation? Can you promise yourself service from them in the spring? When the Enemy find your troops exhausted by fatigue, they will no doubt avail themselves of it. What must then necessarily follow is disagreeable & needless to anticipate—Troops undisciplined, worn-out by service, deprived of every comfort which is necessary to restore health & vigor, cannot be supposed to support an attack against those who thro' the Winter have been in comfortable quarters, constantly trained in Manœuvring & other exercises. That this will be the case, I make not the least doubt.

" A position at Wilmington, I should have no very great objection to, if the troops could be covered in a tolerable compact body, but this I fear cannot be done; & Cantoning by Detachment is a dangerous experiment.—I look Sir, on this Army as the Herculean hinge, on which American Independence turns.—The covering this, or the other spot for the space of three or four months is not a motive sufficient to hazard, or expose this Army for, the object is in nowise adequate to the disadvantages that may result from it: you would in my opinion subject yourself to frequent alarms by taking post at Wilmington, Christiana, Newport & Chester, particularly at the latter. The Enemy are masters of the River, have a numerous Fleet at their command, and within one nights march of you—I should not indeed dread a surprize, but supposing the enemy not inclined to attack you by a sudden march, (which at the same time they would have in their power) but to manœuvre up the Schuylkill & cross above you, should we not be in the predicament we have all this campaign been endeavouring to shun, by keeping their left-flank must we not instantly leave our quarters, perhaps at a season of the year when our magazines could not be got off.—The sick must fall into their hands also, unless we fight them & are success-ful—Should any disaster attend us, by an action with them in this situation, what would be the consequences? a total Annihilation of this Army, & with it, the Liberties of America!—Upon the whole sir, distressing as it is to leave a country uncovered, & at the mercy of an ungenerous Enemy, who no doubt will ravage & plunder the inhabit-ants; yet Sir, we must view our affairs in a more extensive Scale. Subjugating a few individuals who must be left at their mercy, or possessing a small tract of country for a few months goes but a small way in the American cause, while you have this Army in full health.—That we must have another Campaign is, I believe, beyond controversy, prudence therefore dictates a timely provision for the same, the success of it will depend on the health & discipline of your Troops, the care & vigilance of your Officers, and early operations in the Field.—To provide for such im-portant purposes, I give it as my opinion this army be quartered as soon as circumstances will permit, in a country where not only your Officers may have it in their power to make themselves comfortable during the winter, but your troops be relieved from heavy guards, covered from the in-clemency of the weather, *nursed in sickness,* disciplined & restored to their former health & vigor—This Sir, & this alone, will give you the Superiority over your Enemy.— Your Hospitals are now as strong nearly as your Battal-ions: & while you are followed by an army of feeble in-valids, what reward can you expect for your unwearied exertions, by any atchievements such Troops can obtain? The Chain of Cantonments from Reading to Lancaster has been mentioned, I cannot with precision say they are the most eligible, but from the small knowledge I have of the country, should suppose them the most likely to cover the troops, & afford them rest thro' the winter.

"I am Sir y^r very H'bl Servt

"G. WEEDON."

OPINION OF BRIGADIER-GENERAL MUHLENBERG.

" December 1ˢᵗ 1777

" SIR :

" Agreeable to your Excellency's requisition I transmit you my Sentiments on the Question proposed in Council yesterday.

" I would beg leave to premise that agreeable to my Sentiments, the Army should continue in a Position, where they can most effectually Annoy the Enemy, untill it shall be absolutely necessary on Account of the Severity of the Weather to Quit the Field—2ᵈˡʸ That the Preservation of the Army by getting them into good Winter Quarters, will be of much greater Utility, than any small Advantages, which can be gain'd over the Enemy by keeping the Army near their Lines.

" With regard to the place, Propper for the Army to take Winter Quarters, I must confess, I am more inclined to join in sentiment with those Gentlemen who propose Lancaster for the Right of the Cantonment & Reading for the left, than with those who propose Wilmington—my reasons are these. Wilmington &c. are so near the Enemy that there is the greatest probability of their frequent Alarming us, consequently the end intended, that is, the Ease of the Army will not be answered.

" 2ᵈˡʸ Our Army will certainly diminish, at least for the Winter, by a Number of the Soldiers receiving permission to return to the different States they came from which would perhaps enable the Enemy to gain material Advantages over us, especially if it should be found necessary, on account of Covering, to Quarter the Men some distance apart.

" 3ᵈˡʸ The upper Part of Pensylvania would be left entirely to the Mercy of the Enemy, & the Communication with the Eastern States cut of.

" 4ᵗʰˡʸ The Enemy will have it in their power to draw more Supplies from the Jersey, than it would be possible for them to draw from the lower Counties, even if they were entirely given up to them, for if the Army lay at Wilmington, one armed Vessell would be sufficient to prevent us from affording any relief to the Jerseys.

"Perhaps if your Excellency was to order some Person to Reconnoitre the Country from Reading to Easton it would be found more Eligible, to make Reading the right of the Cantonment, & Easton the left, than any other place proposed, especially if the Hint thrown out by a Gentleman in Council, was adopted, that is, to erect Hutts for the more Robust, & let the Feeble be quartered in Houses, &c.—In Reading the Refugees from Philadelphia are less numerous than in Lancaster, Lebanon, &c. Reading, Allentown Bethlehem & Easton lie in a direct line, very near the same distance from Philadelphia—a few miles in front of this Line, is Maxetawny & Macungy, one, if not two Divisions may be Quartered with the greatest ease, & here the Troops would be ready, either to protect our Stores, or prevent any considerable Ravages in the Country. Your Excellencys

"Most obed^t & humble Servt

"P : MUHLENBERG."

OPINION OF BRIGADIER-GENERAL SCOTT.

"WHITE MARSH, 1st Decr 1777

"SIR :

"After Considering maturely the matter Proposed Yesterday with reguard to the Quartering the Troops for this Winter, I have at Length thought that Wilmington and its Neighbouring Villages the most Elligable.

"I would not wish to Trouble your Excellency with my Reasons as it was so very Fully spoke upon Yesterday. I am Your Excellencys

"Ob^t Servt

"CH^s SCOTT."

OPINION OF COUNT PULASKI.

"I leave the choice of Ground to those who are well acquainted with the Country, & confine myself to considering the advantages which will attend a continuance of the Campaign, and the Inconveniences which will flow from retiring to Winter Quarters—Our continuing in a state of activity will give courage to our Friends, be an antidote to the effeminacy of young Soldiers, and enure them to the fatigues which Veterans undergo—keep them in the exercise of their profession and instruct them—Whereas the inactivity of winter quarters will ruin the Army, discourage the Country, leave an extent of Territory for the Enemy to ravage and depopulate; besides how do we know what Reinforcements the Enemy may receive before the next Campaign. For my part therefore I only think that the invalids of each Regiment should be suffer'd to retire where they may under the direction of proper officers be refreshed and recruited—with all the rest collected I would make a vigorous attack upon the Enemy as soon as the Schuylkill is frozen.

" C. PULASKI.

"In case winter quarters are determined upon, I sollicit His Excellency to allow me the body of Cavalry and Infantry to remain near the Enemy's Lines."[1]

OPINION OF BRIGADIER-GENERAL DU PORTAIL.

"By taking Winter Quarters from Lancaster to Reading, we abandon to the Enemy, Jersey, and all the Country adjacent to Derby, Chester, and Wilmington, one of the richest Tracts in this part of the Continent. By establishing them at Wilmington we cover the Country, and do not so completely abandon that part of it which is before Philadelphia, nor even Jersey, because our proximity to the Enemy and the ease with which we could throw ourselves upon the Rear of their Lines in case the Schuylkill should be frozen, will keep them in respect, and put it out of their power to send considerable Detachments on the other side of Delaware from the fear of weakening themselves too much—and the small detachments which they may send will be greatly

---

[1] Translated by Lieutenant-Colonel John Laurens.

restrained by the Jersey Militia—The Position then of Wilmington answers the end of making subsistence very difficult to Gen¹ Howe, who has not only his Army to feed but likewise the Inhabitants of the Town, and who must besides furnish Provisions for the Army of Gen¹ Bourgoyne if he means that they should embark for England.—This position farther deprives him of the means of recruiting in the Country, extending himself in it, adding to the number of his Partisans, in a word gaining the Country. It has besides the advantage of rendering his Communication with his fleet difficult, for I imagine the Vessels will not be able to approach Philadelphia when the Ice prevails—I should not omit mentioning a case in which this Inconvenience would be very considerable—if War should be declared between France and England, and Gen¹ How from a dread of finding himself blocked up in the Spring by a French Fleet, should wish to quit Philadelphia, we shall be within distance at Wilmington for hindering his Embarkation of which we should have timely notice.

" This Position then unites great Military advantages— but it must be confess'd at the same time that these very advantages ought perhaps to prevent our taking it—because the Enemy probably will not suffer us there, and will march against us.—Thus to ask whether the Position of Wilmington is eligible, is to ask at the same time whether it is eligible to expose ourselves to an Action, and perhaps more than one.

" If the season were less advanced, I don't see why we should avoid them—but at present—what end would be answer'd. if we should gain an advantage we should be unable to pursue it—if we Experience a Check, we run the risque of seeing our Army dissipated in the rude marches consequent on a defeat—Consistently with the plan which we ought to form of putting our Army in good condition this winter and preparing it for a good Campaign, we ought not to have it's Repose preceded by a Defeat.

" As to the other points to be consider'd in this Question, whether Wilmington or Lancaster will be the most proper Situation for furnishing the Army with every necessary—I cannot decide, being ignorant of the Country—but it appears to me in general that this point deserves our most serious attention—it is much better to lose Soldiers in Combats with the Enemy to whom we cause a Loss at the same time, than to lose them by Disorders, & Desertion arising from their Misery. Misery destroys a part of an Army and leaves the other without Vigour, without Courage, and without good Will—we should find ourselves then in the Spring with a Body of an Army incapable of any thing, and consequently have no right to expect a successful Campaign.[1]

" Du Portail."

OPINION OF BRIGADIER-GENERAL IRVINE.

" Sir :

" Whether the army should retire into winter quarters in the interior part of this State or to Wilmington and its environs, or whether it ought not to take post nigher to the enemy and remain in huts during the winter, are questions of such importance and the arguments for and against each of those measures so many and cogent that I confess myself at a loss how to decide upon them.—To leave so large a proportion of the most valuable part of the State uncovered as we unavoidably must do should we quarter in either of the places mentioned may have a very unhappy effect upon the minds of the inhabitants, and render it extreamly doubtfull whether much, if any assistance could be drawn from this State the ensuing campaign—few men have a less opinion of the importance of the militia in their present state than myself, but I am apprehensive that should our friends be disgusted as it is highly probable they would be, the executive powers would not be able to make drafts therefrom to fill up the thirteen regiments raised in the state which form no inconsiderable part of the continental army.

" If the observations made yesterday are founded on facts, that so great a part of the army are in a sickly situation, it does not appear clear to me that we should find shelter for more than the invalids, the question then is

---

[1] Translated by Lieutenant-Colonel John Laurens.

whether the remaining part of the army would be more comfortably lodged in huts at the distance of sixty miles from philadelphia, than they could be at twenty or thirty. I am of opinion that they could not, and therefore advise, that the weak and infirm be immediately collected together and quartered between lancaster & reading, that the residue of the army take a strong position on the other side Schuylkill, where wood is plenty, out of surprising distance, and there hut themselves for the winter. I am with the greatest respect, Sir, your most obedient & humb: serv^t

"JAMES IRVINE.
"WHITEMARSH, Decem^r 1, 1777."

CIRCULAR LETTER.[1]
" SIR

" I wish to recall your attention to the important matter recommended to your consideration some time ago—namely —the advisability of a winter's Campaign and, practicability of an attack upon Philadelphia with the aid of a considerable body of militia, to be assembled at an appointed time & place—particular reasons urge me to request your Sentiments on this matter by the morning, and I shall expect to receive them in writing accordingly by that time. I am, Sir, Y^r most Obed^t Ser.

"G^o WASHINGTON.
"Decr 3, 1777."

OPINION OF MAJOR-GENERAL SULLIVAN.

"CAMP, WHITEMARSH, Decem^r 4th 1777
" DEAR GENERAL

" Agreable to your Excellency's Directions I have considered upon the Advisability of making a Winter's Campaign, and the practicability of making an Attack upon Philadelphia with the Aid of a Body of Militia to be called in for that purpose.

[1] For some reason the written opinions just given were inconclusive, and the General again desired an expression of sentiment. It was doubtless owing to some political pressure brought to bear upon him, urging an attack on the British in Philadelphia.

"Though the attacking & carrying Philadelphia is an object much to be wished yet as the Attempt carries with it an Idea of a Winters Campaign I must give my opinion against it—When this motion was first made I was in favor of it, but I was then taught to believe by those who pretended to have view'd the Enemy's Lines that their Redoubts were not Inclosed in Rear but my own observation has since convinced me of the contrary, my own opinion as well as that of a Great majority of the General Officers has been that an Attack upon the Enemies Redoubts in Front & upon the City afterward would be Hazardous & must End in Ruin to the Army; & as we find their Redoubts are Equally strong in Rear, the attempt will be Equally Dangerous—but if not altogether so, it must at Least be attended with great Hazard—and in order to make the Attempt, your naked Army must be kept in the field the greater part if not the whole of the winter. This in my opinion should never be Done but where the object is of great importance and where there is a moral certainty of obtaining the End in view, even when an Army is properly cloathed against the Inclemency of the Seasons: but of your Army one third of them at Least are now confined to their cold Tents & unwholesome Hutts for want of Shoes, Stockings & other Cloathing, a very Large number of them unable Longer to endure the Severity of their Situation have retired (sick) to the Hospitals or to Country Houses. The numbers which Daily fall sick in Camp is surprizing—They have neither Cloaths to keep them warm by Day or Blankets by night. Most of the Officers are in the same Situation. This is what Induces so many of them to Resign. Many Officers who have behaved with Credit have petitioned me for Leave to Retire for a Season, or to resign their Commissions & assigned as a Reason for not waiting on me that they were so naked they were ashamed to be seen, That Cloathing was not to be had & even if it was their wages would not enable them to purchase; I have taken pains to Inquire from the most sensible officers & have conversed with several General Officers upon the

alarming Spirit of Resignation which takes place in the
Army & find they in General say this : ' that they and their
men have been marching and countermarching all the year,
that they have fought no General Action beside Skirmishes,
that the Cloathes & Shoes which they wore out has amounted
to their wages, which leave their Families to suffer at home,
That the Baggage they sent to Bethlehem has been mostly
plundered & they have no possible way of replacing it:
That the price of Articles bears no proportion to their
wages—they further say that their Rank has not been
settled, that they have been told from time to time that this
should be done when they Retired to winter Quarters of
which they see not the Least prospect, & that while they
have contentedly borne all this they Daily see Congress
placing men over their heads without any Regard to their
Ranks or Services.' Dear General, I feel for you when I
tell you that this is not the Language of a few officers of
Inferior Rank, but of high & Low. Such a Disaffection I
never could have conceived had not my inquiries convinced
me. I know it must give you pain as it is not in your
power to Redress these grievances, but Duty oblidges me
to give the information. I am fully convinced and fear the
Event will prove that more than half your officers will
leave you in a month, unless some Remedy is found out to
quiet their minds & relieve their Distresses.—Under these
circumstances a Winters Campaign will in my opinion Dissolve the Army : I know it has been urged that the above
sad state of our affairs should induce us to Risque an Action
as soon as possible and I am myself fully of that opinion—
but can we compell the Enemy to it if they Decline it—if
Mr Howe does not come to attack us when we Lay so near
him it is Evident he does not mean to fight us unless we
attack his Lines—Whoever would advise to this measure
puts the fate of America upon the Toss of a single Die
without Reflecting upon the Dismal Situation our affairs
must be in if unsuccessful in an attempt, where there are
at least twenty chances to one against us—to remedy those
Evils as much as possible, I most sincerely Recommend

that the Army be removed immediately to Winter Quarters; That Congress fall upon some methods of affording a proper support to officers & Soldiers and that the Rank throughout the Army be settled & made known, that in Instances of Rank which give universal Dissatisfaction, the Honor of a few Individuals should be sacrificed to the good of the whole, and every method taken to Recruit the Army collect the scatter'd, Recover the Feeble & Discipline the whole, in order to take the field with vigor early in the Spring which may be by March or April & in the mean while an Apparatus should be collecting to set down before Philadelphia in form so early in the Spring as will enable us by Regular approaches to carry the Town before a Reinforcement can arrive. A Body of Militia may (if tho't necessary) be seasonably notified to join us on the Day your Excellency may fix for opening the Campaign—I know it may be objected to this plan that During the winter we leave a vast Tract of Country exposed to the Enemy, but this may be said in all cases of taking Winter Quarters. Every Army that retires to Winter Quarters must leave some Country exposed & I think it much better to give them all Pensylvania for the winter than to Ruin that Army which must save America, if saved at all. If a winter Campaign is carried on barely for the purpose of preventing the Enemy from Drawing provisions & Forage we shall in my opinion be the greatest sufferers—the Army cannot in a Little time act but in the partizan way. Some of Colo. Steward's Reg^t will soon leave you, nine Virginia Regiments must soon go Home—The Drafts from Connecticut Leave you the first of January—this with what will be taken off by fatigue &c. will render Mr Howe superior to you in the field through the winter, & if our attention is taken up in carrying on a partizan winter Campaign, you will have in the Spring the miserable remains of an Army worn out with Fatigue & totally unfit for any opperations. The King of Prussia speaking of winter Campaigns says that no man having his eyes open will carry on a winters Campaign unless he has Infinite objects in view—this he says of winter

Campaigns generally, but I believe if his opinion was taken upon an Armys carrying one on under our Disadvantages he would adopt a language still more forceable; he says, good winter quarters are to give Tranquillity to the minds of the Soldiers to Recruit your Army, restore Constitutions reduced by Fatigue, mend Carriages, fill up your Regiments, manoeuvre your Troops, refresh your Horse, make your Arrangements & Lay your Plans for the Ensuing Campaign. All This is Essentially necessary for us at present to be about. I am therefore clearly of opinion that no time should be lost in taking the Troops to winter Quarters, & that we should immediately fall upon some method of giving Ease to our Soldiers & Satisfaction to our Officers: unless this is Done & unless all other Considerations give Way to it, I fear the Event of the next Campaign will prove that in striving to do too much we have ruined all. I am confident that if the plan I propose is adopted we shall be able in the Spring to take the field with an Army vastly superior to the Enemy even if our new Recruits should not be numerous, we have a vast number of sick, many have Deserted to their own Homes, there are upwards of a hundred Deserters from the Delaware Regiment only, who are secreted by the Tories. Many other Regiments have almost an equal proportion. these might all be collected in the winter and with the sick which may recover & Recruits which may be added to our Army will be able to take the field with great advantage in the Spring.

" The above is with all due Submission offered by, Dear General, your Excellencys most obed* Serv*

"Jn° SULLIVAN.

" P.S.—The best mode I could Devise for covering the Country I pointed out in my last—Therefore forbear to repeat it in this."

OPINION OF MAJOR-GENERAL GREENE.

" The Subject under Consideration before the board is whether a plan to draw together a large Body of militia in aid of the Continental Troops in the dead of winter to attack General Howe in his winter quarters is eligible or not. However desirable the destruction of General Howe's army may be & however impatient the public may be for this desirable event, I cannot recommend the measure. I have taken the most serious View of the Subject in every point in which I am able to examine it, & cannot help thinking the probability of a disappointment is infinitely greater than of success. We must not be governed in our measures by our wishes—the love of glory natural to man often prompts them to exceed the bounds of human nature in their enterprizes. I am sensible in many instances, that things pronounced impracticable have been crowned with success in the attempt. I know it is justifiable in war to leave something to chance, yet prudence forbids that being made a principle which necessity alone can justify; I am by no means inclined from an excess of caution in a council of war to rob my Country of the happy consequences that may result from a due exertion of the spirit and bravery of the Soldiery—but at the same time let us not flatter ourselves from the heat of our zeal that men can do more than they can. To judge properly upon the subject we must first consider what human nature is capable of when aided by all the powers of art, and what is to be expected when unsupported by those necessary Assistants. In the second place we have to consider how reluctantly people will leave the pleasures of domestic life and engage in a hard and dangerous enterprize at such a rugged season of the year, especially after being out great part of the Summer. In the third and last place let us consider what a combination of circumstances are necessary to give success to the enterprize; weigh this in the Scales of probability and see how far we can promise ourselves a happy issue to the design.

"In the first place supposeing our Soldiery the best of veterans, capable of the boldest attacks, are they cloathed, are they appointed with every thing necessary for such a severe and difficult Attempt? Let any body examine the Condition of the troops, one half without breeches, shoes, or stockings, and some thousands without Blankets, and judge how far men in this situation are capable of enduring the severity of a winter's campaign. The continental troops must be out in the field during all the time the militia are drawing together, and in the natural order of things there must be a great diminution of their Force; the troops must be subject to this evil or else go into winter quarters untill the militia are collected, in which case the officers will be dispersed, which will render it very difficult if not impracticable to draw the troops out of quarters in a condition to undertake the attack. I would not wish to spare either blood or treasure necessary to work the destruction of General Howe's Army; the object is so important that it demands every sacrifice that human nature or national policy can justify, but to make a great sacrifice of men and money without accomplishing the design will be disgraceful to the army and discouraging to the Country.

" The militia perhaps may come together something better cloathed than the continental troops, but the different manner of their living in camp to what they have been accustomed to, together with the extraordinary hardships they must be necessarily subject to in the undertaking, cannot fail of producing a great mortality, or at least some thousands may be expected to fall sick and be rendered incapable of duty. This will not only produce a great diminution of strength, but a numerous sick must be very distressing to those that are well.

" In Europe where they are much older in war than we can pretend to be, and where there are as hardy a race of men as are on the Globe, where the severity of the season little exceeds that of ours and where necessity, ambition and military Glory all conspire to produce winter campaigns, yet they are never undertaken without the soldiers being well cloathed and each furnished with a good watch coat and Blanket. Experience is the best of schools and the safest guide in human affairs—yet I am no advocate for blindly following all the maxims of European policy, but where reason corresponds with what custom has long sanctified, we may safely copy their Example. It must be confessed, and the fatal effects of last winter's campaign will confirm it, that unless men are well cloathed they must fall a sacrifice to the severity of the weather when exposed to the hardships of a winter's campaign.—The successes of last winter were brilliant and attended with the most happy consequences, in changing the complexion of the times, but if the bills of mortality were to be consulted, I fancy it would be found we were no great gainers by those operations.

" There is not only the difficulty of cloathing, but that of covering also. Tents cannot be procured, houses in the country are too scattering to quarter the troops in either for attack or defence. If the troops lye out in the weather they must soon, very soon, be rendered unfit for duty. Such a numerous body of men, hastily drawn together, all unconnected cannot be speedily so arranged as to co-operate in one great and general design. To these difficulties may be added, that of subsisting such a numerous body of troops without having large magazines previously established for that purpose, when such a cold and rigid season, and the variableness of the weather will render transportation by land and water very difficult and uncertain.

" Hospitals proper to receive such a number of sick as we may reasonably expect there will be, will increase the distresses of the army and add to the complaints of the country—especially if the event should be unfortunate.

" The second objection I have to the measure is the difficulty of drawing out such a body of militia from the different States as will be necessary to ensure success to the Enterprise. Those States which are remote from danger, whose militia have been harassed in the Course of the Campaign will be unwilling to call them out without the most pressing necessity, and supposing the Legislators to feel all the military enthusiasm we could wish we cannot flatter ourselves that that spirit will pervade all orders of men which will be necessary to draw out such bodies as will be requisite for the Design.

" Every one that has attended to the difficulties of calling out large bodies of militia, the uncertain success of the most spirited exertions, the impatience they discover to be gone, and the trouble of manageing them when here, may form a good judgment what success we can promise ourselves when we have all those difficulties to encounter in the different stages.

" It is highly probable that a requisition from the Congress to the neighboring states may produce a resolution in each to furnish their quota, but out of the number demanded perhaps not two thirds would actually march and out of the number that did march, ten to one, whether more than three fifths ever arrive at camp.

" The time of the troops being drawn together and forwarded on to camp depends on the coercive power of Government; some being stronger and some weaker, those that arrive first will get out of patience before the arrival of the others—Desertion and Disgust will be the consequence, and if either the one or the other should prevail to any considerable degree, the whole plan would be defeated. I would ask any one if these observations are not founded in truth and human nature, & whether it is not the true history of the militia?

" If it is, what can we promise ourselves from the attempt; when if the whole force was to arrive safe in camp—still there is a great combination of circumstances necessary to compleat the work; the failure of either may render abortive the whole scheme—

" The best way of judging of men and measures at a future period is to recur to their past conduct under similar circumstances—How difficult have we found it to draw the militia of one State to the aid of that of another even where it was necessary to give a check to the enemy from entering the State to which they belong.—

" This measure must go recommended to Congress.— From the Congress after a week or ten days consultation a resolve will take place, recommending it to the different States.—The Assemblies of each one are to be called together, their Deliberations and judgement to be had upon the propriety of the measure, and then an order after ten or twelve Days issues, to assemble the militia,—if the officers are slow and tardy as usual, to collect and march them to camp will be the business of a month.—The continental troops must be out in the field near two months on the most moderate calculation before the Scheme will be ripe for execution—We shall all this time be wasting the very vitals of the army, and risqueing a certain evil for an uncertain good, dependent upon too many contingencies for us to be very sanguine of success.

" The different States will be put to no small difficulty to provide arms for a numerous militia, which must protract the time for collecting it—Consider likewise what delays great and heavy Storms will produce. How distressing they must prove to those that are coming to camp as well as those waiting their arrival there.—

" The third and last objection I have to the measure is the great combination of circumstances necessary to crown it with success, and the improbability of such a multitude of circumstances ever harmonizing together that are independant of each other and originate from such different springs.

" There is in the first place a sufficient force so appointed as to be able to execute the plan of attack, it is highly improbable that such force can be put in motion and still more improbable that they will be properly equipt—Supposing the necessary force to meet properly appointed, they will be a very unwieldy machine, and it must take up a very considerable time to organize the whole in such a manner as to move in concert—Such a numerous militia cannot be drawn together very near the Enemy, where their force is collected, and always ready to take advantage of circumstances, without being very liable to surprize and defeat. Therefore, if they must be drawn together at a considerable distance from the enemy's Lines, and first organized, and then move to the attack the variableness of the weather may interfere— Heavy storms of either rain or snow will put a total Bar to the operations for a time, and more especially the former— but suppose neither of these difficulties interferes, still the operations will be dependant upon the temper of the weather which must be neither too severe or too moderate to enable us to prepare and execute the manœuvre—If the weather is very severe the men cannot live out in the Field long enough to prepare and execute the attack—If the weather is not so severe as to freeze the rivers hard enough for men & artillery to pass over, there can no attack be made only in front of the Enemy's lines—and how far such an attack can be expected to succeed I leave every one to judge—I am told the weather is very variable here and that Storms are frequent—both of which must ruin the platform of our operations; our whole success depending upon the Rivers being sufficiently frozen to enable us to pass over on the ice—

"But suppose all these circumstances should happen to combine to give success to the design, which by the bye is scarcely within the limits of possibility & far out of the bounds of probability can we promise ourselves a victory? Does history afford us an instance as a foundation for such a hope? It is agreed on all hands that there is a very formidable force in Philadelphia and every house is a fortification—can it be expected that young troops unaccustomed to such enterprises will have steadiness enough to push the Enemy from place to place untill they are totally routed from the City?—to make the attack and not totally defeat them will fall far short of the importance of the design or the expectations of the public.

"What aid can be expected from the militia? Will they come up to storm the houses? Let us recur to past experience of the militia & such a militia too as we cannot expect for the present attack and see how far we can hope for success with such troops opposed by such as we have to attack.—I must confess I think it right to trust everything to the spirit & bravery of troops that is warranted by human nature, History or our own observation. Has the present Scheme these Sanctions? Are we not rather drawn into the attempt by the brilliancy of the object than by the probability of its Success founded in either nature or Reason.

" The King of Prussia the greatest General of the age strongly protests against attacking troops by storm in villages, much more in large regular brick cities—He observes, it often proves the ruin of the best part of an army—this was verified in several attacks he made upon towns and villages last war.—Philadelphia is a great object, but I wish our reason may not be seduced from its importance to take measures to repossess it that are not warranted by history or our own observation—An attack of this nature will not depend upon the multitude that attacks, but upon their bravery—for the greater the multitude the worse the confusion when once they are thrown into disorder; and we have no reason to expect anything else from our own or others experience—Men who are brought from home with all their family feelings about them, commanded by officers who in general have little or no ambition for military glory, are not fortified for such scenes of carnage as are generally exhibited in attacks made upon towns defended by a large body of veteran troops.—

" I am not against a winter's campaign if the temper of the officers and the condition of the troops would admit of it, neither have I the least objection to making an attack upon Philadelphia if there was a probability of succeeding founded in human nature or the experience of mankind.—

" Let us consider the consequences that will result from a disappointment in a measure of this nature.—In the first place, it will be attended with a vast expence, and the loss of many lives to no valuable purpose—it will prove a great obstruction to the recruiting service and a defeat will give a general alarm and spread universal discontent throughout the continent—It will expose the weakness of our militia to the enemy and not only to them but to all Europe who now consider them much more formidable than they really are.—

" A winter's campaign in the present discontented state of the officers and an attack upon the city of Philadelphia appear to me like forming a crisis for American liberty which if unsuccessful I fear will prove her grave. If the army goes through a winter's Campaign and the recruiting service is as much injured as I expect from calling out the militia, it will be in a miserable plight to open the campaign with in the Spring; and we may reasonably expect that great britain will rake all the kennels of Europe for troops to repair their affairs in America.

" I have wrote my mind so fully upon the subject of winter quarters, and with respect to a winter campaign that it is unnecessary to add anything further here—I would beg leave to recommend the measure suggested in that paper for recruiting the army—and filling up the continental Battalions—if the measure is adopted the army can be recruited nearly or quite as soon as the militia can be got together—the attack can be made with much more hopes of success & if we are defeated we shall still have a force to carry on a regular siege as soon as the military apparatus can be prepared and the season will permit us to open batteries against the enemy's lines.

" These are my sentiments Sir upon the subject which with all due deference are submitted to your Excellency's consideration, but if your Excellency thinks a winters campaign a necessary measure, or an attack upon Philadelphia, an eligible plan, I will lend every possible aid in my power to carry it into execution; notwithstanding that this is the third year since I have paid the least attention to my own private affairs.   " NATH. GREENE *M. G.*

" CAMP, December 3ᵈ, 1777."

OPINION OF LORD STIRLING.

          " CAMP, Decemʳ 3ᵈ 1777
" SIR :

" Your Excellency's letter of this date requesting my Sentiments on ' the Adviseability of a Winters Campaign,' ' and the practicability of an Attack upon Philadelphia with the Aid of a Considerable Body of Militia to be Assembled at an Appointed Time and Place,' I have duly Considered, and in Answer to the first Question am of Opinion That in order to undertake a Winters Campaign the Troops should be fresh, in good Order and well Cloathed with at least two warm Vests two pair milled Woolen Stockings & mittens, good Shoes, Woollen Overhalls, a Good blanket Coat besides a blanket to Lodge in. Our Troops are not in this Condition, nor are they like to be provided in this Manner, they are already worn out by a long fatigueing Campaign, a Considerable part of them in the Hospitals, above one half of those in Camp are almost naked, and are walking barefooted on the Ice or frozen Ground. In short if a Winters Campaign should be attempted with them, our hopes will be deceived, the Army will be totally ruined; and we shall find ourselves without one in the Spring, the Consequences of which in the Affairs of the American States are too evident to need an enumeration, and therefore must Conclude that a Winter's Campaign [is] extreamly Unadviseable.

" As to the second Question, I have already declared my Opinion (after your Excellency's own view of the Enemy's lines) that it is impracticable on the side Schuylkill with the Troops now under your Command, and were you aided by all the Militia the States on this Continent can furnish by the first of february they would only serve to make the Carnage, or the Route, the greater: the only Chance we have of attacking Philadelphia to advantage, is, over the Schuylkill when it is sufficiently frozen to bear a Column of Troops to pass it; this happens to be the Case in most Winters, sometimes in one Month, sometimes in another, last Winter it was so in the beginning of January, it broke up by the Middle of that Month, and did not get firm again in the remainder of the Winter. this Uncertainty would render the Attempt very precarious. After an Immense expence in Collecting a Great body of Militia we might have no opportunity of passing the Schuylkill; the Men would be disgusted with the Service at that severe Season, without any thing to Cover them, they would return dispirited, the disappointment in the Expedition would bear the Character of a defeat & would have all the bad effects of one, it would increase our sick, hurt the Recruiting Service and prove Ruinous to the Army, but should the Schuylkill prove passable at a proper Season, I should have but little hope of our Carrying philadelphia; to storm the Streets thro' the fire from Redoubts houses & Columns of Men, is too much to expect from any Troops.—to set down before it at that Season, and to drive them out of it by Battering, is to us impracticable, and any Attempt of the kind highly unadviseable.   I am your Excellency's

" Most Obedient Humble Servant

" STIRLING."

OPINION OF THE MARQUIS DE LAFAYETTE.

" The project of calling a large body of militia for such a day, in order to attack the ennemy in philadelphia, seems to me attended with so many difficulties, inconveniences, and bad chances, that if it is not looked upon as a necessary and almost desperate enterprise, tho' it is a very shining and highly pleasing idea, however I cannot think it is a prudent and reasonable one.   The reasons for my rejecting it are as follows—

" 1st I do not believe that any body could advise your excellency to attack only the redoubts in front, whatever could be our force ; such an attack vould be attended with a greater loss but not a greater succés than if we had only continental troops.

" 2° We must therefore expect the moment when the ice upon the Schullckill will oppen to us all the left side of the enemy's line and encampments.   but or the climate makes a great difference between this country and the european ones, or one single fine day may frustrate all our hopes and preparations in putting a way all the ice.   then we schould expect one other moment before dismissing the troops, and in my actual supposition they are to be kept a very schort time.

" 3° in europe ice is brocked every night when it can facilitate the projects of the enemy; if all is not cleared, at least a ditch can be formed in the river. I know that we schould annoy theyr workmen, I know that such an operation would be very hard an[d] troublesome for them. but in the first case I'l answer that everywhere military works are performed with the same inconveniences, in the second the people of philadelphia can be employed there. when I say that we could trouble theyr operation, I suppose that our winter quarters are not in the back country.

" 4° We can't expect any secrecy in our collecting those forces, we can't deceive the ennemy for theyr destination. therefore (untill we could have a respectable body in the jirsay) he can go of before fighting and then we must not entertain the hope of oppressing and destroying all that army, but only of recovering philadelphia.

" 5° Supposing that we could go upon the ice we have only one way of attacking. for if we put the militia in first line, they will fall back upon the continental troops, and we can not depend enough upon our men to believe that we could maintain order and resolution among them. if the militia is in the rear, and the regulars were repulsed, certainly they will not advance where continental troops don't succeed. if amongs us, I don't believe it would do better, therefore our only way should be to make false attacks of militia, and true ones of continental troops, to have a curtain of troops (what we call in French *un rideau*) in the whole lenght of the Schulckill, and on this side of the redoubts, in order to cover the heads of our columns, and our points of attack, and to put the disorder amongs the ennemy by an eavy fire. I wishond [?] too a body should be in the jirsay *in case it would be possible for the ennemy to retreat by the delaware.* and does your excellency think that such a quantity of troops could be raised ?

" 6° When I consider all the difficulties of turning out some militia in interesting occasions, I can't flatter myself that all that people could be sent to your army for such a day, without the utmost difficulties. each state will have an excuse for not sending as many men as they'l be desired. the cold, the rivers, the want of cloathes of every thing will seem sufficient reasons, if not to stay at home, at least to arrive after the time of the rendezvous. every one will trust upon the another, and if we do not succeed all will be against us.

"7° have we in the continent all the cloathes, arms ammunition, &c. &c. which would be necessary for so many soldiers. Would it be possible to find subsistances enough in cattle, forage, &c. All things which I can't know, but however I think worthy of being mentioned, and that principally because the want of exactitude, the necessity of giving to them a light idea of what they are to do will engage us to keep them longer than we think.

"8. I know that all these inconveniences can not be together; because if we keep them some time, then we schall find an opportunity of going over the schulckill in case that we can prevent theyr braking the ice; on the other hand if we have them only for a few days, difficulties of subsistence will be much lesser; and if it is impossible for the ennemy to pass the delaware, certainly a body in jersay is quite useless. I can add that in case we could not go over the ice, it is possible to throw bridges upon the river. but, Sir, I have mentionned all the difficulties which strike me, because my opinion is not to begin such an enterprize unless we shall be certain of succeeding. A great schame for our arms, a great mischief for our cause would attend our being repulsed when we schould attack a part of the british forces with all the united forces of America. europe has a great idea of our being able to raise when we please an immense army of militia, and it is looked upon as our last but certain ressource. if we fall this phantom will fall also, and you know that the American interest has alwais been since the beginning of this war to let the world believe that we are stronger than we can ever expect to be. if we destroy the english army, *our generous effort* will be admired everywhere, if we are rupulsed it will be called *a rash and laughable expedition.* therefore we musst not let a shining appearance and the pleasing charms of a bold fine enterprize, deceive us upon the inconveniences and dangers of a gigantesque and in the same time decisive expedition.

"However perhaps the interest of america, the wish of all the states, the instruction of Congress, the necessity of finishing the war, all these circumstances which are unknown to me, make it necessary for your excellency to hazard something in this occasion. perhaps the difficulties in the physick and moral ressources of this country are not so great as I am affraid to find them. perhaps it is possible to raise, to arm, to cloath, to subsist, to keep together and give some instructions to that so considerable army which according to my opinion is necessary. perhaps the weather is not so changeable in this country as it is in europe, or some other means than going upon the ice could seem eligible to your excellency. but if the difficulties which I fear are indeed true (what you can judge, and I can not know myself) then I am not for that expedition in considering it as only a militar one.

"if however I was deceived, or if politic circumstances schould make it necessary to try such an enterprise, the following precautions seem me to be taken.

"1° I do not ascertain the number of militia to be raised because it must be as large as we can arm, cloath and subsist.

"2° All possible exertions are to be taken for having them at the appointed time which time must be now as soon as it is possible.

"3° Some instructions should take place before the operation, only for some days, because if they were marched to the ennemy without the lest idea of marching together such a disorder would prevent the succés of the less difficult enterprize.

"4° the continental troops should be sent in theyr winter quarters as soon as possible, to take a good rest, to recomfort themselves, to be reinforced by theyr men now scattered everywhere, by some recruits, and the whole to be managed and   by theyr   officers. under that point of vue, and principally cloathes should be delivered to them, and theyr arms put in a good order. it seems to me that this prospect could engage us to be nearer from the ennemy than lancaster is.

" 5° the soldiers and principally the officers of our army schould not be permitted to go home till it would be over.

" 6° proper means for recruiting the army schould be taken as soon as possible. one of the best according to my opinion would be (after having suppressed the substitutes) to annex a part of the militia of each state to theyr continental divisions in order to serve there for twelve months. I think such a regulation is eligible in all cases. for a strong continental army well managed and disciplined, and ready to begin an early campaign, and to make use of all the unforeseen and soudain occasions, would do much greater service than all the militia in the world. and their militia should be made use of only in a less great number or in particular circumstances.

" THE MᵠUIS DE LAFAYETTE

" M. G."

OPINION OF BARON DE KALB.

" SIR

" When your Excellency recommended some time ago the Consideration of the practicability of an attack on the Ennemy, I was already of opinion for such an attack if it was possible to make an attempt on the City behind the lines, either by sending troops in Boats down Delawar River to land on, or below the wharf, or by crossing Schuylkill river below middle ferry either by throwing over Bridges, or upon the ice in great frosts, to fall into the Ennemies rear at the same time the army was to attack the lines in front, with several Colums.

" Sending down Troops Delawar river, seems at least very dangerous if not entirely impracticable.

" The Passage over Schuylkill appears more eligible if attempted by a considerable body of militia, or other Troops. (I say militia, because I think the regulars would be all necessary for the chief attack in front.) Posted along the right bank of said river, on the best and most advantageous spots, from whence the artillerie & even small arms could annoy the Ennemy and protect the work-men for erecting Bridges, and in some places seemingly working. for the better drawing the Ennemy on that side, there ought to be made such seeming or reall attempts in several places at the same time. As this is the weak side, there is no doubt they would considerably divide their forces, and give room to break in upon them either in front or on this side, perhaps on both at once.

" If the necessary Boats and Materials for such bridges could not be provided, or carried to the proper places to be employed, or if there was an impossibility of erecting Bridges, or preventing the Ennemies of cutting a Channel through the ice, in fine if a Passage over Schuylkill should be impracticable, it appears to me, that the attack ought rather to be dropped, then to attack the Ennemies in their strong hold, in front only, this would be running the risk of a repulse, or of a total defeat and the bad consequences thereof.

" If on the contrary the river may be crossed especially upon the Ice, the principal attack could be made on this side with the best troops, and the Militia be drawn up in Battle or in Columns before the lines to make a show, and keep up the attention of the Ennemy. for that purpose a Large body of militia from all States should be drawn to-gether, and such measures taken for their march as to arrive all on the same day or very near, that on one hand, the expedition may take place immediately after their arrival, the Ennemies may be surprised or at least not have sufficient time to collect more forces or to add to their works, and on the other hand that the army may not be distress'd for Provisions, nor the Militia kept a long time in the field, for fear of sickness, or disgust, which is by all means to be avoided.

" Upon the whole this attack is subject to many incon-veniencies, and the greatest of all, will be the necessity of a winters campaign, this will ruin the army by sickness and discontent, perhaps too by desertion, and how will another almost new one be raised, except Congress take such measures as to oblige the militia to serve constantly at least for two years, and to be put into the regulars to compleat the regiments, in fixing a certain number for every State and to be all levied at a Limited time, and there is none to be lost. if your Excellency resolve for a Winter Campaign, the Troops ought to be immediately supplied with cloathing at any rate, if not Winter quarters to take place without loss of time. But in this case where and how to take them is a matter of the highest consideration. if real Winter quarters and rest are intended, they must be taken at a distance (as between Lancaster & Reading, or Reading and Easttown) from the Ennemy. But this would give up to the Ennemy the Jeseys, the whole State of Delawar, the eastern part of Maryland, Chester, Philadelphia & Bucks Counties in this State of Pensilvania, the Ennemy would draw out of these lands, forrage, Provisions, live-stock, and what would be still worse, numbers of able men to bear arms against their country, either by consent, delusion, or by force, besides the bad Effect it would have or produce in Political matters. This may partly be prevented by taking up Winter quarters at Wilmington and Environs with the addition of Hutts, but then there will be little or no rest, and no possibility of sending home many Officers & Soldiers for recruiting their regiments, and at the least movement of the Ennemy on Schuylkill, we must come up with them, in order not to be surprised in some of our quarters or cut off from the neighbouring States and from our Stores; the greatest alertness will be required from all Commanders in those quarters, and the fatigues the army would lie under and the Sicknesses they would be subject to, call aloud on Congress for recruits and Cloathing.

"BARON DE KALB
" *Major General.*"

OPINION OF MAJOR-GENERAL ARMSTRONG.

"CAMP AT WHITEMARSH, 4ᵗʰ Decʳ 1777
" SIR

" In regard to the Advisability of a Winters Campaign, I answer—In keeping the Field, the hardships on both officers and privates are manifestly great, nor is there an alternative presenting your Excellency with less inconvenience, at best you have but a choice of difficulties of which Hutting in the field is in my Opinion the least of the two, and most in charecter for the Army.

" The only semblance of Quarters known to us being so remote from the Enemies Post as to leave a great part of Pennsylvania for several months fully in their power—an acquisition this, too great to be yielded to these cruel & haughty intruders, unless under a greater degree of necessity than has yet reached your Army—To the advantages of the Enemy we must here subjoin the piteous sufferings of the well minded populace, too many to enumerate, too tender to express—I wish Sir to be divested of every local prejudice in the present enquiry where the publick weal is not clearly involved, but most certainly if in present or equal Circumstances the Whole of the Army shall retire to distant Villiages already crowded with her own refugees, Pennsylvania is that moment a publick Sacrifice, her Spirits, her hopes & future exertions Civil & Military, are blasted at once! unhappy State! & well if her diseases do not contaminate some of her neighbours—a mutillated victim cursed of the other twelve—and by Britain too, who for her manyfold services to Congress & to this Army, hath now made her the capital Seat of War.

" To considerations of this sort may naturally be added a train of things relative to the great design uses & reputation of the Army, all pointing against the inelligible quarters, but at present shall omit these.

" Discipline & Œconomy will be better maintain'd in the field than in the villages, where quarters are so far detatched —Health & vigour better maintain'd than in bad Quarters, and liable to debauchery. Hutting in the field in a dry cold winter, is by no means incompatible with health—this hath been experienced. If our Army is remote the lower Counties & some part of Maryland will probably be subject to the like incursions of the Enemy with the uncovered parts of Pennsylvania—In the field favourable Openings for annoying the Enemy may happen & be improved—Great Quantities of Provisions and Forage now convenient to the Enemy may be saved—If in the Field the Enemy will be cautious, if in quarters they will triumph, and their small partys dispersed abroad will serve their purposes & do us much damage.—On the whole I am fully of Opinion however arduous, that the present situation of our Affairs calls aloud for a Campaign, that it is advisable, practicable, honorable and will be found to be salutary.—But as far as possible to reconcile jarring difficulties, suppose one half of the Continental Troops with some Militia alwais in the field, and the other in quarters alternately, by which means some publick good may still be done, whilst all that ease that the nature of things can possibly admit will be granted to the Troops generally?

" With respect to the practicability of an attack on Philad* with the aid of a Considerable body of Militia to be assembled at a certain time and place—'tis a pleasing idea at first view, and ready to elate the anxious mind, in it there is something noble & consonant to the great points in view, and did they assemble in convenient time, the attack might doubtless be made with probable success—Or their very numbers occasion the Enemy to abscond, or a desertion in their Army—Cooper's Ferry wou'd best annoy the Enemy with carcasses—but the Engineers should be knowing, provided with materials, & might throw light on the best means of attack, on whatever side of the Town it might be made. Notwithstanding these wishful things, so many are the contingencies attending the convention of a distant Militia, and the ice serving in proper time, together with the great prejudice of a disappointment, that a measure the efficacy of which must depend on such an exact coincidence of things can scarcely be advised, but must be given up as rather to be wished than expected. Such an attempt with the advantage of Boats might perhaps be matter of consideration for the Spring. I am with perfect Submission

"Yʳ Excellencys Most Obedᵗ Servᵗ.

"JOHN ARMSTRONG."

OPINION OF BRIGADIER-GENERAL MAXWELL.

"SIR,

"Your Excellencys Favour of yesterday I received concerning the Adviseability of a winter Campaign, and the practicability of an attack upon Philadᵃ, with the Aid of a considerable body of Militia assembled at an apointed time and place. I do ashure your Excellency I think the object a verry desirable one could it be put properly into execution and without taking a winter Campaign to it, which in our present circumstances would be sufficient to ruin us of itself.

"It appears to me verry plain that General How does not think himself strong enough now to meet us in the field therefore will give us no opertunity of attacking him but to our great disadvantage. Our expectations have never been verry sanguine that we could prevent our Enemys from taking possession of some of our Seaports but if they cannot meet us in the field they will make verry slow work in conquering the Country. It appears verry plain we must have another Campaign next summer, and the sooner we begin to prepair for it the better by taking every method in our power to prepare our present Armey, and Increase it.

"The Attack proposed on Philadᵃ appears to me to be liable to so many Accidents that the success of it woud be verry doubtfull and should it fail our Armey would be ruined waiting for it.

"I am therefore against the Attack and the Winter Campaign, and am your Excellency's

"Most Obedient Humble Servant

"Wᴹ MAXWELL.

"WHITE MARSH, 4ᵗʰ December, 1777."

OPINION OF BRIGADIER-GENERAL SMALLWOOD.

"CAMP, December 4ᵗʰ 1777

" SIR

" It will be unnecessary to point out the sufferings of the
Continental Troops, from their various hard Duty, & distresses for want of Cloathing, particularly in the Articles of
Blankets, Shoes & Stockings, the most essential part to
enable them to encounter the severity of a Winter Campaign, and the improbability of procuring those necessary
supplies, without which our prospect of success in an undertaking of this Nature must be unpromising and fruitless
—The Army has already & is daily diminishing by sickness,
which has in a great Measure proceeded from the want of
these necessary Articles—The discontent, the disposition
for resigning, & the complaints which so generally prevail among the Officers, arising in some Instances from the
unsettled State of their Recruiting Accounts (which prevents the Draft of their Pay) of their Rank, in other Instances the partial Promotions which have been made, & the
exorbitant Prices paid for what they must unavoidably purchase (overrunning their Pay) renders them destitute &
unable to appear suitable to their Rank, or even decent &
comfortable, which call for redress & respite to regulate &
remedy, this cannot be made or obtained in the course of a
Winters Campaign.

" Your Excellency can be no stranger to their Distress,
and the justice & motives of their Complaints, & desire to
resign, which if not speedily remedied must have a dangerous Tendency, & a Winter Campaign must rather increase
than diminish their Sufferings in, & Objections to the service
—abstracted from which it must lessen, inervate, & render
your troops less formidable, & may give an irretrievable
check to your Advances in the Spring, at a Time when the
Enemy will come out in high Spirits & Vigor, & perhaps
may more than avail themselves of any acquisitions gained
by it—from which, & sundry other Reasons which might
be suggested, I am against a Winter Campaign, tho' at the

same Time I shou'd object to the Troops being canton'd so remote as to afford little or no cover to the Country, this might have a bad Tendency in several Respects, as it wou'd enable the Enemy to procure Supplies without any Risque at the same Time that it wou'd discourage the Inhabitants, & subject them to be insulted & plundered, & the Soldiery being lulled into Security wou'd be inattentive to Discipline, & in all probability so scattered over the Country, as to render it difficult to draw them to a Point, in order to open the Campaign early in the Spring, & prosecute your Measures with Vigor & Success.

" An Attack on Philad⁴ this Winter, I think neither advisable or practicable without subjecting the Army to too great a Loss, this cannot be effected in Front, & an Attempt in Rear & on the left Flank (the only probable way of making an impression) must depend upon Contingencies, which in all probability upon our taking a Position on the other side of the Schuylkill, will be sufficiently guarded against, nor in this cold, dead Season do I think the Aids expected from Militia are at all to be depended on.

" I should therefore judge it more prudent, immediately to take the most eligible Position, for the Security, relief & discipline of the Troops, having in View to cover as much as may be the Country, and awe the Enemy from making depredations, & should the States fall on Measures of filling up their Regiments or supplying you with a formidable Body of Militia early in the Spring, your Prospects of Success wou'd be enlarged & better'd, & it's likely a deep stroke might be made, before the Enemy cou'd possibly be reinforced.   I have the Honor to be &c.

" Your Excellency's most Obed' H^ble Serv'

" W. SMALLWOOD."

OPINION OF BRIGADIER-GENERAL KNOX.

"CAMP, WHITE MARSH, 3ᵈ December 1777

" SIR

" I receiv'd your Excellencys orders to give my sentiments
' upon the advisability of making a Winters Campaign, and

Practicability of an attack upon Philadelphia, with the aid of a considerable body of militia to be assembled at an appointed time & place.' Were it probable that Sr Wm Howe's destruction would be the consequence of a Winter's Campaign I would most chearfully give my voice and opinion for one—I think a Winter's Campaign, under the present circumstances, will be the inevitable destruction, if not of the Liberties of the Country, yet of the present Army; my opinion is founded on the following Reasons.

" Our entire want of Cloathing to keep the men from Perishing by the cold winters season.

" The improbability & impracticability of surprizing 10,000 veteran troops in a well fortified city.

" The impossibility of our keeping the field to besiege their works and city regularly, and being almost totally deficient of any warlike apparatus for so arduous an enterprize.

" The uncertainty of obtaining such a sufficient number of Militia as to make the enterprize warranted by reason, or common Military knowledge.

" My Opinion is for putting the Army in good Winter Quarters, to repair the damages done: to recruit^s reform the Army; to provide Magazines &c. In the Spring we may be enabled to strike the enemy a decisive blow, which by making a Winters Campaign I think improbable and impossible.

" I am Sir with the greatest respect, Your
" Excellency's Most Obed^t H'ble Servant
" H. Knox
" *B. G. Artillery.*"

OPINION OF BRIGADIER-GENERAL POOR.

" Camp, 4th Decem^r 1777

" Dr Sir

" In answer to the question Recv'd by note from your Excellency yesterday—a winters Campain, I am sure it will be attended with Gruel loss of our numbers.

" As to the Militia troops their is but little Dependence

upon them in Case you make an Asolt upon Philid^{her}—
besides if the Rivers should be froze over the Enemy Dout-
less will Contract lines & make their Situation nearly as
strong as it is now.

"I think that if your Army should be Emediatly sent
into winter Quarters—the Absentees Colected, that early
next Spring you'd be able to take the field with Dubble the
numbers that you'l have if a winters Campain is kept up.

"as your men are much fatigued & numbers falling sick
every day for want of Clothing and Comfertable habitations.

"I am Clear of Opinion that it's Best to put your Army
into winter quarters without Loss of time.

"however am Ready to Complie with any Disposition
that shall [be] Concluded upon.

     "I am Sir your Excellency's most obedient
             "H^{le} Servt.
             "ENOCH POOR, *B. G.*"

OPINION OF BRIGADIER-GENERAL PATERSON.
"SIR

"The bad States of our Army at present destitute of
Clothing and many other Necessaries, the Necessity of its
being recruited this Winter, that we may be superior to
Mr How in the Spring, induces me to give my Opinion in
favour of going to Winter Quarters. The Attack on Philadelphia, from the best knowledge I can obtain of the
Strength of their River Works, I must think woud fail,
the Consequences of which would be a universal Discour-
agement to the Country and Army, I find my Brigade
falling sick very fast, and am informed that others nigh me
are equally unfortunate, should therefore think it adviseable
to retire to some convenient Place for the Winter, and
recruit the Army as much as possible, that we may at an
early Day in Spring, take the Field & give Genl How the
so much desired Defeat.

     "I am your Excellencies most
         "humble Servant
            "J^{no} PATERSON.
"CAMP, 4 Decem^r 1777."

OPINION OF BRIGADIER-GENERAL VARNUM.

"WHITEMARSH, 3ᵈ Decʳ, 1777

" SIR

" Having been favored with your Excellencys commands of this day, I shall give my sentiments respecting the subject matters thereof, uninfluenced by any motives but the sincere dictates of my own mind.

" Not being at Head Quarters when the subject of a ' winters campaign was proposed,' in order ' to make an attack upon Philadelphia, aided by a considerable body of militia,' I cannot be acquainted with the reasons offered in support of the proposition : your Excellency will therefore excuse me, if I do not go so fully into the arguments as otherwise might be expected.

" Winter campaigns have not, in modern times, been approved of or practised by great commanders, but upon the most important occasions—Among the ancients they were more common. Two reasons conspired to make them so ; the hardiness of the soldiery, from their abstemious manner of living ; and the small preparations necessary to furnish their military apparatus. The modern use of gun powder, and the tedious preparations in the laboratory, added to the luxury and effeminacy of the times have concured, among other things, to form the modern taste. All Countries, in the same age, equally civilized seem to form their customs and manners upon a similar basis. It is not strange therefore that Americans have, in some measure, imbibed the vices of Europe. And, altho' the living of the American army is necessarily founded upon the strictest frugality, yet a few months service has not given them strength of constitution and patience of mind adequate to the severities of a winter's campaign. This will appear more evident, if your Excellency will be pleased to consider that the army is composed of men from the various parts of an extensive continent ; born in different climates ; accustomed, in some degree, to a different mode of living, and scarcely any of them acquainted with the manner of subsisting in camp. A considerable time is requisite to form them to the same standard. 'Till when, sickness will more or less prevail in proportion to the irregularity of their duty. From this consideration it is in part, that so very great a proportion of the troops are unfit for duty.

"Another and not inconsiderable Cause of the feeble state of the army, is their want of cloathing. From whatever source it is, I shall not decide, but it is a melancholly truth, that the men are naked. And what can we expect from them, opposed to British veterans, well clad, well provided with every necessary, when they are not in a situation to combat the severities of the season? Permit me Sir for a moment to indulge a moral sentiment. The Soldiers, their nearest connections, the country at large, nay, God himself, has committed them to our charge! We are answerable for their safety, their health, their comfort & their lives—If unnecessarily we deprive them of either, a consciousness thereof will plant daggers in our breasts that time cannot remove!—I must therefore conclude that your men are not in a situation to keep the field.

"Where are the magazines necessary for the execution of this great and extensive plan? The commissary's department is in such a situation, that provisions can scarcely be obtained from day to day. I know of nothing like preparations to subsist a large army near the enemy's lines. In that position, we cannot depend upon live stock. Salted provisions and hard bread must be had. Where are they? In the eastern parts of Connecticutt. The horses are extremely fatigued; they want rest and keeping. But, suppose they were in good plight; from what quarter is forage to be drawn to feed them? It is very difficult to obtain it in our present quiet camp. How much more so will it be when near the enemy? In what condition is our laboratory? Where are our battering cannon? Where are our mortars, shells, carcases, &c.? By a general assault upon the City, many of these objections would be obviated; but that I esteem utterly impracticable. The collecting a large body of militia in aid of the continental troops, I presume would be attended with unsurmountable difficulties. The distance from whence many of them must come, would either totally discourage them from attempting it, or protract the time in such a manner, that when they are assembled, arranged, & provided with ammunition &c., the winter season would be past, and your army ruined. They cannot be subsisted on the march, neither could they live here without great alterations. But suppose these difficulties were removed, & we provided with covering and other accommodations for a numerous army, of what service would they be in such a kind of attack as is proposed? I will venture to say, that the scene of confusion, Horror and carnage that must ensue, would only heighten those miseries which result from a total defeat! In this kind of war, I conceive of militia, promiscuously assembled, as an huge unanimated machine, incapable of regular motion or activity; and must infallibly share the fate of that numerous host of undisciplined barbarians, who ventured to fight the Roman Marius. I will beg liberty to extend my Ideas further, and presume we had an army of regular, well appointed troops, sufficiently numerous to ensure victory in the field, even then the attack would appear to me impracticable. It cannot be doubted but that General Howe has strongly fortified the front of the City by a chain of Redoubts, connected by Abbatis, or lines. The flanks are secured by Rivers. The City itself is made up of houses, the walls of which are proof against small shot. Thus securely posted, what probability have we of success? To rush impetuously on certain destruction, would be acting the part of madmen rather than of brave commanders.—It is the duty Sir, of all men to seek their own happiness. In military characters this is derived from glorious actions; from those exploits and successes which claim the approbation and applause of mankind. Rashness and timidity are alike unfriendly. Prudence and real magnanimity form the Hero.

"In matters of great importance, it is the sentiment of byographical writers, that we call to our assistance the

example of shining characters. It is from their experience
we may form our own conduct; and from the success attending their efforts, under similar circumstances, we may
probably conjecture the event of our measures. What
would a Marlborough have done on such an occasion?
' He never besieged a town but he carried it;' but he never
attacked a strong village or town by assault. What would
a Pyrrhus have attempted? He undertook to storm a city—
He lost his army and his own life. Thus, by one rash
manœuvre that dazzling Glory which astonished the universe, was sullied and eclipsed! As many instances of the
like kind will be recent in your Excellency's memory I
shall not trouble you with selecting more; but observe,
that, if your councils are to be formed upon popular opinions, & vulgar prejudices; or even by bodies in high authority, you will be pleased to recollect the misfortune of
the Martial Turenne, who, to gratify the court of Paris,
attacked a town sword in hand; the Event proved their
ignorance and folly.

"Altho' Philadelphia is a splendid object,—altho' a total
destruction of General Howe's army would compleat your
Excellency's felicity in relieving the country from all her
calamities; yet, the consequences of a defeat, would be
attended with miseries beyond Description.

" The salvation of America does not depend upon a successful victory this winter; but a severe defeat would
plunge us into difficulties, out of which we could scarcely
extricate ourselves. In short, I dread the Consequences,
and do esteem an attack, upon the principles proposed, in
every respect unadviseable. However, should your Excellency order it, I shall be happy in relinquishing my own
objections, knowing that if the worst should happen, we
shall fall like the sacred band of Thebes.

> " I am obediently your Excellency's
> " most humble Servant
> " J. M. VARNUM.

" 4th Decr 1777

" SIR

" Having only the last Evening to form, adjust & write my Opinion upon an important Question; Being very much indisposed and full of Pain, I must apologize to your Excellency for the obscure manner in w°h my Ideas are conceived and expressed. But for the Circumstances mentioned, I should have added many more Arguments in support of my Sentiments. I have mentioned in a written Opinion lately, the Uneasiness of the Officers; I hope that may be considered in Connection with this.

" I am as before

" J. M. V."

OPINION OF BRIGADIER-GENERAL WOODFORD.

" CAMP 4th December, 1777

" DEAR GEN^L

" I did not receive your Excellency's Letter till my return from Head quarters last Evening, or I should have comply'd with your requisition sooner.

" I have before given my reasons for being against exposeing this Army to a Winters Campaign in their present condition. I would add to them the present Temper of the soldiery, who I am convinced are very gener'ly against it.

" The practicability of an attack upon Philadelphia I have look'd upon to be entirely out of the question since your Excellency's return from viewing the Enemy's Works.

" As to the Aid of the Militia, I cannot be brought to think they will be of any in such an attempt. I am inclined to think whilst this Boddy were assembling we should loose more Continental officers & soldiers by waiting for them in the Field, then double the value of them that would arrive. Experience shewes that few Militia can be brought to stand in the line of Battle, & it would be deceiving ourselves to expect them upon this creation to march up to the attack of the Enemy's Works.

" If such an attack is to be made, I would advise it to be put in execution Immediately with the Force we have in the Field, because I think we are stronger than we shall be any time this winter. it is possible our numbers may encrease, but our real strength will diminish.

"Without some new light could be thrown upon this matter, or other reasons urged then I heard at the late Council, I am clearly against either making a winter's Campaign, or attacking the Enemy's works.

"I have the Honour to be your Excellencys
"Most Obed^t humble Servt
"W^M Woodford."

OPINION OF BRIGADIER-GENERAL WEEDON.

"DR Sir

"I have from the first moment it was suggested to your Excellency, 'that an attack on Philadelphia this winter with the aid of Militia was practicable and promised success,' kept in mind the desirable object; have compaired and viewed it in every light, and on every ground I could place it, and after mature consideration on the matter cannot promise a single Advantage that would justifie the measure, nor can I see the least prospect of anything honorable or advantagious by adopting it. On the other hand I foresee numberless Obstacles to retard, and perplex that with sober reasoning stares any man in the face who views it with an impartial eye, places it on a military scale, and reflects on what human nature is.—It has been found, I believe, by most of your Officers who you have advised with on the matter, that your Continental Force is far, very far, Inadequate to an attack on the enemies lines, in their present strength and situation.—Operations like those proposed, are of too extensive a nature to carry into sudden execution. Reasons sufficiently cogent, must diminish your force every day you keep the field at this season of the year, and to resolve on the measure, ensures a winters Campaign to this Army, which in their Circumstances also ensures certain destruction to great part of them, without the Aid of an enemy—your principle dependence must then be on the Militia, to carry this important matter into execution. Glory and our Countries good is no doubt what every upright soldier would wish to obtain, but we may be too keen in pursuit of it, and like the Dogs in the fable, suffer the substance to escape while we Grasp at the Shadow.—I would only mention to y^r Excellency some Difficulties that occur in drawing a sufficient force of Militia together for this purpose, and providing for them ; particularly at a season of the year when our Fields, and Rivers are Ice & Snow.—Covering we have not for them when they arrive, Hospital Stores we could not furnish for the numbers that would fall sick by being exposed to the severity of the winter, nor do I know that even provisions & forrage, could be procured with any degree of certainty, which shorely should be rendered beyond a doubt in such cases ; take the matter still on a more extensive scale. Every one that reflects on human nature and considers mankind at large must know how reluctantly they relinquish the ease and more calmer pleasures of domestick & social life to share the hardships & Fatigue of a Camp, even in more pleasant weather than what winter generally affords us. Men that are not taught and compelled to obey, will never render service, and Obedience & perseverance is not to be expected from a permiscuous body of men drawn together from all Quarters of the Globe, ware they to assemble, but you would find one half would desert in their way to Camp, others probably might arive, a day or two before their time of service expired. No object on Earth would keep them afterwards, nor could an [   ] influence them after their time was out. What would follow must be distressing to an exalted mind. You would find your regular Troops by this time much Diminished. They must bare the burthen of all necessary duties, in such cases, while this body of men are collecting,—expensive preparations are daily accumulating. The Eyes of the Continent are turned towards you. Much speculation on the practicability of the expedition terminating with success, which you at last find yourself obliged to relinquish, leaving the unthinking world (who want nothing more to blast reputation than a miscarriage, without inquiring into it's causes,) at liberty to sensure boath you & army.—Your Excellency is perfectly acquainted with my Sentiments respecting this Army—it is Sir the Bullwork of America and should be nursed and cherished as the salvator of her Liberties. The Troops that compose it are not more than mortal, and cannot work Maricles. The bravest spirits may be exausted by uncommon, and constant fatigue. And Sir, there is not in my Opinion an Object on the Continent that justifies subjecting them, at this particular time, to a winters Campaign, unless there was a moral certainty of obtaining that Object, and with it, a perminant and honorable end to any further Hostilities. I give it therefore as my clear Opinion, that keeping this Army in the Field for the purpose of attacking Philadelphia, under the uncertainty of sufficient aid and support of Militia, is by no means Advisable, and am Sir, with high esteem

"Y^r Excellencies most obed^t Servt

"G. WEEDON

"B. Genl.

"CAMP WHITE MARSH
"Decr 4, 1777"

OPINION OF BRIGADIER-GENERAL MUHLENBERG.

"CAMP, Decr 4th, 1777

" SIR

"Your Excellency was pleas'd to desire the Opinion of your General Officers on ' The Adviseability of a Winters Campaign, & practicability of an Attack upon Philadelphia, with the Aid of a considerable Body of Militia to be Assembled at an appointed Time & place.' I must Confess that to me this Question seems so much interwoven, with the Question your Excellency was pleasd to put a few days ago, that I can hardly seperate them: The main point, I conceive, is still, whether a Winters Campaign is practicable; if not, the last Question falls of Course, unless the Time is the Spring. A Winter's Campaign to me, seems not only unadviseable, on account of our Situation, but impracticable, at least if I am to Judge of other Brigades by my own ; one single Reg^t of mine have turned out Ninety Men unfit for duty, on Account of Shoes & other Necessarys. The Sick become Numerous, & the Men, notwithstanding the utmost Care of their Officers, will be Frostbitten, & subject to many other disorders, if they are to keep the Field, until the Militia can be collected, which if we are to Judge from the past, cannot be done in less than two Months—in the meantime it cannot be expected that the Enemy will remain Idle, Their Works will be Continued, Their Vessells who are now before the Town, will not only furnish them with Cannon, but with Marines, Sailors &c., so that in all probability, before the Militia can be collected an Attack will be thought impracticable, upon the same Grounds & perhaps with more reason than at present.—At the Time when this Hint was first thrown out in Council, I was pleasd with it, there seemd a probability of success ; but I had no Idea, that a Winter's Campaign was so closely Connected with the plan, which in my Opinion would prove more fatal to the Army under your Excellencys Comand than an unfortunate Attack on the Town—but I am far from thinking the plan ought to be dropped entirely. If the Army was to go into Winter Quarters where the Men could be refreshd & Clothd, & remain there untill the latter end of March ; the Militia could be Collected in the meantime. Then a Vigorous Attack could be made with a probability of success.

" Thus I have given your Excellency my Sentiments on the Question proposd, as Clear as the shortness of the time I had for Consideration would permit me, which was only a few Minutes this Morning. The utility of hearing a Question debated is great, at least to a Young Soldier— Should the Question be decided otherwise your Excellency may be assured that any part entrusted to me shall be executed with the greatest Chearfullness.

" Your Excellencys Most Obed^t & very humble Servt

" P : MUHLENBERG."

OPINION OF BRIGADIER-GENERAL SCOTT.

"WHITE MARSH, 4ᵗʰ Decʳ 1777

" SIR

" I recᵈ your Excellencys letter of yesterday. I well remember the proposition made. I then thought there was a probability of Success in such an attempt, but after your Excellency returnd from Reconoitring the Enemy's Lines and hearing your oppinion with regard to their strength, I lost every Idea of a Winters Campaign. I must confess I never Promised my self any Certainty of success In it. But the many Waity reasons then given for a Vigorous Execution Induced me to think something possably might be done, but since your Return from the lines, as before mentiond, I have not had a single thaught of such a thing Ither with or without the Militia.

"I am your Excellency's Obᵗ Servᵗ

"Cᴴˢ SCOTT."

OPINION OF BRIGADIER-GENERAL CADWALADER.

"HEAD QUARTERS, 3ᵈ Decʳ 1777

" DEAR SIR

" Whether the Army under your Excellency's command should continue in the field this winter; and whether it is expedient to call to your assistance a great body of militia to make an attack on the Citty, are very important Questions —the determination of which may decide the fate of America—they therefore require our most serious consideration.

" It is certainly usual with all nations, in every cold climate, to retire with their armies into winter quarters— The men want cloathing & want rest; and the army is generally much reduced by inaction, sickness & a variety of casualties. To repair these losses, to nurse & recruit the Soldiers, & to make the necessary arrangements for another campaign are certainly great objects: but, Sir, if the practice of other nations, & the rules laid down in the books by military authors, are, implicitly, to regulate the armies of these States, I cannot help thinking our ruin is inevitable:—precedents may justify us to military pedants, but not to the sensible Citizen.—

"The situation of the American States is very different from that of a nation whose independance is acknowledged & established. It requires great management to keep up the spirits of the well-affected, & to subdue those who have taken a part against us—Imprisonment, confiscation & death are the punishments for those who engage in the support of a revolution—these are terrors not so much dreaded in common wars—To remove these fears, and to secure the inhabitants from danger, appears to me to be measures of the utmost importance. The people of this State had the greatest expectations that the Army under your Excellency's command would have prevented General How from penetrating thro' the country & taking possession of the capital of this State.—They were disapointed!—and it is very evident what conclusions they must have drawn—The superiority of the enemy was easily discovered, and it naturally affected their spirits. Our successes to the northward have enabled you to, draw great reinforcements from thence —our whole force, now collected, gives them new hopes; and tho they may not expect a successful attack will be made on the city this winter, they expect to be protected. The withdrawing your army to a great distance will not only magnify the enemy's strength (in the Opinion of the Inhabitants) but will be construed into an acknowledgment of our own weakness.—The enemy may then detach a body of troops to take post at Bordenton or Mount Holly; another to Newtown on this side, and a third to Wilmington—with these (having possession of the Capital) they have perfect command of an immense country; from which they can draw provision, forage & men.—The State of delaware must be totally subjected—the eastern shore of maryland & virginia left open to be ravaged at will; in short, the inhabitants within this great Circle, must come in for protection, must swear allegiance to the king, & deliver up their arms. Those men who are to compose a very considerable part of your army the next Campaign will be engaged against you; the inhabitants of other States, who are eventually concerned in these misfortunes, will feel very sensibly their dreadful effects—the power of Legislatures will be weakened & the States may find it impossible to enlist, draft, or, by any other means, to furnish their quota's for the ensuing Campaign.—All the manufactures that might be drawn from the Country you desert, will be lost to us.— The depreciation of our money will encrease; and, in a short time, the Credit of the States will be totally ruined— Your army too, cantooned in a scattered manner, at so great a distance from the Enemy, will be dispersed thro' the States, by Leave-of-absence, Furlows, & Desertion—and instead of your troops coming into the Field better disciplined (as some Gentlemen expect) they will become licentious, ungovernable & total strangers to military Discipline.

" Last winter, after repeated ill-successes, you was obliged to retire from post to post, as the enemy advanced, and in addition to your misfortunes, your army was every day reduced, by whole Brigades, leaving you, in sight of the Enemy—When you crossed the Delaware, tho' reinforced with the Philad[a] Militia, you had but a handful of men, & these in a wretched ragged condition—What then would have been the consequence if you had retired to the back-country to nurse & recruit the miserable remnant of your army; and to enlist men for the next Campaign. The Consequences are so evident they need no explanation. By having the river as a Barrier you kept the field till an opportunity offered; and by a well timed, well executed blow, you gave hopes again to all the States—in consequence of this, the Prince-town affair happened, which drew the enemy to one point; and, at once, recovered N. Jersey & set America again on her Legs.

" The King of Prussia (in the last war) overpowered by numbers, had almost lost all his Dominions during the Summer; but by a noble exertion, with those very troops that had been harrassed & almost torn to pieces by repeated actions and constant Marches, he recovered his Losses by a winter Campaign.

"Your men, I know, Sir, are in great want of cloathing, but I conceive they will be sooner equipped by remaining in the field than in winter Quarters—because by being in the field, the necessity will appear more evident, will induce those employed to provide cloathing to exert themselves, and will justify measures that otherwise would disgust & exasperate those from whom they are taken.—Let the robust, & best cloathed, do the duty of Guards; let the Invalids be sent to the most comfortable Quarters; & let premiums be given to those who shall make the best Hutts.

"If you are out of the reach of a surprize, the Duty will be easy; and you may effectually annoy the enemy as if you was nearer.

"I am far from thinking that a winter Campaign will not be attended with great distress to the poor Soldiers, & do not mean to insinuate that good winter Quarters may not be more comfortable; but I am obliged from the necessity of the case to declare, that I think, if your army was reduced by action & sickness, to one half its present number, the consequences would not be so fatal, as if we were to take winter Quarters.

"I have confined myself merely to the Question ' whether a Winter Campaign is adviseable,' but beg leave to make a few remarks on the two Positions that have been proposed.

"To cover our stores, to afford the most protection to the country, to procure the best shelter (& out of the reach of a surprize) where there is plenty of water, forage & provisions—these appear to me to be the considerations that should determine the choice of the position for winter quarters.—Lancaster & the line from thence to Easton, has been mentioned as a proper place for winter Quarters.—Others have mentioned Wilmington & its neighbourhood.—Let us compare them! Lancaster &c., tis said, from the best information, are so crouded with Families from the City & its Invirons, that a traveller can with difficulty get a night's lodging. I cannot conceive that any person can seriously propose to turn out those inhabitants, while their Husbands, Fathers & Brothers are now, perhaps, in the

Field—Hutts then must be substituted in the place of houses.—You have plenty of water, forage, & perhaps provisions, and you leave a vast country exposed as has been mentioned above—You are to live on that country from whence you must draw your chief supplies in the next Campaign, & every article brought a great distance in waggons.

" Wilmington has not its usual number of Inhabitants : & several other Towns in the neighbourhood are under the like circumstances; there are 9 or 10 mills at Brandywine, all these will afford shelter for a great body of troops.— This situation is out of the reach of surprize, & near enough to annoy the Enemy, cover your stores, & a great part of the country, which in the other case is left exposed. Wood, water & forage in great plenty and provisions, as the Com : General informs, may be had in large quantities from Maryland & virginia by water, to the Head of Elk.—Hutts may be built, in such places as will best answer the purposes of defence, for that part of the Army that cannot find shelter in Houses.—

" I am so perfectly convinced, that nothing but success, can keep up the spirits of our Friends, confirm the doubtful Characters, convert our Enemies & establish our Credit, (on which the bringing another army into the Field very much depends), that every Effort ought to be made to procure it—I have not doubt but a successful attack could be made upon the City this winter by calling a considerable Body of Militia to your assistance if the enemy remain in their present position.—But I am apprehensive, that by declaring your Intention (which will be necessary to induce the militia to turn out) it would immediately alarm the Enemy—they would find it necessary to surround the City with works, on the west side, and by drawing their force within a narrow compass, might defeat your Scheme—as they could only be carried by storm, at this season of the year.

" It would probably take two months to collect the Militia from the distant States, which would bring us to the first of February, at which time the Ice is often gone, or at

least, so weak as not to answer our purpose.—I am therefore inclined to think it will not be proper to give the
militia so fatiguing a march at this severe season, or put
the States to so great an Expence without a greater prospect of success.

" I am, Dr Sir, with great respect & esteem,
" Your Excellency's most ob^t very h'ble Servt
" JOHN CADWALADER."

OPINION OF JOSEPH REED, ESQ.

" DEAR SIR

" Tho' the Consideration of a Winters Campaign, & Practicability of an Attack on Philad^a have been so lately proposed, every Gentleman who extended his views beyond the
present Hour, must have turned his Thoughts upon these
Subjects so as to be able to form something more than a
sudden Opinion.   There cannot be any Person, Sir, either
on a publick or private Account, upon whom the Motives
for a Winters Campaign can operate more forcibly.   I have
every Reason to wish it—& yet in the State & Condition
of our Army my Judgment is against it.—The History of
every Winters Campaign made in Europe closely evinces
how destructive they have ever proved : during the Course
of the last War the allied Army under Prince Ferdinand
was almost ruined tho' victorious, & pursuing the Enemy.
—Charles the 12th failed & fell from the very Summit of
Victory, & Success by keeping the Field a part of the
Winter.   It is true, these Climates were more severe than
ours, but the Troops were so well appointed, or at least so
much better than ours, as to give Force to the Argument.
Nay the Experiences of the Enemy last Winter confirms
the Observation—a great Mortality, Discontent among Officers & Men, & considerable Desertions, were the Consequences, tho' they were much better provided than we are.
The Nakedness of the Army, & Temper of the Troops seem
to be insurmountable Objections, possibly the latter might
subside if the former was removed, but as it is, from every
Observation I have been able to make, unless a competent

Supply of Cloathing can be procured all Argument is vain.
—The Dissafection of the Country, Distress to the Whigs, recruiting & refreshing the British Army, a general Despond-
ency & above all,—Depreciation of the Currency stare me
in the Face as the Consequences of Retirement to distant
Quarters : I shall share personally in this Distress—With a
Family I have a Habitation to seek at this inclement Season,
& every other Accommodation to provide, & yet I cannot
desire the Army so unprovided to remain for my Protection. The general Calamity I fear will not be removed by
attempting it. The Credit of the Currency in my Opinion,
will depend more upon an effective Army, than any other
Circumstance. If Sickness, Discontent & Desertion should
disperse or greatly reduce our Army; I think the general
Cause would suffer more than from the Evils I have noticed
before : these Evils will admit of some Remedy, but the
other will not. With a recruited & refreshd Army, we
may recover what we lose, but with a fatigued worn out,
dispirited one what can we expect but that General Howe
will next Spring take the Field with every Superiority—But
in this Case it appears to me, the true & proper Line may
be between such a distant Cantonment as has been proposed,
& taking Post so near the Enemy as to make a Winters
Campaign. The Arguments of disciplining the Troops, recruiting the Army &c. at a distance have little weight with
me; such a Security would afford, & be used as the best
Excuse for going Home, & the Officers Commissions have
not such an inherent Value as to make them fearful of
losing them by Disobedience, or Neglect of Duty. The
surest Pledge of Fidelity, & Attention, would be putting
them in such a Situation as to require it. I do believe a
partial Dispersion of the Army would follow, on putting it
in any other Situation. Military Rules & Maxims laid down
in long establish'd Armies do not allways apply to ours, &
this Case I think is an Exception.

" An Attack upon the Enemy in his Quarters when the
River is froze, has been much thought of—if the Probability of Success was in our Favour, no Exertion ought to

be left untried, & even the present Situation of our Army should be made if possible to bend to it. But if after [*cut*] Efforts, the Chances will be still against us, Prudence forbids our venturing upon a Measure, which if unsuccessful would be attended with very fatal Consequences. Gen¹ Howe from the best Calculation, has now 12000 Men on one side strongly posted with Redoubts & Abbatis, so formidable as to discourage our most enterprizing Genius's, when a large Detachment seemed to favor an Attack—on the others two unfordable Rivers, I fear we cannot oppose a greater Number of Continental Troops to him; but this is to be supplied with Militia from Jersey, Pennsylvania Maryland & Virginia—as to the first they are very fully employed at Home, the second from a Variety of Circumstances we find will not turn out but in two or three Classes & even of these there are Numbers allways unarm'd.—The two latter in Point of Arms are in the same Condition. They are at a Distance & will march in at different Times, those who come early will be impatient, of Delay & hard Service, their Subsistence will be difficult, & after all the very Possibility of it will depend on the Weather—A South Wind with a little Rain will make the Ice impassable in a few Hours, But supposing them to come into Camp in great Numbers, & good Humour, well arm'd, & fed—the Frost to continue—from the Nature of the Thing it can be no Secret —the Enemy will probably throw up Works, or make up other Preparations. On the opposite Bank therefore you will meet with an equal Army ready to receive you: for every one acquainted with our Militia will allow, that the Nature of the Attack will require too much Firmness & Discipline, to expect them to be equal to it farther than as a Support. Upon the whole there are such a Variety of Circumstances each of which are important, indeed essential, all to coincide, that I think it would be almost miraculous if no one of them should fail us.

" We are so circumstanc'd, Sir, as to have only a Choice of Difficulties, true Wisdom will direct us to select that Plan which will be attended with the least.—As to the

main Body of the Army laying on the East Side of Schuylkill, & taking Post between that & Delaware, it is not practicable in my Opinion—as the Country does not supply
Forage or Means of Subsistence.   No Magazines being
established but at a great Distance, nothing, or next to
nothing now to be procured from the surrounding Country,
the Supplies would be too precarious in the Winter Season.
I therefore cannot but join in Opinion with those Gentlemen, who advise passing the Schuylkill with the greatest
Part of the Army.   The left Wing, & as much of it as
could find Cover in Wilmington to take Post there, extending as they can find Accommodation or good Ground
to Hut, as far or farther than Downing-town.   I would also
propose that upon an exact Estimate of our present Force
it be divided into 3 or 4 Parts or Classes.   The most robust,
healthy & well cloath'd to form the first Class; & so on.
The first Class to take the first Tour of Duty on this side
Schuylkill, taking Post at such a Distance from Philadelphia as not to risque a Surprize, having with them only
their light Baggage or even bare Necessaries.   I would
have a Body of Militia advanced between them & the
Enemy, their Line & Parties to extend to Delaware or as
near it, as their Strength would admit.   This Body of Men
will not find Cover sufficient I believe, without going too
far or too near, they will therefore hut, or perhaps Boards
may be procured.—I am very sensible that Objections &
very plausible ones may be framed to this Plan & so there
may be to every other.   this answers the most valuable
Purposes & such as appear to me to require our running
some Risque to obtain.—I will just enumerate a few.   In
the first Place, a very valuable Country, the three lower
Counties & Chester will be covered, & a Degree of Protection afforded to the Country on the East side of Schuylkill.
2ᵈ. The Army will find some Cover; a Country abounding
in Forage, & many other Articles necessary for their
Comfort, those Countries having suffered as yet very little
by the War, & being very fertile.   3ᵈ. The Enemy will be
deprived of this Supply which they will otherwise obtain.

4th. The Troops will be within striking Distance, if Circumstances should favour that Measure without being exposed to a Winters Campaign. 5th. A Tour of Duty will not admit the Officers neglecting the service by going Home, or entering into Scenes of Dissipation, & Amusement, which will in the same Degree infect the Soldiery. 6th. Some Annoyances may be given to the Enemys Intercourse by Ships. 7th. It will prevent any Insurrection in those lower Counties, or the Eastern Shore of Maryland of which every Year has furnish'd us with an Instance. 8th. The Passage of the Enemy has occasioned Wilmington, & that Neighbourhood to be evacuated by the Friends to America, they with many others have retir'd to those very Places some Gentlemen propose to go & occupy—in the one Case you will have empty Houses, in the other you must exercise a Spirit of Hardship by turning Families out to experience every Species of Distress. 9th. You will reserve the Supplies of the back Country for the next Campaign which otherwise you will eat up in the Winter.

" I would farther beg leave to add that the support of the Army, the Success of the Cause & even the Supply of Cloathing & Necessaries for the Troops depends very much on the Opinion & Spirits of the People, they rise or fall according to the Appearances of Success & of our Force; abandoning a large Body of the Country to the Enemy, will to them be a sure Proof of our Inferiority & Inability to oppose the British Army, of course they will seek Protection, take the Oaths, & throw themselves under the Enemys Government.—A Circle of 30 Miles at least including Jersey will be under the Command of the Enemy.

" It is a great Objection & has much Weight that this Post may be liable to Affront from the Enemy & Disturbance in their Quarters, but I do not think our Affairs or Situation will admit of total Tranquillity.—2d. The Schuylkill will afford some Security after the Destruction of the Bridge which must be effected. 3. Some Works may be thrown up for Defence. 4th. The Army will be within supporting Distance of each other, so as to require a great

Exertion & Movement of the Enemy, which they will not be fond of after being settled in their Quarters. These Circumstances in a Degree obviate this Objection.

"2ᵈ Object. That Bucks County & Jersey will be exposed to the Depredations or Practices of the Enemy.

"Answ. This Position will afford a partial Cover & in my Opinion a better than the distant Cantonment. I am confident the Country will esteem it so.

"3. We have Hospitals in this Country & are establishing Magazines at Places that may be exposed by these Movements.

"Answ. These Hospitals are scattered about, they hardly make an Object for an Enemy, but I should think they might be removed as fast as the Patients recover & no new ones sent, so that in a little Time the Difficulty will be removed.

"Upon the whole, Sir, I can think of no other Expedient to reconcile the many Difficulties which present themselves in every view of this important Question. The shortness of Time & a sore Finger has obliged me to throw together these Sentiments with very little Accuracy—they may serve as Hints perhaps for better Heads to improve.

"I am with the greatest Respect & Regard, Dʳ Sir,

"Your obed & affᵗ Hble Servᵗ

"Jos : Reed."

[December 4, 1777.]

OPINION OF BRIGADIER-GENERAL DU PORTAIL.

"3ᵈ December, 1777

" Sir

"I have examined anew with all the attention of which I am capable, the Project of attacking the English and it still appears to me too dangerous—the great Body of Militia with which we might be reinforced for this purpose does not give me any additional hope of succeeding—it is not the number of Troops which is of importance in this case, but it is the quality, or rather their nature and manner of fighting.—The Troops wanted are such as are capable of attacking with the greatest vivacity, the greatest firmness.

—Troops that are not astonished at suffering a considerable Loss in the first onset, without causing any to the Enemy—for this must be the case in an Attack of Intrenchments—although when the Works are carried the Chance turns and the Loss is on the side of the intrenched.—Now, are the Militia or even Continentals capable of undergoing this Trial, in which the best Troops in the World cannot always support themselves—I am very sorry in giving the motives of my opinion to be obliged to speak so unfavorably of our Army—but the Battle of German Town ought to be a Lesson to us—if our Army had proceeded with vigour on that occasion, would not the English have been completely defeated—The Disposition was excellent.—Your Excellency in that instance really conquer'd General How, but his Troops conquered yours.—if then notwithstanding the advantage of a complete surprize, notwithstanding the advantages of ground, we were repulsed, what would happen before a Line of Redoubts well disposed in all appearance, and the Intervals of which are closed with Abbatis.

" There is however a case in which I think we might attack the Enemy with success—I mean if the Schuylkill should be sufficiently frozen below their left to admit of our throwing our greatest Force on their Rear at the same time that we should make an attack in front. Gentlemen acquainted with the Country must decide this point—if indeed the Schuylkill is sufficiently frozen every year to afford a passage for Columns of Troops with Artillery—my opinion is fixed. I think the Army ought to be marched to the other side of Schuylkill, to be reinforced with all the militia that can be collected, while we wait for the favorable moment.

" I would go more minutely into the Subject, if your Excellency did not order me to send my Answer this morning. I did not receive your Excellency's Letter 'till half after twelve, and it is now half after one.

" I am with great Respect, Sir, your &c

" LE CHEV^R DU PORTAIL." [1]

---

[1] Translated by Lieutenant-Colonel John Laurens.

OPINION OF BRIGADIER-GENERAL IRVINE.

" SIR

"If posting the army in a position similar to that I advised in my last letter, be to form a winter's campaign, the measure in my opinion is not only adviseable, but absolutely necessary, as the more I think on the subject the more I am convinced that retiring into winter quarters and leaving the country uncovered will be followed with the ruin of our friends, give ease and plenty to our enemies, and do an irreparable injury to the cause we are ingaged to defend; the aids to be drawn from this State in future will be triffling indeed, the inhabitants of new jirsey will be intimidated, the delaware state lost, and an opportunity given to the tories on the eastern shore of maryland once more to appear in arms against us. When I proposed hutting the army it was not so much with a view of annoying the enemy in their present possessions as to prevent them from ravaging the country; and to give our officers a better opportunity of attending to the discipline of the troops than they could possibly have were they dispersed in extensive cantonments;—how far the former may be effected by drawing together a large body of militia, is a question not easily determined—The idea I confess is a noble one, and could it be reduced to practice might be attended with the most happy consequences, but the great variety of circumstances that must concur to insure those consequences is a strong argument against making the experiment.—I take it for granted that not less than eighteen or twenty thousand militia would be called, it is uncertain whether so large a body could be collected on the short notice they will receive, it is equally uncertain whether the different states could arm their quotas, and their assembling at the place of rendezvous at or near the time to be fixed, still more so, as it may depend upon circumstances not in their power to foresee or prevent: allowing they came in time and properly armed, the ice or weather may be against our striking a capitol stroke for some time, and the difficulty of keeping such a body of militia in the field at that season of the year (when they expected to be discharged in a day or two) is easier to foresee than get over. Upon the whole, I am of opinion that tho' it is necessary for this army to remain somewhere between twenty and thirty miles of philadelphia this winter, it is not adviseable to attempt collecting a large body of militia together with a view of attacking that place.

　　" I am with the greatest respect Sir
　　　　" Your most obedient & humb. Servt
　　　　　　　　　　　　　　　" JAMES IRVINE.
　　" WHITEMARSH, Decem^r 4th, 1777"

　　　　　OPINION OF BRIGADIER-GENERAL POTTER.
" SIR

　　" Your excelancey by your letter of yesterday Requested my Sentements on two points—

　　" first the advisability of a winter Campaign, secondly the Practicability of an Attact upon Philadelphia—Ass to the first of these points my Sentements is that a winter campaign is Practable.—I confess the verey thought of a winter Campaign in our Sircumstances appeers dredfull. But it is liek many other Evels, that befaul us in this life, before we under go them we are Redey to conclud the are unseportable, but when the are over we dont find them so dredfull as we apprehended. I can from experance say so of a winter Campaign—I have not found it, to have so many Evels attending it as I have hard warmly Represented—But on suposition that those evels were Reale, how shall they be remeded　the answer will be by goining into winter Quarters.

　　" I assart winter Quarters is not to be found In the state of pennsylvania　my Reasons for this assartion is, the Capatale is in persession of the Enemy, and there is such large numbers fled from it, and the neghbourhood, adjasant, and the Towns and Viledges along the River Dalawer, that all the Towns and Viledges Back in the Country are full of Refugees all Redey.

　　" What will be dun with those people　Turn them out of Dores to make Room for the Solders, god for Bid it—that would be cruilty unaxamplyfied by General How himself.

"then it Remains that we must Buld Huts, for our soldiers go where we will, in this state—and I take it for granted we will not leave the State Entily to the marcey of the enemy.

" I would Recommend the taking persision of Wilmington and Newport and what other Houses we could find in a Conveneant place in Chester County, and Rais Huts for the Remainder of our Troops, so as to prevent, the enemys furidging in that County by this Station being Ocqupied By us, we will get the furridge and provisions that our enemies would otherwise get, and the Back parts of the Countrey will be Resarved for the ensuing Campaign, and in Case the[y] should be able to force there way into our Countrey in the spring, the furridge and provisions being Acosted [exhausted] will retard there march, and will be mutch in our favour that our stors are safe in our Reer—Another advantige will follow by Quartering in the aforesaid maner it will be In your power to keep a number of men in Bucks and Philadelphia Countys to prevent the enemys coming out in small partys to force the Inhabitance to Take the Oath of Elegance to the King. Nor will the have it in there power to get that suckuer from the disaficted part of the community, if they are closley shut up in the City. I am Convinced a winter Campaign will give Spirits and Viger to all the Inhabitance of these United States and will do Honour to the Army and Good to our cause In genral.—

" Ass to the Provibility of an Attact on the City of Philadelphia with the aid of a Bodey of Militia, it is unsartain when or at what time it would be possible to cross the Rivers to attact them, for that is the way that appeers most provable to me at present.

" If your Enjineers are Confidant that they can set the City on fier from the other side of the Dalawer or Schuylkill in case the Ise did not answer I would be for cauling the Militia to aid the Army, if they could not set it on fier, I think we would be verey liable to a disapointment.

" I am &c.

" CAMP, Decr 4th, 1777"   " JA^s POTTER.

OPINION OF COLONEL LUTTERLOH.

" REMARKS,

" As the present Camp wants Wood & other comfords for the Men, in this Severe Weather, and the Enemys Situation being to strong for an Attaque, I would propose to post our Army into Refreshing Quarters, (as We do abroad in such cases). I have been lucking out where you could forme such a Line, Sufficiently stocked with houses for that purpose & find we would form such a Line between the Two Rivers Schuylkill & Delawar, where we could effectually cover our Country, Stores, & provide the Necessary Supplyes easy, as allso prevent the Enemy from doing our Army any material hurt. To do this we should place our Right Wing allongst the Schuylkill & the left on the Delavar. Our Van Troops in German Town & those hights &c. &c. in [   ] up towards Reading all the Army could lay. Head Quarter to be at Pots Grove which I find a good large Town for it. The great Magazin to be in Reading & in the Trap & Hickery Town the Mooving Magazines & Backerys must be established—to which those places are proper. All that Country is full of Forrage & these Supplyes can be got easy as allso over the Schuylkill. The Right Whing Melitia could be over the Schuylkill as from Mottrom's ford upwards I find the Country very advantagious with hills where no Surprise could happen to them at the Van postes & in each Division some poles must be fixed on it a Caske with Pich & Combustibles which are fired & lightered directly upon the Allarm Gun from the Commander of the Van, by which all the Troops march to their Larm-postes forwards, pointed out to them by their going into the Quarters. All Commanders do keep in the Nights their Troops in their houses together &c. &c. Over Schuylkill must be Two bridges more one by Wolley forge & one near Potsgrove to get quik Communications. When this is done directly we keep our Men in health & are refreshed to stand any attaque & our Supplyes can be good & Regulair.

" H. E. LUTTERLOH.

" Decbr 1ˢᵗ 1777"

INDEX.